# PASTOR HSI

## MRS HOWARD TAYLOR

**Foreword by Floyd McClung**

# AN OMF CLASSIC

© OVERSEAS MISSIONARY FELLOWSHIP
(formerly China Inland Mission)
Published by
Overseas Missionary Fellowship (IHQ) Ltd.,
2 Cluny Road, Singapore 1025,
Republic of Singapore

First published ... 1900
Twentieth edition (revised) 1949
Twentyeighth edition 1989

This edition 1997
ISBN 1-85792-159-3

Printed in Great Britain by
The Guernsey Press Co Ltd, Vale, Guernsey, Channel Islands.

# Foreword

I T is a privilege to write a foreword to this book about a man whose life made such a great impact for God. I have read many biographies, but this one stands out above the rest.

The Bible is filled with stories of God's work in the lives of ordinary men and women who did extraordinary things for the Lord. The stories of Abraham, David, Moses, Paul, and Peter were written not only to give us the truth, but also to inspire us to trust the Lord. These men are the "Heroes of the Faith". We all need the inspiration of what God can do in the life of a yielded man or woman.

Pastor Hsi experienced danger, adventure, persecution, and great power to heal the sick. But what marked his life the most was not the great things he did for God, but his deep and profound awareness of his dependence upon God.

Do you want your life to count for God? I challenge you, as I have been challenged myself, to follow the example of this man. The whole atmosphere and character of his life is characterized by that which can only be attributed to God.

What we read about in the life of Pastor Hsi, we also read about in the book of Acts. This man saw the sovereign in-breaking of God time and time again, yet did not allow it to puff him up into pride or arrogance.

This was a man of strong character, a born leader. With weaknesses, for sure, but also with a tremendous ability to show love to drug addicts and government officials alike. He had great courage and determination and was fearless in the face of evil. His simple childlike faith led him to take the New Testament at face value: he put into practice whatever he read. He fasted, he prayed, he laid hands on the sick and they were healed, and he cast out demons.

Perhaps one of the greatest lessons in this man's life is in the dimension of power encounters with the forces of darkness. Pastor Hsi realized, "We wrestle not against flesh and blood but against principalities, against powers, against the rulers of the darkness of this world, against spiritual wickedness in high places" (Ephesians 6:12).

He not only believed in the reality of evil spirits, but in the victory that Christ had won over them on the cross. This man fought the good fight. Again and again he saw his Lord victorious on his behalf, and on behalf of those in bondage to the power of the devil. The reality of these experiences compels us to search our hearts again and ask if we are availing ourselves of the authority that has been given to us as believers over demon spirits and principalities.

Though he did not dwell on faith healing, nor was consumed with the spectacular, he regularly saw healing miracles in his ministry. These are reported in a very factual way, so much so that one longs for the same kind of reverence and caution in the reporting of miracles in today's Christian world.

Pastor Hsi also walked a life of faith through his daily needs. Again and again we read of wonderful, thrilling stories of the Lord's provision at the last minute. It is true what has been said, that God will never let us down, but sometimes He takes us right down to the wire.

Pastor Hsi lived his life in the "radical middle". He was a man of great balance: while he prayed for the sick, he was also a practicing doctor, using drugs and other medical means at his disposal. While he was very strict and disciplined, he was also loving and kind, particularly to the opium addicts of his day. Though he had great vision and faith, he also exercised patience, being willing to wait for others to catch up with the vision that he had in his heart.

We are indebted to Overseas Missionary Fellowship for making this book available again to us. I believe the book will be a great inspiration to many believers, and will be a channel through which God will call many into missionary service.

If you dare to be changed, read on!

FLOYD MCCLUNG JR
INTERNATIONAL EXECUTIVE DIRECTOR
YOUTH WITH A MISSION
1989

# Contents

# Introduction

*From the author's original Preface, "A Traveller's Journal"*

THE following pages trace some outlines of the story of the notable Chinese pastor, Hsi Shengmo. It has been difficult to gather material for a connected narrative, specially of his early days, for he was ever reticent in speaking of himself. When we were with him, we urged his making some record of the past, if possible from childhood; and after thought and prayer he promised to do this. The result was a brief but deeply interesting manuscript, written in Chinese character by his own hand, in which, touching lightly upon personal experiences, he magnifies the grace of God in every step of the way. Upon this simple autobiography the following story has been based. Further information has been added by those who knew him best, especially Mr. D. E. Hoste, who for the last ten years of Pastor Hsi's life was his fellow-worker and most valued friend.

Not to magnify our friend has this story been written. Pastor Hsi, like most of us, had many faults, especially in his early Christian course, and to the end he may have retained some of the defects of his outstanding virtues. But he wonderfully matured as years went on, and to those who knew him best his life was fragrant of the indwelling Christ, who through him did many mighty works. The spirit of the man, as well as the purpose of this book, may best be judged from a few characteristic sentences of his own that close the introduction to his modest manuscript. After referring to the difficulty of the task he had undertaken, and to the unsuccessful attempts he had already made towards its accomplishment, he says—"Then I set myself to prayer and fasting beseeching that the precious blood of Christ might wash my heart, and that He would cause me to write to His glory, speaking only of how He had used me, this unworthy man, to open these refuges and carry on His work, and of how the Holy Spirit's power had been manifested in leading many souls to obtain salvation, causing all the glory to revert to my Father in Heaven. I desired that there should not be the least bit of self in this story. By the help of the Holy Spirit I was enabled to write all that follows in three or four days from the time of thus waiting upon

God. But during all these years so many things have happened that I cannot remember them completely  because in doing the Lord's work I seek to forget the things that are behind, and to press on to those that are before. I have not kept any record, nor have I lightly informed others of my doings, lest I should receive praise of men and not obtain God's gracious favour. This by way of preface."

# Extracts from the Introduction written for the First Edition by D. E. Hoste

AS time goes on, China will certainly produce men whose zeal and gifts will fit them to take a leading part in the evangelisation of their own countrymen, and the building up of the native church. A story therefore such as this will repay the thoughtful study of all interested in the development of the kingdom of God in that country. Should it not also awaken in those who read it a solemn searching of heart before God as to how far their own aims and practice in life can compare with the unremitting toil and unreserved devotion recorded in these pages, in the case of one whose advantages were far less than their own?

The subject of this biography possessed in more than ordinary measure the qualities that fit men for leadership; combining that comprehensiveness of mind and foresight which enable men to frame measures on a large scale, with the strength of will, practical resourcefulness, and capacity for the management of others, essential in carrying such projects to completion. At the same time there were points in his character which rendered his co-operation with foreign missionaries a matter of difficulty. By nature and by training, his temper was autocratic and independent. It was difficult, therefore, for him to give due weight and appreciation to the counsel and co-operation of other workers. His confidence was not easily won; indeed, a tendency to over-mistrust and suspicion concerning those whom he did not know well, was a distinct weakness in his character.

The transition period, in which leadership and initiative are transferred from foreign missionaries to native workers, demands the careful and prayerful forethought of all concerned.

One thing is certain from the character of the people: that with the growth of Christianity in China, men and women will increasingly be raised up to initiate independent enterprises. What is to be our attitude toward them? The life and work recorded in this volume surely answer that it should be one of cordial recognition of the gifts and position of the native leader, coupled with the patient, earnest endeavour, by winning his love and confidence, to enrich and elevate his views; and so, through him, the work he is carrying on. The relationship between the missionary and such a Chinese will not be of the official nature that characterises his connection with paid helpers under his own supervision, but will depend for its power and usefulness on the measure of influence that by tact, humility, and sympathy he may be able to win over his native brother.

In developing such a friendship the foreign worker may learn many useful lessons, not only in respect to the practical conduct of affairs among the Chinese, but lessons also of a directly spiritual character. Among the latter he will become impressed with the fact, that while in many respects his own acquaintance with the Scriptures and his standards of Christian life are higher and fuller than those possessed by his Chinese fellow worker, the latter may nevertheless, in other important particulars, be his spiritual superior, and far more effective, under God, as an active instrument for good, both among the heathen and the native converts.

In conclusion, a few words as to the general impression made by Pastor Hsi, upon one who was intimately associated with him for nearly ten years, may not be out of place. His remarkable energy and force of character, coupled with an entire devotion to his Lord, and to the work to which he was divinely called, were the features about him that most impressed a close and constant observer. His Christian experience was deep, and was of the strenuous rather than restful type. His life was an unceasing warfare with the powers of evil. He was habitually burdened in heart about the sins and sorrows of those under his care, and his tears and fastings on their behalf were almost constant. He was a born leader; nothing escaped his keen eye, and he was ever ready to rebuke, instruct, or succour as occasion required. And with these sterner characteristics he possessed also a deeply affectionate heart, and true humility of spirit that could only be fully recognised and appreciated by those who knew him well. As years went by, his masterful character grew more and more mellowed and softened; until, when he passed away, it is no exaggeration to say that hundreds wept for him as for a father or elder brother.

May the Christian reader of this book be stirred not by the interest, merely, that its style and matter will naturally excite; but to an abiding resolve, by prayer and practical consecration, to hasten the day when China shall be evangelised and her Church cared for by her own sons.

# The Home of His Childhood

THERE was quite a flutter of interest and excitement in the Western Chang village, that sunny autumn day. Something had happened to call forth smiles and congratulations; and from one to another the exclamation went—

"Have you heard the happy matter? What good fortune for the old gentleman, Teacher Hsi!"

It was not that Mr. Hsi had gained a law-suit or inherited a fortune, not even that he had obtained a high degree at a recent examination, or had received an official appointment. Outwardly his circumstances remained unchanged, yet he was a prouder man at that moment than ever in his life before. For had not Providence that day bestowed upon him *a fourth son*! What virtue, what merit were his! The honour of his old age, the comfort of his declining years were now ensured; and, more important still, the supply of his wants after death, and the worship of his memory to future generations were fully provided for. One son, or even two, might die or prove unfilial, but the possession of *four* sons was a security to be envied indeed. And so the neighbours, as they met the fortune-favoured man, were loud in their congratulations and good wishes, the report of which penetrated even to the inner apartments, where, in the back courtyard of Mr. Hsi's house, the women gathered round the little stranger.

No one came to see the mother, of course. That would not be manners, nor would any woman risk the disaster that might follow. For a full month she would receive no visitors, nor dare to enter a neighbour's door. But all the same she knew that every woman in the village was envying her good fortune, and that sympathy and admiration would attend her when she went with her offerings to the temple to give thanks for her boy.

Meanwhile, she was well satisfied with the pretty and useful gifts that daily appeared for "the little scholar": pieces of gaily coloured silk for baby garments; charms and amulets; silver ornaments; velvet shoes, beautifully embroidered; and elaborate satin head-dresses of wonderful design, adorned with tremulous butterflies, bats, dragons, or tigers, as the case might be. Baby's birth—the day and hour—were accurately recorded, for upon this would depend the arrangements that might any time be entered upon for his betrothal.

It was in the fifteenth year of the Emperor Tao Kuang, just before the accession of Queen Victoria, that "the little scholar," whose birth called forth such jubilation, came to the ancestral home at the foot of the mountains. He was born of a reputable stock, into a family of more than average means and culture. Both father and grandfather were scholarly men, and had built up the family fortunes by careful management of their property and diligence in the duties of public life. For several generations medicine had been a favourite profession among them, and the valuable recipes thus gathered were handed down from father to son. At the time of which we write, the head of the family was known and respected throughout the countryside, having done much to encourage education and promote the healing art. Filial to his parents, and generous as a brother, it was fitting that he should be rewarded with four sons of his own, to revere his memory and reproduce his virtues.

The boys, as they grew up, all gave promise of ability, and Mr. Hsi had the satisfaction of seeing them complete their university training with unusual success. The eldest brought honour to the clan by carrying off a high degree, and the second and third obtained their B.A. with distinction.

Meanwhile the youngest brother, with whom we are chiefly concerned, was bidding fair to follow in their footsteps. He was a bright, merry little fellow, though serious at times beyond his years. Even in early childhood strange questions perplexed him, and the fear of death shadowed the future with mystery and terror. Nobody knew it. Children do not speak of these things.

Sometimes on sunny days the boy went with his brothers to the grim temple on the mountain, near his home. Leaving the populous plain, they crossed the sloping uplands, covered with wheat and barley, or the autumn cotton, hemp, and maize. A little higher, village homesteads give place to ruder dwellings. Caves are utilised for houses, and where these are wanting, the hillside itself is tunnelled, and excavated hamlets shelter under protecting cliffs. Five thousand feet above the sea the mountain ridge is gained, whence from a lonely summit the grey old temple looks on the scene beneath.

Far below, amid fields and orchards, lay the home of his fathers. Beyond it stretched the plain, dotted with towns and hamlets; watered by the winding river; and guarded by the wall-encompassed city of Pingyang. A scene of wonderful fertility, unbroken by fence or hedge, the park-like landscape extended, far as the eye could see. Beautiful in summer with a wealth of golden corn amid fields of variegated poppy-blossom,[1] or groups of flowering fruit-trees and darker foliage where the houses stood; in autumn it was clothed again with verdure, from the creeping tendrils of the ground-nut and sweet potato to the broad-leaved tobacco plant, the white down and graceful foliage of the cotton, the red stem and feathery flowers of the buckwheat, and tall-growing heads of millet bending in the mellow light.

A few years later, and Hsi, with childhood left behind him, would find a new and deeper charm in that fair scene. For there lay not only the home of his fathers, but the cradle of his ancient race. Far back in the dawn of history, that rich peaceful valley had been the birthplace of China's earliest civilisation. There, more than a century before the birth of Abraham, the famous monarchs Yao and Shun had reared their capital, and won all hearts by their beneficent rule. There Kao, the Lycurgus of China, drew up his Code of Justice, and framed laws, that in modified form govern the nation still. In those long-past days the arts of agriculture flourished throughout the plain; religion and education were well established, and good government ensured universal peace. Inhabitants of the district still cherish the tradition that "in the good old days of Yao and Shun no one bolted his door at night, for thieves and robbers were unknown"; and if the traveller dropped any of his belongings by the wayside, the first passer-by considered it his duty to mount guard over the lost property till someone else came along, who in his turn took charge, to be relieved by the next comer, until the owner reappeared, to find his possessions intact. Traces of those famous times still linger in the temples dedicated to Kao, the ancient law-giver, and to the now-worshipped emperors Yao and Shun. Often, in years to come, the young Chinese would wander with admiration through those broad enclosures and noble halls, recalling the memory of that distinguished past, and of more recent days, when, during the Ming dynasty, literature and learning flourished in Shansi, and its cities were the resort of wealth and fame.

[1] Opium was much grown in Shansi.

But of all this the child as yet knew nothing. Far more interesting to him, when he climbed the mountain, was the grim old temple on its summit, than the historic associations of the plain. Not without awe would he enter the massive gateway, guarded by warlike gods, and pass in silence through those gloomy chambers, where, amid dirge-like music, the shaven priests were chanting their unintelligible prayers. Incense perfumed the heavy air. Low notes of deep-toned bell, or loudly resounding gong, re-echoed through the dim and dusty halls. Hideous idols glared upon him grimly from either side, while the impassive features of the central Buddha gazed into vacancy beyond. Chilled and uneasy, the boy would soon escape into the sunshine, glad to hasten back to the cheery simplicities of home.

Awesome as were the precincts of the temple on the mountain, still more so were the courts and cloisters of the city god, with their horrible depictions of the tortures of the Buddhist hell. There, in deep alcoves, stood eighteen groups of brightly-coloured figures, striking terror into his childish heart. The punishments represented were dreadful beyond description, some of the least revolting showing victims hung up by the feet and flayed alive, or pounded in a mortar, sawn in pieces, eaten by dogs, or boiled in oil. The expression of the faces, crude but realistic, was sufficiently agonised to fix itself indelibly upon the mind, and the child went home to live it all again in tortured dreams, never for a moment doubting that such experiences awaited him in the unknown of mystery and terror beyond the grave.

Sometimes on summer nights the little fellow wandered off alone, pondering his unanswered problems, searching with tear-dimmed eyes the starlit depths of unresponsive blue. When only eight years old he questioned with himself—

"What is the use of living in this world? Men find no good. And in the end——?"

Dimly he felt he had a soul that came from heaven; and with a child's hopeless sorrow he turned away and wept, because he knew no way by which he might escape the Here and the Hereafter.

But generally, with other boys, he was all life and animation. His bright intelligence and force of character made him his father's favourite son. The elder brothers, though jealous, were proud of his ability, and urged him to study hard at school.

"You can win wealth and fame," they said, "and in the end become a great mandarin."

"What good is there, after all, in being a mandarin," thought the child, when alone. "Sooner or later one must die."

He went to school, however, and worked hard for his degree. But always, in quiet moments, that unspoken fear came back. Nothing could shake it off. It only grew with his growth.

Meanwhile, across far seas, in an English cathedral city, another child was growing up amid surroundings of Christian culture. While little Hsi was weeping over his unanswered questions, this boy, five years his junior, was learning at his mother's knee Truth, profound yet simple, the Divine solution for life's mysteries. More than thirty years later, led by an unseen Hand, those two must meet. In that walled Chinese city, Hsi, the proud, opium-smoking scholar, must look at last into the face of David Hill, saint and missionary: the face that always bore such radiance of the light and love of God. Not yet, not for long, weary years. But surely, even then, God was preparing his own answer to the child's unconscious cry.

# 2

# Wedding an Unknown Bride[1]

YOUNG Hsi had been some years at school, when the good old father, who was drawing near the end of his journey, became impatient to see his favourite son settled in marriage. He had secured for his boy the advantages of a good education, and had provided for his future as far as his means allowed. It only remained to discharge the last paternal duties, and carry through the wedding in proper style. The little bride had been selected long before; and though none of the bridegroom's family, much less the boy himself, had ever seen her, presents had been exchanged, and the elaborate red papers filled up that made them irrevocably one.

At last the day was chosen, and the bridal chair sent to bring the weeping girl to her new home. Great excitement prevailed in the village of the bridegroom, everybody crowding to witness the gay proceedings. Lavish preparations were in progress for the wedding feast. Friends and relatives had gathered from far and near, and the hubbub and commotion that prevailed defy description. With difficulty could the elder brothers preserve order and protect their household property amid the ever-increasing excitement.

A room had been made ready for the bride with fresh-papered windows and much ornamentation of red scrolls and hangings. Upon a handsome table in the courtyard were placed the ancestral tablets, and two small cups of wine for the marriage ceremony. By and by, sounds of approaching music caused a general rush to the great outside doorway to receive the returning cortège. With a final explosion of crackers, shouting of children, and crowding of onlookers, the gay bridal chair was carried into the courtyard and set down. The silent and unwilling girl, met by the women-folk, was dragged[2] rather than escorted to the table in the open air, where the bridegroom was standing with his father

[1] The wedding described is one that the writer witnessed in northern China, and is introduced in default of information as to the actual marriage of young Hsi himself.

[2] To go willingly would be considered a shameful lack of modesty.

and friends. He had never seen her face, and even at that moment could form no idea of what she might be like; for a long coarse-looking outer garment enveloped her; a large red cotton cloth covered her head, and nothing would induce her to look up. Let go by the women, she went down upon her knees before the table, knocking her forehead thrice upon the ground, in worship of Heaven, Earth, and the Ancestors. The bridegroom simultaneously went through the same proceeding. Then she was seated on "the lower side" of the table, and handed a tiny cup of wine, which she was made to sip, while the bridegroom, in the seat of honour, also tasted his. The cups were exchanged, and again tasted; and the marriage service was complete.

Hustled by the crowd and supported by the women, the girl was then dragged off to her own apartment, as many spectators as possible crowding in to see her dressed and make remarks upon her appearance and belongings. Seated in the middle of the excited throng, she had to submit to being examined all over, while her sisters-in-law unfastened and rearranged her hair in the approved style for married women, and robed her in her gayest clothing and wedding ornaments. Everything she had or did was the subject of freest comment. Her long black tresses, her little feet, her complexion, temper, trousseau, all passed under review, while she maintained unbroken silence, looking down upon the ground and trying not to laugh or cry.

Meanwhile the bridegroom and his friends were feasting in the men's apartments. Did he think of his young wife, whose face he had never seen? Did he want to shield her from so trying an ordeal, to comfort her in her loneliness, for the first time away from home? Plenty of remarks would be made in his hearing, and comments freely passed about his bride, children and others running from room to room to carry all sorts of exaggerated rumours. But he cannot go to her. Not for many a long day will he venture to be seen speaking with her in public.[1]

By degrees the excitement passes off, and the first strangeness wears away. Visitors still come crowding in for a few days to look at the bride, who must sit silently, dressed in her best, to be stared at as long as they please to stay. But between times she begins to talk a little to the women of the family, and may even

[1] In some parts of northern China it is customary for the husband's mother to prohibit, and to prevent, any conversation at all between the young couple for the first three years of their married life.

be persuaded to take food, until by the end of the first week things settle down, pretty much, into the regular routine. Soon the girl becomes sufficiently at home to take her share of household duties, and wait upon her husband's parents.

At the time of his marriage young Hsi was only sixteen years of age, and his bride probably a year or two older. But little change was necessary in the family arrangements. He lived on still in his father's house, and continued his studies as before. He seems to have become much attached to his gentle wife, who, no doubt, understood the Rule of the Three Obediences laid down by Confucius:

"Woman is subject to man. She cannot herself direct any affairs. At home, before marriage, she must obey her father. When married she must obey her husband. After her husband's death she must obey her son. She may not presume to follow her own judgment."

Also, "Reverential obedience is the great duty of a wife. The husband should lead, and the wife follow. This is the correct relation."

Young Hsi, undoubtedly, was born to lead; and this would make for peace in domestic relations. For in China, a woman would far rather have a husband who might be hot-tempered and violent, if he only made others fear him, than a man, no matter how kindly, who could be set aside and imposed upon. The husband's duty to be strong is taught as clearly as the wife's obligation to be yielding. Thus:

"The union of husband and wife resembles the relation of the superior and inferior principles which permeate all things, and influence the earthly and heavenly intelligences. The virtue of the superior principle is inflexible firmness; that of the inferior principle is pliable weakness. So man's strength is his honour; while woman's weakness is her excellence. . . . Heaven takes precedence of earth: the king takes precedence of his ministers: the man is superior to his wife."

About this time also the young husband was promoted to a public school, and went in for special coaching, with a view to his first examination. He won his degree[1] at sixteen, covering himself with glory and rejoicing his father's heart.

Of the years that followed we have little record. Gradually

[1] In Chinese polite language, "Entered the Dragon Gate and swam in the great waters."

there came changes in the old family home. The mother had long since passed away, her place being filled by a second marriage. Then the father also died; and the tablets of both parents were erected in the ancestral hall, and reverently worshipped by their children. Later on, the property was divided, each of the four brothers taking his share. The youngest settled in a comfortable house on the outskirts of the village, with fields and farm buildings around him, and bright prospects of a scholarly career ahead.

# 3

# Winning a Reputation

PROSPEROUS and respected, young Hsi grew into manhood, steadily acquiring influence in the village and district. He was clever and ambitious. His aim was to get on in the world and attain the rank of a mandarin. Outwardly successful and carrying all before him, no one would have imagined that deep in the young man's heart still lay the underlying consciousness of soul unrest. The world, at its brightest, could not satisfy. He still longed, as in earlier years, to escape from it all; from himself, his fears, the future. On the surface, however, he was a man of character and determination, wholly absorbed in the pursuit of power.

In China, if a man has sufficient ability, others will unquestioningly submit to his authority and follow his lead. In a large village there are many matters of common interest, such as arranging for theatricals or fairs; repairing embankments; protecting the crops; collecting dues for the temples; and questions of taxation and government. The man who can manage affairs, and knows how to deal with others, and how to meet the official classes, gains great power, and his opinion is regarded as decisive.

Such a leader Hsi readily became. Fearless, resourceful, and determined, he combined shrewd judgment with powers of ready speech, and possessed a temper that was the terror of all who had the misfortune to rouse it.

As his character became known, he was constantly entrusted with the management of difficult matters and the settlement of local quarrels. Whenever there was a law dispute, he would be called upon to write out the accusation, and frequently went before the mandarins on such business. Mixing among the gentry of the neighbourhood, he also had a following to the lowest class of hangers-on at the mandarin's office. Not overscrupulous, and prepared either to argue or terrorise as the case might require, he was equally ready to create or to settle disturbances, as long as he could see his way to personal profit.

Sometimes the cases brought to him were simply family matters, and personal disputes; sometimes the whole community would be in difficulty, and his courage and energy were taxed to the utmost.

On one occasion the heads of his own and adjacent villages came to consult him about a longstanding trouble. It was connected with an annual fair in the neighbouring market-town. In country districts these large fairs are of great importance, most of the buying and selling of local commodities being reserved for such occasions. People flock into the town in thousands. The streets are crowded with stalls and booths, the tables of fortune-tellers and medicine vendors, and the tempting wares of the pedlar, laid out upon the ground. Often a large theatrical stage is erected over the main thoroughfare, and a troop of actors engaged, who perform for three days and nights in succession. All sorts of property changes hands at the fair, from grain of various kinds, and farm produce, to household furniture, clothing, new and second-hand, and articles required in the worship of the gods. This is the great opportunity of the year for the village people to obtain hard cash in exchange for their goods, and upon the fair they depend for the ready money they need to pay taxes and purchase whatever they do not themselves produce.

This particular fair in the neighbouring town had got into the hands of a powerful ring of bad fellows, who for some years past had managed it exclusively for their own advantage. They were typical specimens of that formidable class known as "the Chinese bully." Of such characters the people have a saying: "The bean-curd bully rules a square territory; and the carrying-pole bully rules a strip." Cakes of bean-curd being square, and carrying-poles long, these objects are used to represent the sadly universal tyranny of this objectionable class. In the case in point, a number of these men had banded themselves together to shut out all the villagers, by armed force, from the control of their own annual fair. They alone decided who should be allowed to rent stores and standings, and who should have the best places. They settled the value of goods, and kept in their own hands all the details of management upon which the success of the fair depended. And as a matter of course they pocketed most of the profits.

Although the grievance was serious, the village people dared not venture to seek government protection. The cure would be worse than the disease. To go to law would simply mean to be fleeced by mandarin and underlings alike, and the issue would depend, not upon the rights of the question, but upon who could pay the highest bribes.

In this dilemma, hearing of young Hsi, the village elders felt they could not do better than put the case into his hands. They trusted entirely to his common sense and force of character, and begged him to make an effort to break up the objectionable clique. To their great relief Hsi undertook the matter. He kept his own counsel as to the means he would employ, and his neighbours were satisfied to ask no questions.

When the time came for organising the fair, Hsi quietly went down to the neighbouring town and took his place on the board of management. As a scholar and one of the local gentry, he had a right to a voice in the matter, though hitherto ignored. Now he simply said—

"The majority of the country and village people have asked me to undertake the arrangements for the fair for this year, and I am come to control it."

The oppressing party were completely taken aback, and in their consternation could hit upon no plan of united action. It was all unexpected! Hsi, with marked ability, ran the whole concern, and his temper and fearlessness were such that no one dared oppose him. He carried everything through, no doubt in a high-handed way, and with a good deal of forceful language, but the arrangements he made were fair for both parties. The country people responded gladly, and the townsfolk bided their time. The "bullies," with their following, were ready when the fair came off to make an armed attack and clear their opponents from the field. Hsi had boldly bearded the lion in his den, but more likely than not he would pay for it with his life.

Meanwhile, however, the scholar had been perfecting his arrangements. He had written letters to friends in distant places, and had received satisfactory replies. The fair opened stormily, but just at the critical moment a group of twenty men suddenly appeared on the scene, all strangers, and armed with swords.

"Oh," said Hsi, "and where have you come from?"

"We heard," was the reply, "that you might be having some trouble here, and have just dropped in to look after you."

"Dear me!" ejaculated the scholar, in well-feigned surprise; "there is nobody here who would think of molesting us!"

A little later another party came in, and still another, all with the same story, which spread like wildfire—

"We heard it reported that there were certain ill-disposed men who were likely to give trouble, and thought we would come in and protect you."

At last there were no fewer than a hundred men, all armed and watchful, scattered about the town to protect Hsi's interests. This unexpected and formidable turn of affairs thoroughly intimidated the bullying party. They practically retired from the field. The fair went off successfully, and a compromise was arranged with the townspeople by which impartial representation was secured for the whole county. When the danger was past, Hsi's armed supporters vanished from the scene as mysteriously as they had come, and the excitement subsided. Therein lay the skill of his management. If he had used local men, the irritation would have been kept up indefinitely, and worse troubles might have developed. In this and similar ways he was constantly able to serve his neighbours, while increasing his own reputation.

As time went by, Hsi acquired an extensive practice as an irregular advocate at the law courts, and his name was known all over the countryside. Yet he was not happy; not at rest. No little children came to gladden his home. And, worst of all when he was still quite a young man, the wife whom he loved sickened and died. In deep sadness Hsi was driven more than ever to the consideration of the old problems that had pressed upon his heart as a child, when he used to wonder, wistfully, how he had come to be, what he was in the world for, and whither he was going. The study of the classics had brought no answer to these questionings. Confucianism had not satisfied the hunger of his soul. It had given him no light to illuminate the darkness of the grave; no comfort for an aching heart.

But there were other systems of faith and teaching round him. The classics of the scholar were not the only ancient writings to be found. Lao-tzû, sage of the Taoists, had lived as long ago as Confucius, and had left philosophical works of great importance. The priests of this religion abounded in their temples and communities throughout the district. They professed to be able by their magic arts to avert the ills of life; to abolish want and sickness; and to procure for their votaries the blessing of immortality.

Beside these, were there not the Buddhists; multitudes of yellow-robed monks, in monasteries and temples? Had they not brought sacred writings from India, dating back almost as far as the days of Confucius? Of course no educated scholar could for a moment credit their absurd fables, or look otherwise than with contempt upon their idol-worship. And yet in their teachings about the "Western Paradise" there was much to attract the world-weary soul, and many of their doctrines closely resembled the philosophy of the ancients.

And so the question came, why should not even a scholarly Confucianist examine into these strange systems, and see whether, in them, any truth or help might be found? To one of Hsi's vigorous nature, inaction was impossible. How could he rest content with uncertainty until he had at any rate examined every religious system within his reach? Little though he guessed it, even then the hand of God was upon him, permitting him to wander further into darkness, that he might be more ready to welcome the dawning of the one true Light.

But like many another before him, Hsi sought vainly in such teachings for the light and help he needed. Well might he have echoed the sad utterance of Lao-tzû himself, when, grieved that his doctrine made but little progress, he exclaimed—

"I am forlorn, as one who has no home. All others have and to spare; I alone am like one who has lost all. In mind I am like a fool. I am all in a maze. Common people are bright enough; I am enveloped in darkness. Common people are sagacious enough; I am in gloom and confusion. I toss about as if on the sea. I float to and fro as though I were never to rest."

Pathetic cry of a heart that never heard the supreme invitation, "Come unto Me, and I will give you rest."

# 4

# The Swift Descent

"It is not the man that eats the opium, but the opium that eats the man."—*Saying of a Chinese Mandarin.*

GRADUALLY, as years went on, a change began to be noticeable in the once proud Confucian scholar. Still a young man, only thirty years of age, he was beginning to realise that he had come to an end of himself and had failed to attain his ideals or shape things as he would. By all his searching he had not found out GOD; and the stern stress and temptations of life were closing in upon him.

Hsi's position at this time was more critical than he or anyone else supposed. He had reached a turning-point in life, from which the swift descent was to begin that soon would plunge him into depths of sin and misery it had once seemed impossible he should reach. Following his experiences during these sad years, from 1865 onward, one trembles to see how nearly the enemy of souls had compassed his destruction before he had ever had a chance of hearing of the power of Christ to save.

After years of loneliness, Hsi married again, when about thirty; his second wife being a bright young girl of sixteen or eighteen, from a neighbouring village. Slight and graceful, she was attractive in appearance, and possessed no little natural intelligence and force of character. A warm attachment grew up between them, which deepened through all the years of their united life.

Long-continued soul-unrest, combined with the excitement of his occupation as a lawyer, began seriously to tell upon Hsi's health, which failed perceptibly after his second marriage. Feeling so much the vanity of life and emptiness of earthly things, he had long devoted a good deal of attention to the study of Taoism, hoping for something to satisfy the hunger of his soul. It was the promise of immortality held out by the Taoists that attracted him. Gradually, however, as health began to give way and the strength of his young manhood seemed ebbing from him, his eyes were opened to the falsity of such pretensions.

"What," thought he, "is the meaning of this? Before taking up

Taoism I had good health. Now I am sickly and weak. Is this becoming an Immortal?"

Startled and disappointed, he had to acknowledge that it was all a terrible delusion. Confucianism had left him unsatisfied; Buddhism had brought him no help; but Taoism had given him worse than nothing. Undeceived, he came to realise what he ever afterwards maintained, that the whole system is a dark mystery of spiritualism and devil-worship. He found its priests to be mediums having extraordinary mesmeric power; and he firmly believed their hold upon the people to be due to their familiarity with evil spirits and the way in which they make use of Satanic agency.

Thus in the prime of his manhood Hsi began to fall behind in the race of life. Gradually he was seen less and less at the law courts; and when clients came to him with their troubles, instead of meeting the vigorous man whose fame they had heard, they found a scholarly gentleman indeed, but one spent and worn, and prematurely old. By degrees his illness increased so much that he had to take to his couch. Things went from bad to worse. His income began to suffer, and the future looked dark indeed.

It was then a new temptation met him. Doubtful of any cure, his friends began to urge that he should try what opium would do for the relief of his sufferings. Just a few whiffs of the pipe, and he would feel so much better! No one would think any harm of it. Public opinion had entirely changed of recent years, and instead of being regarded as a vice, opium-smoking had become quite fashionable. So many people seemed to find relief from pain and depression through the magic of this drug. It would be sure to do him good. In fact his case was now so serious that there was no other hope.

For some time the unhappy man held out. He had seen enough of opium-smoking among his neighbours to feel doubtful about tampering with so dangerous a habit.

"But try it, only try it," urged his advisers. "You need not smoke it constantly. Just take a little until you are better. It will then be quite easy to give it up."

This sounded reasonable; and at length the sick man yielded, and the opium-tray found its place beside him on the couch.

Rapidly then the downward path was trod. In his enfeebled state Hsi had no power to resist the ravages of the poison. At first, after each dose, he felt better; his spirits rose, and everything looked bright. But all too soon the exhilaration passed away, to be succeeded by deeper depression that nothing could shake off till he turned to the opium pipe again. The more he smoked the worse his sufferings became. Appetite failed him; sleep forsook him; all interest faded out of life; nothing seemed to matter but the satisfaction of his growing craving for the drug.

"It is not the man that eats the opium, but the opium that eats the man," now became the unfortunate scholar's experience. Studies, business, care of his property, pursuit of his profession, all alike were forgotten. He lived but to smoke opium. The inevitable result followed. He became a complete wreck, and for a whole year and a half never left his couch. During lucid hours between the intoxication of the poison, he was plunged into depths of misery, remorse, and despair. At times he struggled to conquer the craving that was killing him but in vain. Relentless as a vulture, the vice to which he had yielded had him now in its grasp.

In more hopeful intervals he turned to the practice of medicine for support, and at one time opened a second-hand clothes shop in a neighbouring town. But such efforts only resulted in the opium-smoker's perpetual failure. At last, all hope abandoned, his emaciated figure, sallow face, and changed bearing too plainly told their own sad tale.

His original illness, instead of getting better, gradually increased in severity, until it seemed the end was near. On one occasion his wife and friends, thinking all would soon be over, dressed him for death, according to Chinese custom, in the handsomest clothing they could command. It was then a curious experience came to him, of the reality of which he never had any doubt. He was lying evidently at the point of death, his family all wailing round him, when, in some strange way, he became distinctly conscious that his spirit was leaving the body. With a delightful sense of relief he seemed to be free from the weary, worn-out frame, and was just going to quit the room, when suddenly a voice of great authority called to him—"Go back! Go back!" and with sorrowful reluctance he had to return. Though in later life he rarely alluded to this strange occurrence, he always believed that it was no dream or delusion, but that God Himself in mercy to his soul had sent him back.

Years passed on, in which the opium-smoking scholar tasted to the full the bitterness of his degradation. In many an hour of anguish he cursed the folly that had led him into such a snare. What would he give now to be free: to go back to the manhood of other days! He hated and loathed himself and the habit that enslaved him; seeing with terrible clearness, at times, all that it meant, not for him only, but for the young wife and aged mother he was involving in poverty and shame.

Too well he knew what the end must be. He had seen it often enough in his own village and district of recent years. What a change had come over things since he was a boy. Then opium-smoking was prohibited, and only indulged in with the greatest secrecy. Now it was common everywhere, and with what fatal results.

Often at night, waking from heavy stupor, with aching head and burning thirst, he would think about these things as he lit the opium-lamp and held his pipe over the little flame to prepare another dose. He could not live without it, and yet the shadows round him seemed crowded with horror, as he waited to inhale the sickening fumes. Forms and faces he had known in youth were there, changed, sunken, degraded like himself, honour and manliness all gone, eyes without lustre, parched and yellow features, livid lips, thin and tottering figures, clothed in rags. From the opium-suicide's dishonoured grave they had come back to haunt him. And beckoning in the darkness, "You are one of us" they seemed to say.

But they were not alone. The midnight silence was dreadful with other voices: voices that wept and pleaded and reproached in vain. Pale women he had seen, and little children—toiling to keep body and soul together and supply the opium that husband and father must have; always hungry; always cold in winter; often beaten and abused; never knowing any moment but that a worse fate might overtake them—sobbed out their pitiful despair. He could see again the anguish of girl-faces, young wives and mothers, or unmarried daughters, sold away for money into life-long slavery, worse, far worse than death, that men, lost to all sense of shame, might have the opium without which they could not live. Little wonder the trembling smoker hastened to banish unwelcome consciousness once more.

Or in the morning, when the sun was high, rising depressed and miserable, faint for want of food but hungry only for more opium, the realisation would rush over him, at times, of the depths to which he had fallen and the hopeless wretchedness that lay ahead. Far off and unattainable now seemed the days of his fame and scholarly ambition. Never again could he take his place as a man among men. Even his darkest hours of doubt and sorrow were enviable, looking back from this living death in which nothing was left him but remorse and fear. One thing only seemed necessary now—opium, and plenty of it. Sometimes he wondered, shudderingly, what would happen if for any reason he could no longer supply himself with the drug? He had heard of beggars, once men of good position like himself, dying in the open street, pleading with the scoffing crowd for opium, any dregs of opium, to stay the awful craving that was rending them with anguish. Would he ever lose the memory of one such miserable creature, lying half-buried in the dust and filth of the city gate? For days the man had lain there dying in the sultry summer heat. Worn to a skeleton; covered with disease and dirt his rags no longer hid; worried by dogs and flies; his lower limbs dead already and corrupting; exhausted by hunger; parched with thirst; the wretched sufferer had but one entreaty, following with tortured eyes each passenger that hurried through the gateway— "opium, opium; only one mouthful of opium." And, with that gasping cry, he died.[1] Could it be that he himself should ever come to such a fate?

Sometimes, on better days, when his spirits rose a little after an extra pipe, he would go out and wander round his farm, once well-cared-for and productive, thinking sad thoughts about it all. With apprehension he noticed how much of his best land, once bearing rich crops of wheat, was now under opium, and realised that his reserve store of grain was lessening year by year. All around him over the plain the same condition prevailed, for he could see wide fields of poppy-blossom everywhere curtailing the food-crops. His neighbours, like himself, had too readily succumbed to the seductive poison; and those who did not as yet smoke opium were glad enough to grow it for others and pocket the large profits that otherwise would go to the importers of the drug.

And this awakened other thoughts often present in his mind. How had it come about—all this fatal relaxation of prohibitions against the growth and use of opium? Whence flowed this flood of poison that was devastating the land? Alas, the story of the

[1] The writer saw the man described, lying in that condition, in the gate of the city of Pingyang, a few miles from Mr. Hsi's home.

conquest of China by the opium-habit was only too familiar to the scholar in whose lifetime the tragedy had come to pass. When he thought of the black record, his blood boiled, and his hatred of the unscrupulous oppressors from over the sea, who for the sake of gain had wrought the ruin of his country, became intense.

He knew that retribution lay ahead. The bitterest drop in his cup of misery was the conviction that somehow, somewhere in the Unknown Beyond, just and terrible requital awaited his sin. Dimly he wondered whether the vengeance of High Heaven was visited on *nations*, and if so what must be the portion of those who had wilfully disregarded the cry of a great people, and, in mad haste to be rich, had consigned to such sufferings as his, millions of the human race?

He had never seen an Englishman; but he knew well who had brought opium to China; who had bombarded Canton; who had burned the palace of the Emperor, drained his country of millions of money as indemnity for two unjustifiable wars, and bound the hands of the nation while slowly driving them to suicide. He knew well why the imperial regulations against the growth of the poppy and the use of opium had been so fatally relaxed, and how it came about that his own beautiful province, in common with all the rest, had come to be so prolific in producing the poison. Himself a victim to the opium-habit, in the prime of his manhood a helpless slave to that which he detested and knew only too well was working his ruin, he had good reason to feel bitterly against the Western power but for whose action these things had never been. Is it strange that he should share the indignation of his fellow-countrymen in Canton, who, in a spirited paper denouncing the guilt of England, exclaimed—

"*If you wish to purify their crimes, all the fuel in the Empire will not suffice, nor would the vast ocean be enough to wash out our resentment.*"

# 5

# Dark Days in Shansi

HSI had been an opium-smoker about ten years when events began to transpire that were to change not only his entire future but the fortunes of the great province in which he lived. Up to that time, shut off completely from contact with the Western world, Shansi was about to become the scene of a tragedy that should command the attention of all civilised nations, an eventual outcome of which, however, should be deliverance and uplifting for the opium-smoking scholar and many others like him.

Fifteen years had now elapsed since the close of Britain's second war with China—years in which the rapidly-spreading opium-habit had wrought havoc with the old-existing order of things. Shansi had been going steadily down hill, and was ill-prepared for the calamity that was about to fall.

It was New Year's Eve in the scholar's home (1877–78), and never a sadder new year had dawned for Shansi. Bleak whistled the wintry blast over the desolate country. Wrapped in his wadded gown, thin, pale, and suffering, Hsi stood in the doorway of his outer court, looking down the village street. Snow lay deep on the black-roofed houses, and drifted against the long blank walls. Now and then a shivering figure, in garments all too few and thin, came into sight, or a passing neighbour stopped to salute the well-known scholar.

"Alas, Honourable Teacher Hsi, your sufferings too are great! What is to become of us this winter? Surely everyone must perish! Heaven no longer cares for men."

Little comfort could the scholar offer. And, as he turned away, his own heart echoed the sad question, "What is to become of us?" shuddering at the probable answer.

It was two or three years now since the drought had set in. At first people hoped for the best, and spoke of former seasons of scarcity that had soon passed away. Not until crop after crop had failed did the growing anxiety break out into painful distress. Then crowds flocked to the temples to entreat the Higher Powers. Theatricals were arranged, to propitiate hard-hearted gods, whose images were carried out into the open street and respectfully enthroned where the best view could be obtained of the stage. Processions were daily made to wayside altars and city shrines, led by Taoist devil-worshippers, frantic with excitement, or mediums under the influence of spirit-possession. At great inconvenience city gates were barred to shut out unpropitious influences from the south. Village elders gathered in little groups to devise plans for obtaining the longed-for showers. Men and lads wandered over the dried-up fields, whistling and calling to the winds for rain, scanning with anxious eyes the clear blue sky from which the clouds seemed gone for ever. But all without avail. Until at length famine—gaunt, relentless, awful—stared them in the face.

Hsi, in his well-built house, surrounded by the remains of former affluence, was not among the first to feel the pinch of poverty. True, his store of grain was less than formerly, and much money had gone to buy opium; but his family was small, and his wife a careful manager. He hoped with strict economy to be able to tide over the difficult time. With most of his neighbours, however, it was very different; and as winter drew on sad rumours began to reach him of the state of things in all the country round.

Soon he dreaded to go down the village street. Haggard, anxious faces met him at every turn. He could not speak to anyone without hearing heartrending stories of distress. Everywhere groups of people loitered idly about. Occupation they had none; for spinning-wheels were silent, household affairs at a standstill, and nothing could be done with fields as hard as iron and garners empty of grain. Beggars, foreseeing trouble, had vanished off the scene; and theatrical troupes had disappeared from the district.

Availing themselves of his position as a scholar, the village elders resorted to Hsi in their troubles. It was impossible any longer to pay taxes. Would he write a statement, on behalf of his neighbours, to the local mandarin? Everything that could be sold for food was gone. People were already living on coarse black millet bread, and suffering for lack of bedding and winter garments.

One day fresh rumours reached the scholar of excitement in the neighbouring town. A most unusual thing had happened. Was it a portent of still worse disaster? Suddenly, without any previous warning, two foreigners had appeared in Pingyang. Such a thing had only once before been heard of when, eight years previously, the English teacher, Williamson, and his friend passed through, staying only a night or two on the way. But these young men[1] were different. They wore Chinese dress; said they had come to learn the language; and were going to stay! Gradually it appeared that they also were teachers of a religion from England and had nothing to do with commerce or opium. Hsi, with others of the leading gentry, was displeased at their arrival at so critical a juncture, and was much relieved when they left the district, though he heard afterwards that they had taken up their abode at the capital of the province. He had not seen them, nor did he wish to do so. What could their coming mean but trouble? Surely there was evil enough abroad already, without further provoking the anger of Heaven.

A new religion indeed! Indignant, and yet interested in spite of himself, he sometimes could not help wondering what it could be about. Some teaching, not a pure system of ethics like Confucianism; not a philosophy like that of the Taoists; nor yet an idolatry such as the Buddhists brought—what then could it be? He heard that the foreigners had spoken about worshipping the one true God, unseen but everywhere present. But anyone with a moment's reflection could see that the Supreme Being was far too distant and exalted to be worshipped by common men. And as to His answering everybody's prayers, the idea was absurd! Even the local mandarin was too busy with matters of importance to be able to attend to personal complaints. The thing was self-evidently false and foolish.

And yet it could hardly be worse than the gross idolatry around him. Surely people would *now* begin to wake up to the falsity of the idols, from whom no answer came, in spite of all their prayers and pleadings and anguish of distress. It was amazing, the length to which credulity would go! He had seen his neighbours first fêting their gods, to try and please them; getting up theatricals for them, and spreading feasts; and then, when the drought still continued, and no signs appeared of coming showers, they had tumbled them unceremoniously out of the temples, and put them to bake and blister in the burning sun, that they might realise from experience the desperate condition of affairs, and in self-defence send the needed rain. But this too was without effect!

[1] Messrs. Turner and Drake, pioneers of the China Inland Mission.

What more proof could people want of the folly of making and worshipping idols?

Yet surely there must be Higher Powers? Gods that had made man, did they not pity him? He remembered the noble prayer of the Emperor Tao Kuang, when Peking was threatened with drought some tens of years before. With heart-searching and self-humiliation he, The One Man, had poured out his petitions before Heaven; and that very night the copious showers fell. But now, alas! the Emperor, as yet only a child, could not intercede for the nation in its extremity, and they were practically bereft of a high priest. Ah, if only it were true, as the foreigners declared, that the heart of the great God was full of love toward men, and that even common people might approach Him in prayer and be sure of His attention—what would he give for such a faith as that!

But too evidently there was no pity in that unresponsive Heaven. Month after month the agony had increased; and now the winter was again upon them, and millions were on the verge of starvation. In his own village, Hsi could number house after house, empty and deserted. Famine fever raged over the populous plain. Old people and children were dying off in thousands. Crowds of refugess'had left their homes to try and gain the more favoured regions of the south. And in many cases, despairing of relief, whole families had committed suicide rather than face the horrors of another winter. People hardly dared to enter forsaken houses now; it was so common to find them ghastly with the silent dead.

But worse than this were the tragedies, now become so common, in the lives of women, once happy and sheltered, in all parts of the province. Strangers from the south had come: men with carts going round from village to village. They seemed to have plenty of silver. It was young women and little girls they wanted. And soon the carts began to go away full. Young wives and mothers, girls, and little children disappeared in hundreds. Where they had gone, no one could tell. One thing only was certain: they would never come back.

And yet Hsi managed to live on and keep his home about him. When the winter was at its worst, just before the dawn of that terrible New Year, he heard that English missionaries from the capital had passed through the district on their way south. They could speak the language, and, when interrogated, told of the appalling condition of things all along the route they had travelled.[1] The barren country, swept by bleak, piercing winds, everywhere bore traces of the fate of famine-stricken multitudes. Men and women who had left their homes in search of food, fallen by the roadside, were frozen as they lay. Dogs preyed upon the dead, and were devoured in their turn by the living. In many places where, a few months before, the young men had been followed by crowds of starving people, wailing for bread, all was now silent and deserted, heaps of human bones and skulls alone revealing the horrors that had transpired. Cart-loads of women and girls were still met with, travelling south. And in some districts terrible tales were current about human flesh being in use as food.

Shudderingly the scholar listened to the story brought by the strangers, filling in many details from his own knowledge of the sufferings around his home where the famine was at its worst. All that they said was true, and far, far more. He was glad they did not seem to know everything. For in his neighbourhood not only the dead had been devoured for food. As the awful agony went on, parents had killed and eaten their own children, and even children their parents. In almost every village such things were happening, so that the wretched survivors scarcely dared

[1] "During that journey," wrote Mr. Turner, "we saw scenes that have left an indelible impression of horror on the mind. . . . We passed men, once strong and well dressed, staggering over the frozen ground with only a few rags to shield them from the piercing wind. Their feeble steps, emaciated bodies, and wild looks told only too plainly that they were about to spend their last night upon earth. As we passed along the road in the early morning we saw the victims of the preceding night lying dead and stiff where they fell. Upon that road we saw men writhing in the last agonies of death. No one pitied them; no one cared for them; such sights had long ago become too common. There were hundreds of corpses lying by the roadside. We saw them. Some had only just fallen; others had been there longer and were stripped of the rags that had covered them. As we drew nearer we saw hungry dogs prowling about, only waiting for one bolder than the rest to commence the attack. Many of the corpses were fearful to behold. Birds and dogs had been feasting upon them, and the soft parts of the body were all devoured. Others were mere skeletons, with here and there a piece of bleeding flesh. Men, women, and children were among the victims. Outside some of the cities we saw a heap of skulls, bones, rags, and pieces of human flesh; and very often, away across the open country, we saw numbers of corpses lying side by side, evidently the remains of wanderers, who, exhausted by their weary search after food, had huddled together to die. Families are broken up: the wife sold, the children sold or cast out on the mountain side to perish, while the men wander about in the vain search for food. The whole district through which we passed (three or four hundred miles) was in the same condition."

venture, unarmed, beyond their homesteads. In one place, not far away, five women had been seized and burned alive by the authorities, for killing and eating children they had kidnapped. Evidently the foreigners had not heard the worst.

But what was to be the end of these things? Surely it meant the extermination of the race![1] Seventy-five per cent. of the population had already perished. Unless Heaven intervened, who could survive? At times the scholar did not wonder when he heard prayers turn into curses, and the ceaseless groaning of the sufferers to their gods give place to bitterest maledictions.

Meanwhile he knew that the authorities were doing all they could to meet the crisis. Government relief was being distributed in the cities, and Hsi had even heard of foreigners at the capital giving away large sums of money sent from outside lands. But no such help had reached his district; and the scholar knew that in the year that opened upon such scenes of anguish, multitudes more must inevitably perish.

But there were things he did not know nor dream of. He did not know that the young English missionaries had safely reached the coast, after the perils of that awful journey; that their story had awakened deepest sympathy; that letters had been written home, and money telegraphed from England; that one of them was coming back, accompanying another, older missionary, with means to succour multitudes of the distressed; that already David Hill was on his way to Pingyang, and the time was drawing near when they should meet.

[1] The London *Times*, early in 1878, wrote as follows:

"It is stated on authority which cannot be questioned, that seventy millions of human beings are now starving in the famine-stricken provinces of North China. The imagination fails to cope with a calamity so gigantic. The inhabitants of the United Kingdom and the United States combined hardly number seventy millions. To think of the teeming populations of these lands, all crowded into an area very little greater than that of France, starving and eating earth, with no food to be had, and with no hope of succour, is enough to freeze the mind with horror."

# 6

# Light at Last

STILL the famine was at its height, when, one day in early
summer 1878, startling news reached the Western Chang
village. Foreigners were coming to Pingyang: coming not on a
passing visit, but actually to settle in the city! And, more wonderful still, they were coming not as merchants or speculators in
mines, but as doers of good deeds to distribute food and money
among the famine sufferers, and to preach a religion from the
West.

Great was the consternation that prevailed. Not among the
poorest of the people, for they were too suffering and imperilled
to care much, even about so unprecedented an event. Nor among
the official classes for the mandarins were glad to welcome anyone with power to help. But in scholarly circles, and among the
gentry who were still able to hold their heads above water, there
was a good deal of indignation against the authorities for allowing
foreigners to take up their abode in the city.

Meanwhile the friendly, yellow-robed priests, in the Temple of
the Iron Buddha, were persuaded to give the strangers accommodation. There were a number of unused apartments within the
precincts of the temple, and the most suitable of these were slightly
swept and garnished, for the reception of Mr. Li and Mr. Teh.
In the end of the month of May they arrived; and people were
relieved to find that they were dressed in civilised, that is to say
Chinese garments, and had heads properly shaved, and hair
plaited behind in the becoming queue. The teacher Li (Mr. Hill)
seemed the older of the two, and had the conversation and
manners of a gentleman, through long residence in the country.
Mr. Teh (Turner), his companion, had been seen before in the
city. He also was familiar with the usages of polite society, and
seemed possessed of energy and ability. They were like elder and
younger brothers in their relationship to one another, and were
never heard to quarrel. So far so good. But they must be carefully
watched.

Their activity, at any rate, was praiseworthy. They spared no
pains in searching out the most needy people, and were prompt,

generous, and systematic in their distribution of relief. They were inoffensive also in their conduct towards the priests of the Iron Buddha, neither insulting the gods not profaning sacred buildings. In fact they were constantly occupied in deeds of mercy, and seemed to live virtuous lives, neither indulging in wine nor tobacco. Of course many rumours were afloat as to their ultimate motives in coming to Pingyang, and giving away so much money. It certainly was incomprehensible! Some said they were fools; some vowed they were knaves, enriching themselves out of the funds they disbursed. Time alone could prove; and meanwhile they were undoubtedly rescuing hundreds of people who must otherwise have perished.

Before long, the fame of the strangers began to reach the scholar Hsi, in his village home, ten miles from the city. Sick, sorrowful, and impoverished, the once proud Confucianist had still enough of the old spirit left, hotly to resent the idea of foreigners coming to his very doors, to pry out the condition of his people, and cast over them their seductive spells. Had they not done harm enough already, with their wars and their opium? What were they wanting now, when money was no longer in the question, unless it were to bewitch people's hearts, and take the whole country for themselves? He, for one, had no curiosity to see the strangers, nor would he receive their pauperising gifts. Had he been in authority, they would never have been able to settle in the province at all. What good could come of their so-called religious teachings? By far the safest policy was to keep them at arm's length.

Too busy to care much as to what reports were being spread about them, Mr. Hill and Mr. Turner worked on through the long hot summer days, praying for rain to come, and set a limit to the sufferings of the people. The mandarins of the district were grateful and friendly, doing all in their power to help the missionaries, while leaving them a free hand. Temples were everywhere put at their disposal, and lists given them of the families in each village they took up. These were then personally visited, the missionaries going from house to house, sometimes giving away tickets, which the people carried to the temple to be cashed, and sometimes making careful notes and forwarding the money through the headman of the neighbourhood. In one case, when the silver was sent to a more distant village in this way, the messenger came back to return the shares of no fewer than twenty people who had died of starvation in the few days since the lists had been made out.

Heartrending scenes were constantly witnessed as the missionaries went about their difficult work. People were reduced to living on the bark of trees, and chaff cut up and boiled with weeds, without even salt to make it more palatable. In some places they were making cakes out of a soft stone, ground to powder, mixed with millet husks and water, and baked in the embers of whatever fuel they could find. Many haggard faces had become strangely dark, almost black, through feeding upon such horrible concoctions, and severe disorders supervened in those who managed to survive.

Human flesh, also, was still being eaten in the neighbourhood of Pingyang. In some places it was even publicly exposed for sale. So terrible was the condition of things, that people dared not go beyond their own towns and villages, for fear of being hunted down for food, and any who wished to secure their dead from such a fate, had to wall up the corpses in strongly-built houses over which they could keep guard. But a general impression seemed to prevail that those who fell so low as to feed upon human flesh could not long survive. Whether from physical or mental causes, certain it was that death soon closed the scene, and this was regarded as sufficient condemnation of the revolting practice.

Many lives were lost in these dreadful days through the attacks of wolves, grown desperate with famine. Scarcely a village was without experiences of their ferocity. In open daylight they would spring upon children, and even grown-up people, and devour them within sight of horrified onlookers. Mr. Hill was one day passing through a village and noticed traces of blood that seemed quite recent. Upon inquiring the cause, he was told that a girl of eighteen, walking down the street with an older woman, had just been dragged away and torn to pieces by a wolf in the presence of her neighbours, who could do nothing to save her. Sad comment upon the enfeebled condition of whole communities.

Mr. Hill himself almost lost his life on one occasion through a wolf. He was lying awake one night, in his gloomy quarters in the temple, tired after a long day's work, when he heard a low, sad sound that immediately attracted his attention. Quick to respond to any cry of need, he sat up and listened, wondering who could be outside at midnight. The piteous moaning was unmistakable. Someone must have fallen down at the door to die. Sights and sounds of sorrow, though so common all round him, never became matters of indifference to that Christ-filled heart. He was up at once, and made his way across the courtyard to the great doors of the temple, from which the sounds had come. He intended to go out and call the stranger in, but to his surprise the door was shut and fastened. One of the priests had evidently locked it, and taken the key away. Not hearing the sounds any longer, Mr. Hill went back to rest. In the morning, upon inquiry outside as to who had been moaning during the night, he learned that a great wolf had been prowling about the doors of the temple in search of prey.

During the summer the mandarins, finding Mr. Hill would prefer it, arranged for him to rent a house of his own in a quiet part of the city, and he no longer had to be guest in the Temple of the Iron Buddha. Thankful for the change, he and Mr. Turner set up housekeeping for themselves in the commodious premises put at their disposal, and thus established the first Christian home, the first mission-house and station in southern Shansi. From that simple beginning how much was to grow!

Picture a quiet street, a wide entrance, leading into a good-sized courtyard, square, and paved with stones. Round the four sides of the court, well-built rooms open on a raised pathway, over which the projecting roofs are supported by a row of wooden pillars. The whole frontage, consisting of woodwork, is elaborately carved and ornamented, right up to the roofs. Occupying the north end is a large apartment used as a chapel, and the handsome reception-room or guest-hall is on the east. From the first courtyard enter a second, through an ornamental doorway. It is the same in size, shape, and arrangement, only a low-roofed second story gives additional accommodation, and a quaint verandah, on which the doors of the upper chambers open, adds artistic effect.

Lodged in one of the empty rooms on the back courtyard, Mr. Hill's time was mostly spent out-of-doors, in caring for the distressed; or in the guest-hall, receiving interested visitors, many of whom came for medical help. Probably one of the upstairs rooms was set apart as a place for quiet waiting upon God, and very earnest were the prayers that went up during those summer days for a plentiful rain upon the stricken land.

Already the drought had lasted three, and in some places four years, and it almost seemed as though it never could rain again. But as summer wore on, great clouds began to gather, and at length all over northern China the saving showers fell. Then the despairing survivors of those terrible years began to pluck up heart once more, and the missionaries redoubled their efforts, encouraging the people, and providing them with money for grain, that they might sow their fields and take advantage of the promise of better days.

But in many places even when the rain did come, it brought little or no relief, for men were too feeble to put the seed into the ground; ploughs were no use without animals to draw them; and sometimes whole families had died out entirely, leaving the land without owners, and the villages without inhabitants. In one hamlet no fewer than seventeen families had become extinct, and out of fourteen hundred (Chinese) acres belonging to the village, only a little over a hundred could be put under cultivation when the rain came. For the rest the people had no seed, and no strength to sow it even if it had been given them. The rain, however, saved the province. Wealthier people put in their crops, and the poor had more wild herbs, grass, and weeds to mix with the bark and roots they were able to gather. They were a long way still from the edge of the wood; but the worst of the famine was over; and gradually hope returned to many a broken spirit.

# 7

# Fishers of Men

IT was Christmas Day in the great city of Taiyüan; the first
Christmas ever kept in Shansi. True, there had been a solitary
Englishman in the city the year before (1877),[1] but the famine was
then at its height, the missionary was all alone, and amid the
pressure of his difficult work Christmas passed almost unnoticed.

But now a change had come with brighter days. The famine
was passing away, and a new era had dawned for Shansi. Quite a
little community replaced the solitary worker; and in the reception-room of one of the mission houses a family party gathered to
celebrate the Christmas season. Mr. Richards was there with his
bride; the lonely days over in which he had held the fort single-
handed at Taiyüan. Turner and James were there, who two years
previously had been the first Protestant missionaries to settle in
the province. David Hill had come up from Pingyang. And the
latest reinforcements were a party of ladies, including Mrs.
Hudson Taylor, who had recently arrived from England.

Far from home and loved ones, buried deep in the heart of
China, this little pioneer band represented a new movement, then
just commencing, for the evangelisation of the great interior—
the nine important provinces still without the Gospel. Shansi was
the first of these to be entered by women-workers; and that group
of English ladies, wearing Chinese dress, and already quite at
home among the women of the capital, was full of significance
and promise.

Uppermost in all their thoughts that Christmastide was one
supreme question: how to accomplish the task they had undertaken; how to carry the Gospel to every creature in Shansi? They
were a little company for so great a work. Eighty populous
counties, with as many governing cities and numberless towns
and villages, lay around them, waiting for the light. How were
they to reach the millions of so large a district, and make known
everywhere the message they had come to bring?

One outcome of their conference and prayers was the preparation of a large supply of books and tracts specially suited for

[1] Mr. Timothy Richards, of the Baptist Mission.

distribution in Shansi. The missionaries were few, and could not possibly go everywhere, but they could visit the important cities, the governing centres of all the eighty districts, and leave in them these permanent witnesses for the truth. So Mr. Richards took the district north of the capital, and the China Inland Mission went south, and in every county town throughout the province they distributed Christian literature from house to house, each pamphlet stamped with the address of the nearest place at which further information could be gained.

The blessing of God rested upon this systematic effort to spread a knowledge of the Gospel. The Holy Spirit, in many instances, followed the Word with His own life-giving power, and the missionaries were cheered by finding fruit after many days.

Passing down a street in the city of Pingyang a few months later, Mr. Hill met an old man, fully seventy years of age, carrying his bedding on his back and looking inquiringly about him.

"Sir," said he, accosting Mr. Hill, "can you tell me where a teacher lives of the name of Teh? I have come twenty miles to-day to seek him."

"Come with me," was the friendly reply, "and I will take you to the house. Mr. Teh and I live together."

Seated in the guest-hall, over a refreshing cup of tea, the missionaries soon learned the old man's story. He had come across a tract, some time before, telling of a strange new doctrine that had interested him greatly. The essay had one fault, however; it was far too short. But on the back of it he saw a sentence, to the effect that anyone wishing to learn more of the Christian religion was invited to go into the city to the house of Mr. Teh, who would be happy to give the fullest instruction. So he had rolled up his bedding, and made his way twenty miles into the city to seek for fuller light.

Needless to say, he met with a cordial welcome. For several days he stayed in Mr. Hill's house, and in many long conversations, they put before him simply and fully the way of salvation in Christ. Full of joy the old man went back to his home, with a fresh supply of books, leaving behind him hearts cheered and thankful.

In another place a younger man was arrested by a street tract pasted upon a blank wall in the city. He read it; wanted to learn more about the doctrines it taught; noticed the same invitation to the house of the teacher Teh, and went at once to find him

out. What was his surprise, when Mr. Teh appeared, to see that
he was a foreigner! He had not thought of that. However, he
was deeply interested in the Gospel, and went home declaring
himself a Christian.

In a remote and lonely village another man was found daily
worshipping God. He had never seen a missionary, nor met a
fellow-believer; but from books and tracts he had gained a considerable knowledge of the truth, and morning and evening he
knelt down in his house to pray in the name of Jesus, whom he
had learned to trust.

As time went on, Mr. Hill was increasingly possessed by the
conviction that something further should be done to reach the
*literati* of the province, the proud Confucian scholars, in their
strong antipathy to Christian truth. Frequently meeting these
men, he could not but be struck by their contemptuous attitude
toward the Gospel, their hatred of foreigners, and their prejudice
against missionary work. His whole heart went out to them in
genuine sympathy. He saw all the power that such men could be
if only laid hold upon by Christ. He longed to win them to at
any rate a fair consideration of Christianity, and pondered much
how this could best be done.

At last the thought came to him—why not offer prizes for first-
class literary essays upon Christian themes? Only scholars could
compete, and the study necessary for such writing would bring
their minds under the influence of the Gospel. With the instinct
of a true "fisher of men," David Hill saw at once the value of the
idea, and decided to act upon it. He knew that in the early
autumn, the great triennial examination would be held at the
capital of the province, and that thousands of scholars, holding
their first degree, would be going up to compete for the second—
corresponding to our Master of Arts. What an opportunity! It
must not be lost.

And so, long before the scholars began to start for the capital,
the eager missionary went on ahead to make all arrangements for
carrying out his project. With the help of his friend Mr. Timothy
Richards, who was heartily in favour of the plan, several tracts
were carefully prepared, to accompany the prospectus offering
four valuable prizes for the best essays upon given subjects taken
from the Christian classics—the Scriptures.

In the middle of the eighth month, when the moon was full
(September, 1879), the graduates began to gather from every

county in the province: the very flower of the intellectual life of Shansi; men who were everywhere looked up to as the natural leaders of thought and action, and future rulers among the people. The ranks of the competitors were markedly thinned by the sufferings of the recent famine. Still, six or seven thousand students were enrolled, and entered the examination hall for their searching test.

Three days later, when the doors were opened and the weary scholars trooped out, thankful to be through with the first part of their examination, they were met at the great gateway by a few foreigners in Chinese dress, who rapidly handed to each man a packet containing papers of some sort. The surprised scholars received them courteously, and some even seemed pleased and friendly.

Thousands of books and tracts were thus put into the hands of the men the missionaries were most anxious to reach. On the cover of one of the pamphlets was printed a map of the world; and all were stamped with the indication that further literature could be obtained from any of the missionaries whose addresses were given, who would welcome visits from the graduates.

Little did those Confucian gentlemen guess the hope and longing hidden by the quiet exterior of the men who handed them those books. Much prayer had been made by the missionaries that God would, through this effort, draw to Himself some, whom He purposed not only to save, but to use in the salvation of others. Eagerly they scanned the faces of the students as they hurried by: strong faces, clever faces, some thoughtful and refined, some coarse and heavy, many pale and tired with the strain they had been through, some thin and worn from the distress of famine. If one seemed more courteous than another, would not the missionary's heart throb with sudden hope. But though many of the students showed signs of interest, and not a few came to inquire more about the truth, and held long conversations with the missionaries, the man in whom, especially, those prayers were to be answered did not come out of the great examination hall that day.

For there was one Confucian scholar, in his home in the south of the province, who had not come up at all to the triennial examination. His interest in literary studies had faded as the years went on. Opium had enslaved him; sickness and trouble of mind robbed life of its spring; famine had brought him to poverty, and ignorance walled him in with an impassable barrier of prejudice. No man in all the province at that time seemed more beyond the reach of the Gospel than Hsi of the Western Chang village. He had given up the search for light and truth that had so impelled him in earlier days. He had not the slightest desire to acquaint himself with the new religion, though brought to his very doors. Foreigners and everything connected with them stirred his deepest animosity. He really believed the dreadful things that were said about them, and thought that even to have received help at their hands in the famine was a thing to be ashamed of. Had he met the missionaries at the entrance of the examination hall, he would probably have passed them by with contempt, and certainly one glance at his hard, proud face, with its too evident traces of opium, would have made them turn sadly away, hopeless at any rate of him.

Yet that very man, out of all the thousands of scholars in Shansi, was the one whom God purposed to save and bless. Whether Hsi came up to the examination or not, the net cast there so skilfully was to draw him in; for God has ways of working beyond our ken, and with Him nothing shall be impossible.

# 8

# Drawing in the Net

THE great examination was over, and thousands of scholars, successful and unsuccessful, were travelling back to their homes throughout the province of Shansi. Along the way, respectful congratulations greeted the new M.A.'s, pleasantly anticipating the ovations that awaited them in their native places, where they soon would be the heroes of the hour.

Among the little companies travelling southward, some were making their way over the hills to the neighbourhood of Ping-yang, carrying tidings of all that had transpired at the capital; of who had passed and who had failed; and especially of the unprecedented action of the foreigners in offering valuable money prizes to be competed for by literary men. Speculation was rife as to what possible object the missionaries could have in view. The prizes promised amounted to scores of *taels*.[1] What could they be expecting to gain in return? Surely there must be some sinister motive; some trap laid for the unwary.

Among the more cautious of the graduates, not a few were ready to warn their companions of the extraordinary power the foreigners undoubtedly possessed. There was no fathoming their motives. It was well known that they could cast spells over people in the most mysterious ways, and bewitch men with a glance. Even their books carried a peculiar odour,[2] no doubt some medicinal ingredient of potent influence. A wise man could not do better than avoid all contact with them, and thereby the common people would be warned to keep out of their way. But to others, more daring spirits, the opportunity of winning thirty ounces of silver for writing a single essay seemed a chance not to be lightly despised. It was too good to lose. For whatever might be wrong with the foreigner, his silver at any rate was above suspicion, and his word was as good as his bond. In spite, therefore, of risks, scores of men made up their minds to go in for the competition.

[1] A *tael* = 1⅓ ounces of silver.
[2] Due to the oil with which our printer's ink is mixed. The Chinese only print with Indian ink and water.

Great excitement prevailed in many a county town and village
as the scholars began to reach their homes, and the papers distributed by the foreigners were spread out for inspection, fathers
and brothers gathering round with interest and surprise. In the
Western Chang village, at the foot of the mountains, this was
especially the case. One of Hsi's elder brothers had come back
from the city, full of the strange news.

"Old-Four, Old-Four,"[1] he cries, "where are you? Just come
and look at this. You are the man for literary essays. No one
better! Here's your chance; if you are not afraid."

"What is it?" responds the scholar, coming slowly out of the
inner room, strong with the fumes of opium. "What's up now?
Have you heard news of the examination at the capital?"

"News—yes, indeed! Several of the fellows have returned,
with degrees, as proud as can be. But look at these papers they
have brought. Some announcement by the foreigner Li of
Pingyang. Read it out, and let us hear what you think of it."

So, to the wondering group of neighbours who had crowded
in, the scholar reads in loud, impressive tones:

## NOTICE

Wishing to make plain the knowledge of the Heavenly Way, I have determined to propound six theses,[2] and respectfully invite the scholars of Shansi
to express their sentiments concerning them, and, treating each one separately,
to write essays upon them.[3]

The six theses are as follows:[4]

*The Source of True Doctrine, or the Right Way*. The great origin of the Right
Way is said (by Chinese sages) to be from Heaven. The sages of antiquity,
both in China and in the West, "inquired into the lucid decrees of Heaven."
But the tradition of the Right Way was not transmitted. Later, ancients composed scriptures and precepts, supplementing books of ceremony and music.
They spoke of transmigration, rewards, immortality, and so forth. Now again
one meets with those who proclaim a Right Way.[5] If one inquires whether it
is from Heaven, or of men, what definite evidence is there to decide its source?

[1] A familiar way of addressing the fourth son in a family.

[2] There were four prizes offered, the first amounting to thirty taels, then
about seven guineas.

[3] A packet of Christian books and tracts was supplied with each copy of the
theses, so that the subjects might be studied.

[4] The wording of the theses may seem peculiar. They were purposely expressed in as Chinese a form as possible, in order to commend them to Confucian readers.

[5] Referring to the preaching of missionaries.

*The Regulation of the Heart.* The Confucianist desires to make his faults few; the Buddhist to conquer his passions; and the Taoist seeks to obtain the elixir of immortality. The Mohammedan acknowledges only one God. And all attach supreme importance to rectifying the heart. But what is High Heaven's method for the Regulation of the Heart?

*On Prayer.* Man's virtue is limited; the grace of Heaven is infinite. How should those who wish to receive the favour of Heaven, sincerely seek that they may obtain it, and avoid calamity?

*Rewards and Punishments.* That good is to be rewarded and evil punished is a great principle with wise rulers. God loves all men; and, to lead into the way of virtue, rewards and punishes the people of every age. How does He offer happiness in place of retribution, in order to lead men to avoid the sufferings of hell and gain the blessedness of heaven?

*Images of the Gods.* Is it permissible that those who worship the Supreme Ruler and follow the right way of Yao and Shun (ancient Chinese heroes) should bow down before idols?

*On Opium.* Those who wish to see the opium evil conquered, and thus to carry out the wise desires of the Government, know well the injury caused by this drug. What good methods are there for stopping the cultivation of opium, restricting its use, and curing the craving it causes?

The 5th year of the reign of Kwang Hsü, the 8th month and the 15th day. The English missionary Li issues this.

Many were the exclamations and comments that accompanied the reading, the last subject especially calling forth emphatic approval.

"That's the theme for you, Elder Brother," some one suggests, mischievously.

"Yes, but why not write on more than one? You have ability. Are there not four prizes? Write one essay for yourself and one for me, Honourable Nephew."

"And for me, Great-Uncle," put in another. "To write an essay and win a prize cannot surely lead anyone astray."

"It certainly does seem a capital chance to make money out of the foreigners, Brother," said the man who had brought the papers. "But what do you think about their magic arts? The whole affair is curious. Are you not afraid of being bewitched, if you have anything at all to do with them?"

The younger man thought long and carefully, and looked through the papers again and again. There must be something uncanny behind it all; but for the life of him he could not make out what it was. The subjects seemed natural, and properly worded, and they were certainly full of interest. Mr. Li, the foreigner, was well known by reputation, living in the city only ten miles away. To be sure, the reports about him were strangely conflicting. Some maintained that he was a doer of good deeds and a man of great benevolence, while others could find no words strong enough in which to express a contrary opinion. But in any case there would be no occasion to come into personal contact with the foreigner. To study and write quietly in one's own room could surely do no harm. So, by degrees, Hsi made up his mind that he would go in for the competition, and at the same time do his neighbours a good turn by writing four essays instead of one reserving, of course, the best for himself.

This determination reached, Hsi had to begin work in real earnest, reading up the literature that accompanied the theses. Something of the old scholarly enthusiasm seemed to return to him that autumn evening, and, even in spite of himself, as he read on, he could not help being interested. Had he met with such teachings long before, how different his life might have been. But now it was too late to change, even if the new doctrine were true. After all, it was easy enough to talk about the Right Way and the Regulation of the Heart; but, practically, who could attain it? Prayer might be right enough for those who had the favour of the gods: they might be able to avoid hell and aspire to the happiness of heaven; but what could he, a helpless opium-smoker, expect—in this life or the next? As to any power that could make it possible for a man to break off opium and begin life afresh—if such a power existed—neither he nor anyone else had ever heard of it.

But sometimes, as he wrote his essays, chiefly at night, because the house was still, he seemed to have a sense of some unusual Presence; and several times he was conscious of a strange, bright light, that came distinctly from above and rested over the doorway of his room.

"See," whispered his wife, "the gods have sent you a token! Certainly you are to win the prize."

"Yes," thought the preoccupied scholar, "it must be a sign from the gods."

But afterwards he used to say, on the rare occasions when he alluded to this experience: "It must have been a Divine intimation of the enlightenment of the Holy Spirit, that so soon was to come from above."

Meanwhile Mr. David Hill had returned to his home at Pingyang, and was busy with arrangements for awarding the promised prizes. A hundred and twenty essays had been sent in from all parts of the province. These were first read and arranged by competent native scholars, who carefully selected the best, which were then submitted to Mr. Hill and Mr. Richards, who awarded the prizes. When the final results were declared, great was the delight of Hsi and his friends to find that his essays had been successful. Under different names, he had carried off three out of the four prizes.

The next step, of course, was to go to Pingyang for the money; and this, though apparently simple enough, was the cause of much anxiety in the family of the successful scholar. So far, no serious risk had been run, for there had been no actual contact with the foreigner; but to go in person to his house, and receive the money from his hand, was a very different matter. That, Hsi determined he could not and would not do, if it could possibly be avoided. The only way was to get a substitute, and a suitable one was soon forthcoming in the person of his wife's brother, who was a daring sort of fellow and quite willing to undertake the job.

But then a new difficulty arose. The young man was ready enough to go and get the money, but whether he would be equally willing to transfer it to the rightful owner seemed more than doubtful. So an arrangement was come to that, as the sum was considerable, Hsi should go with him to the city, and wait outside the house while he obtained the silver; and that then they should take it to the silversmith's together, and have it weighed and examined; by which means Hsi hoped to get into his own hands at any rate the larger portion.

Accordingly the two men travelled into Pingyang, half a day's journey over the plain; and Liang, the brother, presented himself at the foreigner's house. Mr. Hill, well pleased to hear that the prize-winner had come, went out to receive him courteously. He had been interested in the successful essay, and desired to obtain an interview with the writer. But as soon as he saw the young countryman, he knew there must be some mistake.

"Have I the honour of addressing the distinguished scholar Hsi?" he inquired kindly.

"No, sir," replied the young man; "my unworthy name is Liang. I have come on behalf of my elder brother to receive the honorarium bestowed on his paltry composition."

"Sir," was the unexpected reply, "the silver can only be given into the hands of the gifted writer himself. I fear it will be necessary to trouble him to come in person."

This being final, the only way out of the difficulty was to inform Hsi, who was not far away, and to convince him that he must go himself if he wanted the money. Very reluctantly the scholar yielded, and followed his guide to the house in the quiet street. A handsome doorway entered a spacious porch, from which a view could be obtained of the courtyard beyond. Seeing nothing to arouse his fears, Hsi ventured in, and called for the gatekeeper, when, to his immense relief, a pleasant-looking Chinese appeared. Bowing politely, Hsi inquired his name.

"My unworthy name is Sung," replied the old gentleman, who was Mr. Hill's first convert and devoted friend. "But forgive me; I have not yet inquired your honourable title."

"My insignificant name is Hsi," replied the guest. "May I hope for the honour of an interview with the English teacher Li?"

"Mr. Hill will be delighted, sir. He is anxiously awaiting your coming. Pray enter the guest-hall and drink tea."

A good deal reassured by the presence of Sung, and one or two other Chinese who dropped in, Hsi began to look about him, and ask a few questions as to the foreigner and his manner of life, keeping an eye on the door, however, by which Mr. Hill must appear.

"Are you not afraid, old teacher Sung, to be so much in company with the foreigner, by day and by night?"

"Why, sir, what should I fear?" was the smiling reply. "Do you see anything alarming, or feel conscious of magical influences? I see you do not venture to drink our tea. But indeed, sir, such fears are ungrounded."

Annoyed at being caught, Hsi lifted the cup to his lips, bowing politely; but nothing would have induced him to drink a drop of the foreigner's tea. Still things were not so bad as he had expected. He must be on his guard, however, and make his escape at the first opportunity.

Presently, steps approaching caught his alert attention. A rather tall, slender man, in Chinese dress, entered the room. Hsi heard someone say:

"The teacher Li."

He rose at once, and met the stranger in the middle of the room with a profound bow, which gave him time to notice the blue cotton gown, white calico socks, and native shoes worn by the missionary; but for a moment he dared not raise his eyes to the face he almost dreaded to see.

Mr. Hill, returning his salutation, constrained him to occupy the place of honour, taking himself a lower seat at the opposite side of the table. The pleasant voice was prepossessing; and as the missionary turned to pour out fresh tea for his guest, Hsi at length looked up to take him in with one swift, searching glance.

How much may be compressed into a moment. A whole lifetime of prejudice and suspicion melted away from that proud, cold heart, like snow before the sunshine, with just one look into the quiet, radiant face of David Hill. Years afterwards, Hsi said of that moment:

"One look, one word, it was enough. As daylight banished darkness, so did Mr. Hill's presence dissipate all the idle rumours I had heard. All sense of fear was gone; my mind was at rest. I beheld his kindly eye, and remembered the words of Mencius: 'If a man's heart is not right, his eye will certainly bespeak it.' That face told me I was in the presence of a true, good man."

So, after weary years, those two were brought to meet. Side by side they sat at last: the Confucianist, disarmed of all antagonism, friendly and satisfied; the missionary, his whole heart filled with sympathy and longing for the soul he had come so far to bless. "God's clocks keep perfect time." Through all the years, the moment had been fixed. For that hopeless, opium-smoking Chinese, life would never be the same again; and for David Hill, to all eternity a star of singular brightness lit up the crown that he should lay at the Master's feet.

Kindly and courteously the missionary complimented his guest upon the admirable essay that had won the prize, saying that some learned scholars at the capital had seen the paper and commended it highly. Tea having been drunk, the silver was produced and handed to Hsi, who received it with many polite protestations of his unworthiness. As soon as the money was in his possession he felt impelled to go, and the thought flashed through his mind:

"Perhaps, after all, this foreigner is just bewitching me! Better leave at once and see him no more."

Noticing his uneasiness, Mr. Hill made no effort to detain him. He was far too wise to be in any hurry. Letting him have plenty of line, he bade him a friendly farewell, and said nothing about meeting again.

Greatly pleased, Hsi went home with the silver. Thirty taels was a small fortune in those hard times. His wife and family were delighted to find that he had succeeded in getting the money and come back none the worse. And there, for the time being, the matter rested.

# 9

# The Living Christ

A FEW days passed, in which Mr. Hill did nothing further, though he waited much upon God. And then, one sunny morning, a stranger arrived at the Western Chang village, asking for Mr. Hsi. Upon going out to meet him, the scholar to his surprise found Sung, with a message from the missionary, who desired to see him on important business. With characteristic promptitude Hsi started at once. The invitation pleased him; and this time he felt no fear. After apologising for troubling him to come in to the city, Mr. Hill opened the subject by saying:

"I have a favour to ask of you, Mr. Hsi. I am needing scholarly assistance. Will you come and help me in my work?"

"Sir," replied the amazed Confucianist, "I fear I have no understanding of foreign matters."

"It is not in foreign matters that I seek your help," returned the missionary, smiling. "I want to have essays written. Can you do that?"

The visitor bowed assent.

"I want help in studying the classics and other books. In a word, I want you to be my teacher. Can you come to me in this capacity, Mr. Hsi?"

"Certainly," replied the gratified scholar. "That office I will gladly undertake."

Picture then this proud Confucianist, this opium-smoking scholar, in middle life, with all his sad, dark past, his heart hunger, his disappointed ambitions, his bondage to sin, brought near to Christ, the living Christ, for the first time. Thoroughly sickened with self and disillusioned with the world, he is at last face to face with Truth as it is in Jesus. In his hand he holds the Word of God, and before his eyes from day to day he has its best exponent.

From the commencement, the quiet, happy life of that Christian home made a profound impression upon Hsi. Unobtrusively, he noticed all that was taking place with searching keenness. Privacy is rarely to be secured in a Chinese *ménage*, and the life led by Mr. Hill at Pingyang was entirely Chinese in this respect.

Whether alone in prayer, or occupied in preaching; whether conducting daily worship, or Sunday services; reading and studying,
or preparing books and tracts; taking his meals with chopsticks
in Chinese style; caring for opium patients; writing letters;
attending to housekeeping; or receiving his guests; the missionary
was ever under the observation of his silent, courteous, but
watchful teacher, who lost no opportunity of forming his own
conclusions.

Hsi did not join the household at morning prayers or evening
worship. He had no desire to be identified with the little company
of his fellow-townsmen, mostly illiterate people, who were
already enrolled as Christians or inquirers. When not studying
with Mr. Hill, or conversing with gentlemen who visited the
guest-hall, he spent most of his time alone, smoking or reading in
his own room on the front courtyard. And all the while, how
little he suspected the eagerness with which his missionary friend
was watching him.

But though he prayed much, the missionary was wise enough
to say but little. He trusted the power of another Voice that he
knew was speaking to the heart of the proud Confucianist in those
days. Upon the table in Hsi's little room lay a copy of the New
Testament. It was but natural that he should keep it there, for to
that book Mr. Hill invariably turned during study hours, and the
teacher needed to make sure beforehand of any doubtful characters. But was it this necessity that led him to take up the book
so often? Was it to refresh his memory only, he would pore
over its contents for hours, losing all count of time as he slowly
turned the pages? No: it had become more than a book to him;
it was a revelation, telling him all his heart for long years had
hungered to know.

Gradually, as he read, the life of Jesus seemed to grow more
real and full of interest and wonder, and he began to understand
that this mighty Saviour was no mere man, as he had once
imagined, but God, the very God, taking upon Him mortal flesh.
Doubts and difficulties were lost sight of. The old, unquenchable
desire for better things, for deliverance from sin, self, and the fear
of death, for light upon the dim, mysterious future, came back
upon him as in earlier years. And yet the burden of his guilt,
the torment of an accusing conscience, and bondage to the
opium-habit he loathed but could not conquer, grew more and
more intolerable.

At last, the consciousness of his unworthiness became so over-whelming that he could bear it no longer, and placing the book reverently before him, he fell upon his knees on the ground, and so with many tears followed the sacred story. It was beginning then to dawn upon his soul that this wonderful, divine, yet human Sufferer, in all the anguish of His bitter cross and shame, had something personally to do with *him*, with *his* sin and sorrow and need.

And so, upon his knees, the once proud, self-satisfied Con-fucianist read on, until he came to "the place called Gethsemane," and the God man, alone, in that hour of His supreme agony at midnight in the garden. Then the fountains of his long-sealed heart were broken up. The very presence of God overshadowed him. In the silence he seemed to hear the Saviour's cry—"My soul is exceeding sorrowful, even unto death": and into his heart there came the wonderful realisation—"He loved me, and gave Himself for me." Then, suddenly, as he himself records, the Holy Spirit influenced his soul, and "with tears that flowed and would not cease" he bowed and yielded himself, unreservedly, to the world's Redeemer, as his Saviour and his God.

Words can tell no more. The mighty miracle was done. The living Christ had come, Himself, into that silent room. There, all alone, the stricken soul, with eager faith, had touched the hem of his garment, and straightway was made whole.

"With tears that flowed and would not cease," the pardoned, renewed, rejoicing man knelt there before his Lord. Time, place, circumstance, were all forgotten. He was alone with God.

Then, gradually, there rose upon his soul another supreme revelation. As to Saul of Tarsus, long ago, Jesus Himself was revealed from heaven; a Light above the brightness of the sun, blinding him thereafter to all other, lesser lights; so to this man, in the first hour of his new-born life, came the vision of the risen Christ. It was not that he saw a visible form or heard an actual voice, but, alone in that quiet room, the living, present, personal Jesus was so wonderfully revealed to him by the Holy Ghost, that he was ever afterwards as one who had seen the Lord. Silently, and with deep solemnity, the very presence of the living Christ overwhelmed his soul. He saw Him then, not only as his Saviour, but as his absolute Owner, his Master, his Lord. And to the first glad, wondering consciousness—He has redeemed me, succeeded the deeper, more adoring conviction—He has enthralled me: I am for ever His.

There, then, let us pause and leave him. The place whereon we stand is holy ground.

So real and wonderful was the experience in the life of Mr. Hsi that, years afterwards, those who knew him best used at times to be quite solemnised by a sense of the reality to him of the Heavenly Vision. "The more one saw of him," writes his most intimate friend,[1] "the more one felt that Christ had taken possession of his life—the real Christ, the living Christ. Nothing else, nothing less, could have accounted for the change that came over him from that hour. For he was a strong man, and such a typical Confucianist, full of the pride and prejudice of his race, and with a natural contempt for the whole form of our religion and the 'foolishness' of the Cross. But the living, present, personal Christ, revealed by the power of the Holy Ghost, will break any man down. This was the root of the whole matter with Mr. Hsi: the great reality of all his after life. No amount of argument or education could ever have brought about that change. It was just one vision of the living Christ—and down he went; melted in a moment; to become, oh, such a fusil Christian! Yes, melted to the very core, and recast in Christ's own mould."

> "A Man of Sorrows, of toil and tears,
>   An outcast Man and a lonely;
> But He looked on me, and through endless years
>   Him must I love—Him only.
>
> And I would abide where He abode,
>   And follow His steps for ever;
> His people my people, His God my God,
>   In the land beyond the river.
>
> And where He died would I also die,
>   For dearer a grave beside Him,
> Than a kingly place amongst living men,
>   The place which they denied Him."

[1] Mr. D. E. Hoste, of the China Inland Mission.

# 10

# Stronger than all the Power of the Enemy

WONDERFUL indeed was the change that had come over life, brightening everything with fresh hope and gladness, for the man who left his little room that autumn evening, a new creature in Christ Jesus. In the first wondering joy of salvation, the impulse was strong upon him to find someone who could understand, to whom he might speak of what Jesus had done for his soul. How altered were his feelings toward the humble men whose company he had shunned before, because they were illiterate and Christians. Now he too is a Christian. And eagerly he seeks old Mr. Sung to claim him as a brother in the Lord.

With characteristic energy and determination it was now Hsi's chief desire to confess Christ before men, by openly uniting himself with the little band of Believers meeting daily for worship and instruction. Feeling unworthy to ask in person for this privilege, he went about it in correct Chinese fashion, and requested Sung, as his senior in the faith, to lay the matter before Mr. Hill and obtain his permission.

Hastening to meet the returning messenger, what was his disappointment to learn that Mr. Hill thought it early yet to take so pronounced a step, and counselled him to wait a little.

"Wait!" exclaimed Hsi, with surprise. "But what do the missionaries come for? Is it not to lead men to believe in Jesus? Why, then, reject me? I earnestly beg the teacher to reverse his decision."

"Mr. Hill is afraid," returned the old man, "lest, taking this step suddenly, you should afterwards regret it."

"Tell him," urged Hsi, "that I now worship God, not because of any outside influence, but through the teaching of the Holy Spirit. I understand for myself, having read His Word. I know my sins are great, and deserve the punishment of hell. I know too that Jesus has forgiven all my sins; that He will save me from them; and grant me to live with Him in heaven for ever."

Mr. Hill, though full of thankfulness, still hesitated. He was afraid of hindering, by over haste, the good work he could see was begun.

"Perhaps, Mr. Hsi," he said kindly, "you might enter the

religion of Jesus very zealously and go back again just as quickly. Had we not better postpone it for a few weeks?"

Sadly then and reproachfully the new convert made reply: "From this day until death and beyond, I will never, never draw back."

Moved by his deep sincerity, Mr. Hill hastened to reassure him, saying, with warm affection—

"Come with us, then, by all means. We rejoice to bid you welcome."

Never to be forgotten was that first hour of fellowship in Christ. The prayers, the hymns, the teaching from the Word, all seemed so satisfying to his new soul-needs. Young as he was in the faith, Hsi could feel and appreciate the warmth of divine love flowing through Christian hearts. Years afterwards he remembered it and recalled with the old freshness—

"Returning from worship, Mr. Hill was extremely pleased. Oh, how kindly he treated me! I loved him as a father; he loved me as a son."

But it was not all calm sunshine. Conflict and darkness lay ahead in the valley of humiliation and the shadow of death, where Apollyon waited, determined by some means or other to recapture his escaping slave.

Immediately upon his conversion the conviction came clearly to the scholar's mind that his opium-habit must at once be broken. There seems to have been no parleying about it. Ever since he first entered the missionary's household, his conscience had troubled him on the subject. Mr. Hill's kind but sorrowful words would not leave him, and their reproach was burnt into his soul.

"Mr. Hsi," he had said, "you are a distinguished member of a scholarly family. I deeply regret to see you brought to so en-feebled a condition through opium. If you do not cleanse yourself, how can you be an example to others?"

But at that time he knew no power that could enable him to cleanse himself from the degrading vice. Now all was different. He belonged to Christ, and there could be no doubt as to the will of his new Master. It was thoroughly in keeping with the charac-ter of the man to come to this clear decision at once. Of course he knew well what leaving off opium-smoking would involve. But there was no shrinking; no attempt at half measures. He saw it must be sacrificed at once, entirely, and for ever.

Then came the awful conflict. It was as though the great enemy of souls, seeing his prisoner escaping, fell back upon his opium-habit as an invincible chain with which to bind him. How critical was the struggle, how momentous the issues, Hsi himself hardly realised. Upon its outcome all his future power and usefulness depended. As angels lingered near the Saviour tempted in the wilderness, may we not believe the watchful care of God encompassed this young believer, as he went down into his terrible fight with the flesh and the devil?

Mr. Hill, knowing his teacher had ceased to smoke opium, and was consequently in a good deal of suffering, at once prepared the usual medicines for his relief. Hsi took them gladly, thankful for any help; but nothing seemed to do him good. His opium-habit was of long standing, and his whole system thoroughly impregnated with the drug. All remedies failed to alleviate his distress, and what he endured in the days that followed, words cannot tell.

As hour after hour went by, his craving for the poison became more intense than the urgency of hunger or thirst. Acute anguish seemed to rend the body asunder, accompanied by faintness and exhaustion that nothing could relieve. Water streamed from the eyes and nostrils. Extreme depression overwhelmed him. Giddiness came on, with shivering, and aching pains, or burning thirst. For seven days and nights he scarcely tasted food, and was quite unable to sleep. Sitting or lying, he could get no rest. The agony become almost unbearable; and all the while he knew that a few whiffs of the opium-pipe would waft him at once into delicious dreams.

Determined, by the power of God, never to go back to it, the suffering man held on. Mr. Hill and others did what they could to help him. Medicines were given in larger doses, and native as well as foreign drugs were tried, but all without avail. Prayer was constantly made on his behalf, and Hsi himself, as far as he was able, cast himself upon the Lord.

At last, in the height of his distress, it seemed to be revealed to him that the anguish he was suffering, arose not merely from physical causes, but that behind it all lay concealed the opposition of some mighty spiritual force; that he was, in fact, hard pressed by the devil, who was using this opium craving as a weapon for his destruction. In his sufferings, Hsi became increasingly conscious of the presence and power of Satan; and the conflict was then one of the soul, strengthened by Christ, against the malignity and might of the evil one seeking to overwhelm it. Then how utterly did the helpless man cast himself on God. Refusing to be dragged away one step from his only refuge, he fought out the battle in the very presence of his new-found Saviour. Praying and clinging to Christ, he made his terrible adversary come, as he says himself, "before the Lord's face daily," and there cried out repeatedly—

"Devil, what can you do against me? My life is in the hand of God. And truly I am willing to break off opium and die, but not willing to continue in sin and live!"

In his most suffering moments he would frequently groan out aloud: "Though I die, I will never touch it again!"

At last, after many days of anguish, his attention was attracted by some verses in his open Bible telling about "the Comforter"; and, as he read, it was borne in upon his mind that He, the Holy Spirit of God, was the mighty power expressly given to strengthen men. Then and there, in utter weakness, he cast himself on God, and cried for the gift of the Holy Ghost. He did not understand much, but he had grasped the supreme fact that the Holy Spirit could help him, making impossible things possible, and overcoming all the power of the enemy.

And there as he prayed in the stillness, the wonderful answer was given. Suddenly a tide of life and power seemed to sweep into his soul. The reality was so intense that from head to foot he broke into a profuse perspiration. Anguish and struggle ceased; the conflict was completely ended. The Holy Spirit came, flooding his heart with peace.

"He did what man and medicine could not do," records the liberated soul. "From that moment my body was perfectly at rest. And then I knew that to break off opium without real faith in Jesus would indeed be impossible."

In later years it always seemed to Mr. Hsi that there had been a special purpose in the sufferings he endured at that time, and in the manner of his deliverance. He often said—

"I see now why I was permitted to pass through such a severe ordeal. It was in order that I might thoroughly understand the true nature of the conflict, and the only power that can deliver."

In all his subsequent dealings with opium patients, the perception of this truth guided him and inspired the methods he used for their cure. He never had the slightest faith in medicine only, though he always used medicine and appreciated its value. What he saw so clearly was the necessity for cutting at the real root of the matter, by overcoming first the spiritual difficulty, if one would effectually conquer the physical habit.

"Truly," he would say, "the opposition of evil spirits can only be met by the power of the Holy Ghost. Sooner or later, the man who is trusting in medicine is certain to go back, because the devil has not been driven out. If you would break off opium, don't rely on medical help, don't lean on man, but trust only in God."

# Called to Life Service

FROM the time of that first prayer for the gift of the Spirit, Hsi made sure and rapid progress in the heavenly way. The power of opium was completely conquered, never again to return. But more than this, he seemed to be specially taught of God, and his growth in spiritual things was remarkable.

The Divine method of working in the soul, as in other realms, is often slow and gradual up to a certain point, and then extremely rapid. One day is sometimes with the Lord as a thousand years; and then a thousand years as one day. The day of the Lord had come in that man's life; and where a slow, negative process had been unfolding, a positive work now proceeded with great rapidity. Through all his early exercise of soul, his sense of vanity of life, his fear of death, and consciousness of sin; through all his searching for truth, his failure and disappointment, self-condemnation, and despair, a preparatory work had been accomplished. He had been more and more cut off from hope in himself or others, shut up to the light that was to dawn. And when at length that great Light rose upon him, his whole being responded, transfigured in a moment. Suddenly the man was caught up into the sphere of the spiritual kingdom and instantly and truly born into the family of God.

While the long preparatory period is in progress it is useless to attempt to hurry matters in the soul. As well try to bring spring in the middle of winter, or produce the warmth of summer by lighting a fire out of doors on a snowy day. Each Christian is a divine mystery, and only as divine wisdom is obtained can one know rightly how to deal with even the least.

Too often there is a conventional sort of idea that because a man has been brought up in the midst of heathenism, with centuries of darkness and idolatry behind him, therefore, in the nature of things, it must take years before he can apprehend much of spiritual truth. We do not expect him to grasp what we can grasp, or rise so rapidly into the experience of divine things. As well might one argue that because Christianity has been in Europe now many centuries longer than in the days of Paul, therefore we are on a higher level and realise loftier spiritual attainments than he. Few mistakes can be more foolish and pernicious, and few more calculated to hinder the work of the Spirit of Truth. We need to be often reminded that all spiritual illumination is of God, and He is not limited in His working. He can make a Christian out of an unconverted Chinese just as easily and rapidly as of an unconverted European, moving directly on the spirit of the man. Did we but adequately realise this fact, we should pray more, while not preaching less; we should depend more, and with larger expectation, upon the Holy Spirit, and reverence more the mystery of the divine life in the soul of even the youngest child.

One night shortly after his great deliverance, Hsi was alone in his room in prayer. The hour was late, and all around him silent. Though so young a Christian, only a few days converted, he had already perceived some glimmering of the great truth about the full indwelling of the Holy Ghost. In thought and prayer over the Word of God, he had learned that there is a baptism of the Spirit different from the regeneration of the soul at conversion. Already, in the hour of his helplessness and anguish, he had cast himself upon the power of the Holy Ghost, and had been lifted out of his despair and carried into a new life of victory and rest. But this experience seems only to have convinced him that there were yet further possibilities open to faith. The story of Pentecost had raised his expectations, while it quickened his longings; and for this fuller baptism he prayed.

Alone in that midnight hour, as he waited upon God, with dim perception but sincere obedience and simple faith, the answer came. Heaven itself seemed opened over that little room as once again the promise was fulfilled, "I will pour . . . My Spirit upon him that is thirsty, and floods upon the dry ground." For there upon that untaught, newly-converted Chinese, so recently rescued from heathenism, opium-smoking, and sin, was shed a wonderful outpouring of the Holy Ghost. Life, divine and more abundant; life that is joy, light, victory, and love, triumphing over self as well as sin, flooded his soul.

"Three times in the night," reads the simple record, "the Holy Spirit descended, filling and overflowing my heart."

Pardoned and delivered, he was now possessed and satisfied, filled for a life of service that should grow brighter and brighter unto the perfect day.

For with this baptism of the Spirit there came a clear and definite call to the work of God. Just as Paul, the once bitter persecutor, was filled with the Holy Ghost and received his apostolic commission three days only after the vision of the risen Christ had changed his life, so in that hour was given to the transformed Confucianist a vivid and deeply solemn consciousness that he was called of God to the ministry of the Gospel. Unmistakably, as though a voice had spoken, he was impressed with the conviction that his life was to be spent in labours for the salvation of his fellow-countrymen.

The call was so definite and the outpouring of the Spirit so real, that the whole experience left an impression on the life of Mr. Hsi that never passed away. From that time forward he was as a man set apart, with an apostolic sense and conviction of being chosen of God for some special service. At the time he said nothing about it, feeling deeply conscious of his unpreparedness and ignorance in spiritual things. He realised that, so far, it was but an indication of the Divine will, and that only in after years could the full purpose of God be unfolded.

Overflowing with new love and joy, Hsi's first desire now was to hasten back to his own people with the glad tidings of the power of Christ to save.

Obtaining a brief leave of absence from his duties, he made his way to the familiar village; a new man in a new world. But there an unexpected difficulty awaited him. On former visits his family had been delighted to see him and find that he was well and like himself, unharmed in any way. Now there was a change. They felt at once that he was different, and immediately concluded that their former fears were realised—he was bewitched at last!

For a while their wondering surprise was chiefly directed to the fact that he had broken off opium-smoking. It seemed incredible. Surely it could not be true. What about his former weakness, that had induced him to take the drug? What about the inevitable craving so few had any power to resist? The foreigner must be possessed of strange magic indeed if he could accomplish such unheard-of results. It was in vain that Hsi told them of the mighty power that had brought the change to pass. The more he spoke about the living Christ, the one and only God, the more concerned and angry they became.

At length he broached the subject of taking down the idols: the god of riches and the god of war, the pictures of the goddess of mercy and the kitchen god, and any other that the house contained. Then anxiety was replaced by fear and indignation. What! profane the image of the gods? Cease to burn incense and paper? No longer worship the Higher Powers? Clearly he had fallen a prey to the deceptions of the "foreign devil."

It was only by exercising the greatest firmness Hsi was able to carry the point, and rid his house of at any rate the outward observances of idolatry. He realised that the matter was one in which he dared not yield, and that delay would be fatal. Very patiently and gently he tried to explain his reasons to the wife he truly loved and to the other members of his family; but he was met by torrents of abuse and accusation, and had to wait for time to put things right. And yet all the while his wife was conscious of the great improvement that had taken place in her husband's appearance and temper. She had never seen him so bright and loving, quiet and kind, before. Certainly something very strange had taken place. So for the time being the storm lulled, though it was far from over. Hsi took down all his idols and burned them before returning to the city, and committed his house and family to the care of the living God.

Then followed two quiet, happy months in which Hsi remained on as teacher in the missionary's household. His appreciation of the character of David Hill deepened as the days went on. There was a gravity and dignity about Mr. Hill that entirely satisfied the scholarly instincts of his companion. For the first time in his life Hsi felt that he had found a living embodiment of the high Confucian ideal of "the Princely Man." All that had seemed to him most excellent, though unattainable, he felt was realised in the life of his friend. And this gave Mr. Hill an unusual influence over him for good.

Perhaps nowhere is the great law of heredity—like father, like son—so clearly seen as in the relationship between the missionary and his spiritual children. They have practically no other standard, and can imagine no higher ideal than the life he lives before them, and unconsciously his example becomes the limit of their expectation and attainment. "Your character is your message": a profoundly solemn truth in the experience of the Christian missionary.

Certain it is that those weeks of delightful intimacy with David Hill left an impression on the life of his teacher that was never afterwards effaced. But the happiness of that fellowship was shadowed by the knowledge that very shortly his friend must leave him, and that in all probability they would never meet again on earth. Keenly Hsi felt the sorrow of this separation long before it actually took place. For the love between them was of that rare spiritual quality found in no other relationship to the same degree. Meanwhile, as long as they could be together, Mr. Hill sought to impart all he could of teaching and help to his friend, and Hsi profited by his forethought with eager appreciation.

Life had now become so new to the once Confucian scholar that he felt impelled to take a new name, the choice of which was eminently characteristic. Instead of selecting some elegant literary title, such as men of his position usually adopt, he chose the two characters *Sheng-mo*, meaning "Demon-overcomer." Intensely practical and thorough-going, Hsi felt from the first that the Christian life must be one of conquest. To him the devil was a personal foe, a terrible reality, and the power of Christ an equally tangible fact. In the strength, then, of his new Master he threw down the gauntlet to his old enemy. Never for a moment relying on his own sufficiency, but hidden in Christ, he went forth to real conflict and real victory, and in faith in Him who overcame, he wished henceforth to be known as "Conqueror of demons."

Another characteristic thing was that he began, a few weeks after his conversion, definitely to seek the good of others by spreading a knowledge of the truth. His idea was that a candle was meant to shine from the moment it was lighted. He could not preach as Mr. Hill did, or go about telling of Christ among his neighbours and friends. His duties kept him in the city. But he had a good deal of leisure time, and some talent for essay-writing. This he determined to use. His mind was naturally full of the wonderful salvation that had come to him, and of the principles of the new kingdom into which he had been introduced. So he wrote two tracts entitled "How to obtain Deliverance from Calamity," and "The Ten Commandments of God," which were widely circulated.

Thus, full of happy work and fellowship those too short months passed away, and the time arrived when Mr. Hill must leave for the coast. Winter was over (1879), and the wheat was springing fast for a new harvest. The terrible famine had passed away. Missionaries had come, and thousands of copies of the Word of God were already in circulation in Shansi. Better still, souls had been saved that were becoming in their turn saviours of others; lights had been kindled in the darkness, never again to go out. David Hill's work was done; and after an absence of two years the needs of his mission in Central China[1] claimed him once more.

During those last days at Pingyang the missionary's heart was much drawn out in prayer for the little group of Christians he was leaving behind him. Mr. Turner had come down from the capital to take charge of the station, so that the young converts would not be uncared for; but the man who had first led them into the light, who had so truly loved them, lived in their lives, and spent himself in prayer on their behalf, felt like a father parting from his own children. Thinking and praying much about their future, there gradually came to him a strange and very marked impression that one of that little band was chosen to be used of God in quite a special way in the spread of the Gospel throughout that region. He did not clearly know which: whether old Mr. Sung, who had a natural gift for pastoral work, the heart of a shepherd; or one of the younger men, full of love and zeal; or his teacher Hsi, educated, cultured, with unusual force of character and evident enduement of the Holy Ghost; but that one of them was set apart for special service he felt convinced.

The last night came, and they assembled once more for worship. Looking round upon the little company, Mr. Hill's heart was deeply moved. With the impression strong upon him that one of them was called of God to be a leader in their midst, he felt he must tell them of it, and earnestly warn them never to allow a moment's jealousy or any spirit of rivalry to come in and hinder blessing. Very solemnly he urged them, when the Divine will should be made apparent, gladly to recognise the chosen leader in the position that God's purpose designed.

Deeply impressed by the words of his friend, Hsi at once recalled the experience of a few weeks before, when he had been conscious of a Divine appointment to the work of the ministry. He could not but feel that Mr. Hill's words confirmed his own definite impression. The circumstance came to him as a second call from God, a re-emphasis upon the solemn conviction already given. But he said nothing. Though his heart was all the more drawn to his beloved teacher and friend, he could not, even to him, speak of a matter so sacred.

At early dawn the following morning preparations were all

[1] The English Wesleyan Mission at Hankow.

complete for the long journey, provisions packed, the cart loaded, and the little group of Christians waiting to bid farewell to the loved friend who was leaving to return no more. From full hearts the last words were said, the last prayers offered, and Mr. Hill turned his face toward the city gate. But not alone. Not there, not then, could his sorrowing teacher leave him. Together they passed through the silent streets and left the city, following the cart along the great north road down to the river. Neither could say much in those last moments, but their hearts were one in the deep love that united them.

At length the old stone bridge is reached and crossed, and still they linger, till the carter becomes impatient. The sun is rising and the traveller must be away. In silence the last courteous bow is made, the last long look taken. Then the distance widens between them as the heavy cart rumbles slowly away. For long a solitary figure leans against the old stone coping of the bridge, watching until the travellers have passed out of sight. Years afterwards the sorrow of that hour was still fresh in the memory of the man who walked back alone to the city in the early morning light.

"We dwelt together rather more than two months," he records. "When Mr. Hill was taking his departure he could not restrain his flowing tears. I, also weeping, accompanied him outside the city to the north of the great bridge, and there we parted. Returning, my heart was straitened as I thought of the people round me in great darkness, like sheep without a shepherd; and I feared it would be extremely difficult to find another pastor like him."

# 12

# The Great Change

WITH the saintly Davil Hill gone, Hsi felt indeed bereft. But it had to happen if there was to be life and growth and strength. The eagle had stirred her nest and was going to teach her young to fly. She would be there above them to watch their first attempts, and be in readiness to swoop beneath to uphold them if they should so need the help. Nests are for fledglings as nurseries are for babes. Hsi was necessarily a babe in Christ; but he was not to remain so. He was to become a man of God.

In the days of His flesh our Lord had cast out the legion of evil spirits from the poor demoniac, who, in his gratitude, had made request that he might stay with his deliverer. But the divine plan for him was that he should make His wondrous power known to many more; and He sent him home to his friends to tell them how great things the Lord had done for him. So Hsi returned home, to the little Western Chang village at the foot of the mountains, to give and live his testimony to all about him.

"Many changes had taken place within the memory of that little town. Some of its inhabitants could recall days of wealth and prosperity, before the "foreign smoke"[1] was known in Shansi; could tell of disastrous wars waged against their country by "outside barbarians"; of the fatal growth of the opium-habit; and of the drought that had led to the famine in which millions of people had perished. But nothing like this had ever been known before, and over their pipes the village elders discussed the situation.

Yes, it was only too true, the scholar Hsi had become a Christian, or, to put it plainly, had been bewitched by "foreign devils." From the beginning two years before, when the preachers of this new religion appeared in the district, thoughtful men had foreseen that some among "the foolish people" would doubtless fall a prey to their spells. But who could have imagined that the first to be entrapped would be the scholar Hsi, a man of position and influence, a cultured Confucianist, the leader of their own set. Herein lay the surprise and bitterness of it all, and loud were the lamentations.

[1] The term commonly used in North China for opium.

For beyond doubt it was a serious calamity, this becoming a Christian; the delusions involved were so powerful and far-reaching. Now, in the case of Hsi, if there was one thing for which he had always been noted, it was his antipathy to foreigners and dislike for everything connected with them: a laudable and patriotic feeling that now, alas! had given place to extraordinary interest and affection. His long-venerated idols were discarded; rumour even whispered that they had been taken down and burned. His sacred ancestral tablets were no more worshipped. The very fragrance of incense had departed from his home. Strangely enough, his opium craving was gone too. This was indeed mysterious, for he had been a slave to the habit, and, as everyone knew, in such cases deliverance was well-nigh impossible. Yet, with surprising suddenness, and nothing to account for the change, Hsi's opium pipe was laid aside, and even the need for it seemed to have left him.

The time he used to spend in preparing and smoking opium was now devoted to the peculiar rites of his new religion. Day and night he might be seen poring over the books the foreign teachers had brought; sometimes singing aloud in the strangest way; sometimes quietly reading by the hour together; sometimes kneeling on the ground, his eyes shut, talking to the foreigners' god, who could neither be seen nor heard and had no shrine to represent him. And whatever Hsi might be doing, the remarkable thing was that he seemed continually happy; overflowing with satisfaction. If he had come into a fortune or discovered the elixir of endless youth, he could scarcely have been more elated.

And yet it did not appear that he had improved his circumstances by "eating the foreign religion." If the missionaries had bought his allegiance with large sums of money, as everyone believed, he at any rate managed to conceal the fact. Far from living in greater luxury or the idleness that became his position, Hsi had suddenly developed quite the opposite tendencies, and, forgetting the dignity of a scholar, was now frequently engaged in menial pursuits. Reasoned with, he simply replied that he was learning farming with a view to the better care of his estate. But whoever heard of a literary man hoeing in the fields, herding cattle, winnowing grain, or gathering fuel with his own hands? No doubt his home and farm were improving under the process, but what compensation could that offer for loss of social standing and the angry alienation of equals and friends?

Yes, there could be no doubt of it, Hsi in becoming a Christian had outraged the feelings of the community, and the prominence of his former position only served to increase the offence. The gentry, as soon as the fact became known, ceased to recognise him as of their number. He was socially "done for"; at once blotted out. But any hope that such treatment might recall him to his senses was doomed to disappointment, for it shortly transpired that he had even submitted to the ceremony of baptism, thus receiving full initiation into the "foreign devil sect." Rumours as to the nature of this mysterious rite did not tend to improve matters, and the villagers, now despairing of his reclamation, became more than ever watchful and suspicious.

One thing at any rate was certain; brave it out as he might, the renegade scholar could never escape the judgment of Heaven. He was free and independent, a middle-aged man with no one to control him, and of course could do as he liked; but in the long run he would find it impossible to defy the anger of the gods. In some way or other, vengeance must fall upon him. He would inevitably come under evil influences, and suffer either in person, family, or estate. For the present he might scorn such apprehensions, and even appear to be improved in health and vigour. But that was clearly illusive. The terrible nature of his offence would soon appear.

Meanwhile, Hsi of the Western Chang village went quietly on his way; a new man in a new world. For him a great light had arisen, above the brightness of the sun. All the perplexities of former years, his doubts and painful questions, the burden of his sins, his dread of death and the unknown Beyond, had passed away. The chains of his opium-habit had fallen from him. Renewed in spirit like a little child, his heart overflowed with love and joy. Already he was beginning to possess his new possessions, to enter into the glorious liberty of the children of God.

In the seclusion of their ancestral dwelling, the women of his household were first to appreciate the change. Though fully as prejudiced as the outer circle of his acquaintance, they had better opportunities for judging as to the results of his new faith. "The mean one of the inner apartments," his gentle little wife, saw and felt most of all. Life had brought her grievous disappointments. To have no son, in China, is a calamity beyond thought; a cause for which many a woman is divorced or sold into slavery. And her only child, a boy, had died in infancy. For long years her life

had been shadowed with this sorrow and shame. But her husband
was different from other men. He did not sell her, or take a second
wife. Of course he was free to do so at any moment, and her heart
often trembled at the thought. Quick-tempered and imperious
even in his kindest moods, he was a man to be feared, and his
outbursts of passion were terrible. But how wonderful the change
coming over him: new gentleness, now, in all he said and did;
new self-control and thoughtfulness for others; and, towards herself unwonted affection, and strange solicitude that she should
enter into his new faith.

Day by day as she noted these things, Mrs. Hsi could not but
modify a little her first anger and scorn. Though mistaken, her
husband was evidently sincere. Others might scoff; but she began
to feel curious about the secret they had failed to find. Waking
at night she often wondered to see him still poring over the Book,
or kneeling absorbed in prayer, talking to that invisible God
whose presence seemed to him so real. And then what could
account for his persistence in assembling the household daily for
this new worship, unless some good were likely to follow?

After all, this was the most trying aspect of the whole affair.
If only he would keep his religion to himself and be dignified
about it. If he could be just respectably "bewitched," and not let
everybody know. Why must he propagate these new notions,
making his change of faith so ostentatious and offensive? No
wonder the whole neighbourhood made fun of them.

And besides, he had adopted a new, most singular name. In the
strength of the God he now worshipped, far from being terrified
of evil spirits as before, he had actually called himself "Conqueror of Demons!" What could be more reckless, more certain
to incur disaster? No one in his senses would venture even to
speak of such beings, far less arouse their ire. Surely this alone
would be enough to bring down retribution.

In these days there is a tendency, in some quarters, to doubt the
very existence of a personal devil, a malignant spirit of evil, with
hosts of emissaries to work his will. This perhaps is hardly to be
wondered at in Christian communities, where the power of
Satan is restricted, and it is clearly inexpedient for him to appear
in his true colours. To us he comes as an angel of light, veiling
his true nature often with consummate skill. Not so in heathen
lands. There, with undisputed sway, his tactics are open and his
aims apparent. It would never occur to a Chinese to question the

existence of demons; he has too frequent proof of their power. We may regard such ideas as superstitious, and dismiss them without further thought, but facts remain; and some facts are startling as well as stubborn things.

When Hsi at his conversion took the new name, "Devil Overcomer," he unconsciously expressed an attitude that was to characterise his entire Christian life. For to him Satan was ever a personal foe, a watchful, mighty antagonist, keen to press the least advantage, always designing fresh onslaughts, without or within. But so real was the power of Christ in his life, that he was made more than conqueror; not without frequent struggle and occasional defeat, but with growing certainty as he more fully yielded to the Holy Spirit.

With such convictions it was no wonder that his experience, from the beginning, was of the strenuous sort. Prayer, to him, was a necessity, and he early discovered the benefit of special seasons of fasting, that he might better wait upon God. Naturally of a resolute character, he acted under the new conditions with all the old decisiveness. To keep in subjection the body, and triumph over sin and every difficulty, in the power of the Spirit, became now the passion of his life, combined with an absorbing desire to make this wonderful salvation known.

Thus it was impossible for Hsi to be silent about his Saviour. As well might the sun keep from shining, or the heart that loves and is loved, from rejoicing. He could not but speak of Jesus; and speak of Him he did until his latest breath. But, though definitely conscious of a call from God to preach Christ far and wide, he recognised from the first that soul-winning must begin at home. The testimony of his life must appeal to mother, wife, and friends. And for this, love and patience were needed.

To the women of his family, it was no small surprise that he should be so eager for them to understand. In old days he never thought of teaching them anything. They could not read or write, much less enter into his Confucian studies. But this new doctrine—were it the greatest good fortune in the world, he could not be more anxious for them to possess it!

And somehow, strange as it might seem, the things he talked about were beautiful, at times, and corresponded unexpectedly to the heart's need. The book he read was not like other books. There were comforting words in it that could not be forgotten, and stories about people so like ourselves to-day. A strange, warm feeling seemed to touch the heart as it told of Jesus blessing little children, and folding them in His arms; saying to the widow, "Weep not," and bringing back her son again; caring for the happiness of a wedding feast; and healing with tender touch so many sick and broken-hearted.

One could not help loving Jesus. One could not keep back the tears as the wonderful story moved on to the Cross. Why so good a man should die like that was mystery indeed. Could not the gods have delivered Him? And what could be the meaning of His rising from the grave, as the book said, and being in these days alive and near us, with the same love and power? Strangely attractive, strangely perplexing, this foreign religion! Who could understand it? And yet, the more one heard the more one longed to hear.

# 13

# "Conqueror of Demons"

AND now came a painful experience. For some months all had
gone well in the home of the ex-Confucianist, and the excitement aroused by his conversion had to some extent subsided. It
even seemed as though the tide were beginning to turn, and he
might gain ground in popular favour again. This in large measure
was due to a practical way he had of applying the teachings of
Christ to daily affairs.

His first concern, for example, on becoming a Christian, had
been to seek out the aged stepmother, driven from his home years
before, and living still in poverty and neglect.

"Only return to us, Mother," he urged, "and see how changed
my heart has become. All that is possible, now, I will do to atone
for the past. You shall have the best our home affords, and the
handsomest coffin and funeral I can provide."[1]

At first the old lady was frightened, and thought he must have
lost his senses. But by degrees it dawned upon her that he really
meant what he said. And then with joy and wonder, she went
with him and was reinstated in the old home.

"See," said the village women, "to be a Christian cannot be
so bad after all!"

And then there were his brothers, clever, unscrupulous men,
with hot tempers like his own. Though all of them Confucian
scholars, well drilled in "the five relationships," they had found
it impossible to live together, and long ago the family had been
broken up. Time only added bitterness to the quarrel, until
everybody knew that the brothers were at daggers drawn.

But Hsi read in the teachings of his new Master, "first be
reconciled to thy brother"; and this he felt must mean just what
it said.

It was a difficult undertaking; but he prayed much about it,
and frankly confessed where he himself had been wrong. Publicly

---

[1] When parents reach middle age in China, it is a son's first duty to present
them with handsome coffins, as a token of filial affection. These are highly
appreciated, and are placed in the guest-hall, the old people frequently calling
attention to them with much satifaction.

to sue for peace, for nothing of that sort can be private in China, meant not a little humiliation, and at first he was only laughed at for his pains. But by degrees he conquered the difficulty, and friendly intercourse was resumed.

"Surely," thought the onlookers, moved to approbation, "the teachings of the Western Sage have power."

Thus, little by little, the new faith won its way. A Chinese knows how to appreciate a good thing when he sees it, though it usually takes some time to open his eyes. And all the while Hsi was preaching as well as practising the Gospel. Daily worship in his household had grown into a little service, often attended by outsiders. Among his relatives not a few were interested, and his wife and stepmother were almost ready to declare themselves Christians.

And just then this new trouble arose: the strangest. most unexpected thing that could have happened.

It all concerned Mrs. Hsi, and thus touched her husband in the tenderest point. For he had been so full of hope and joy about her. Always receptive and intelligent, she had grasped the truth with clearness. Her life had brightened and her heart enlarged, until it seemed as though she would become her husband's real fellow worker and friend.

Then, suddenly, all was changed; and her very nature seemed changed too. At first only moody and restless, she rapidly fell a prey to deep depression, alternating with painful excitement. Soon she could scarcely eat or sleep, and household duties were neglected. In spite of herself, and against her own will, she was tormented by constant suggestions of evil, while a horror as of some dread nightmare seemed to possess her. She was not ill in body, and certainly not deranged in mind. But try as she might to control her thoughts and actions, she seemed under the sway of some evil power against which resistance was of no avail.

Especially when the time came for daily worship, she was thrown into paroxysms of ungovernable rage. This distressed and amazed her as much as her husband, and at first she sought to restrain the violent antipathy she did not wish to feel. But little by little her will ceased to exert any power. She seemed carried quite out of herself, and in the seizures, which became frequent, would use language more terrible than anything she could ever have heard in her life. Sometimes she would rush into the room, like one insane, and violently break up the proceedings, or would fall insensible on the floor, writhing in convulsions that resembled epilepsy.

Recognising these and other symptoms only too well, the excited neighbours gathered round, crying:

"Did not we say so from the beginning! It is a doctrine of devils, and now the evil spirits have come upon her. Certainly he is reaping his reward."

The swing of the pendulum was complete, and in his trouble Hsi found no sympathy. There was not a man or woman in the village but believed that his wife was possessed by evil spirits, as a judgment upon his sin against the gods.

"A famous 'Conqueror of Demons,'" they cried. "Let us see what his faith can do now."

And for a time it seemed as though that faith could do nothing. This was the bitterest surprise of all. Local doctors were powerless, and all the treatment he could think of unavailing. But prayer; surely prayer would bring relief? Yet pray as he might the poor sufferer only grew worse. Exhausted by the violence of more frequent paroxysms, the strain began to tell seriously, and all her strength seemed ebbing away.

Then Hsi cast himself afresh on God. This trouble, whatever it was, came from the great enemy of souls, and must yield to the power of Jesus. He called for a fast of three days and nights in his household, and gave himself to prayer. Weak in body, but strong in faith, he laid hold on the promises of God, and claimed complete deliverance. Then without hesitation he went to his distressed wife, and laying his hands upon her, in the name of Jesus, commanded the evil spirits to depart and torment her no more.

Then and there the change was wrought. To the astonishment of all except her husband, Mrs. Hsi was immediately delivered. Weak as she was, she realised that the trouble was conquered. And very soon the neighbourhood realised it too.

For the completeness of the cure was proved by after events. Mrs. Hsi never again suffered in this way. And so profoundly was she impressed, that she forthwith declared herself a Christian and one with her husband in his life-work.

The effect upon the villagers was startling. Familiar as they were with cases of alleged demon-possession more or less terrible in character, the people had never seen or heard of a cure, and never expected to. What could one do against malicious spirits?

Yet here, before their eyes, was proof of a power mightier than
the strong man armed. It seemed little less than a miracle.

"Who can this Jesus be?" was the question of many hearts.
"No wonder they would have us, too, believe and worship."

Some did follow Mrs. Hsi's example, and turn to the Lord.
Regular Sunday services were established and idolatry in many
homes began to relax its hitherto unquestioned sway.

But it was Hsi himself who learned the deepest lessons through
all this strange experience. More than ever confident in the power
of Christ, he devoted himself afresh to the spread of the Gospel,
and came to believe with stronger faith in the efficacy of prayer
in His name under all circumstances.

# 14

# Early Success and Failure

AMONG the hills that skirt the plain toward the sunrising, lay a group of villages in which, about this time, Hsi began to take a special interest. Up there in the hamlet of Yangtsun lived two farmer brothers named Li, who had been led to Christ by David Hill, and baptized on the same occasion as Hsi himself. And now they were in trouble. Their beloved father in the faith had left the province, and the remaining missionaries were too much occupied with their work in the city to be able to visit these outlying places. The brothers were discouraged on account of long-continued persecution. What more natural than that the Christian scholar from his neighbouring village should go over and help them.

Thus, week after week, Hsi turned his face toward the mountains, and cheerfully traversed seven miles of rough road, either way, to conduct a little service in the farmhouse at Yangtsun.

They were informal meetings, and many were the queries and exclamations that interspersed the proceedings, especially from heathen neighbours who dropped in to join the little circle.

"But is all this true, Teacher Hsi? Did Jesus really heal that demoniac among the tombs? Or is it only an honourable fable? Did He indeed open the eyes of the blind, make lame men walk, and cure even lepers?"

"Why do you not respectfully invite Him to our neighbourhood? There are plenty of sick people here. We should like to see your Jesus, if He can do the things you say."

It was indeed a strange, new story, and Hsi was never more happy than in explaining it to those who had not heard. Sin, the incarnation, and atonement, faith, and Christian living all had to be made plain in the light that streams from Calvary. And the word preached was with power. For when his listeners asked him:

"Can Jesus do those same things now? You say He is living near us. Can He heal the sick and cast out devils here, to-day?"

The answer came with equal simplicity and directness:

"Of course He can. He healed me after long years of sickness, and took away my opium craving too. Did you not hear how He delivered my wife from demon-possession, only the other day? There is nothing Jesus cannot do for those who turn from sin and trust Him fully."

That was satisfactory so far. But then followed the practical application.

"Will you then pray for me, Teacher Hsi? My mother is ill; my wife; my son. Do come to our house and get the Lord Jesus to make them well again."

It was a searching test. But Hsi welcomed it. Wherever he saw real earnestness, and found people willing to put away their idols and give up sin to follow Christ, he gladly laid his hands on their sick and prayed for immediate recovery.

Hsi's Bible knowledge of course was most defective, and his ideas crude and incorrect in many ways. But he had learned some things; amongst them, that the Book means just what it says; and he had not learned to doubt or discount what it does say, by an unsatisfactory, God-dishonouring experience. And so in the simplest, most natural way, he expected the Lord to do as He had said.

Up in the little village of Yangtsun, he knew that he could pray in the name of Jesus; and he believed that that name had lost none of its ancient power.

Wonderful were the scenes those simple homesteads witnessed, recalling days in Samaria, Lydda, and elsewhere, when the Apostles' message was—"*Jesus Christ maketh thee whole.*" And seeing these things with their own eyes, it was little wonder that men and women turned to the Lord. Nor was it strange that antagonism should be aroused; for the powers of darkness had never been so challenged in those upland valleys before. That too seemed natural, and in keeping with the experience of the early Church.

But persecution went on and grew more serious, until the Christians and inquirers had hard work to stand their ground. False accusations were made against them to the mandarins. Some were robbed and beaten, and others threatened with danger to life itself. At length the time for a great festival drew near, and the heathen villagers decided that all who would not worship the gods as usual should be taken to the temple and strung up by their hands tied together behind them, the ropes drawn over the beams in the roof, until they retracted their faith in the foreign religion.

This was too serious an outbreak, and the Yangtsun Christians determined to escape while they might. And so in the middle of the night, Hsi of the Western Chang village was aroused by persistent knocking at his gate. He stumbled out in the darkness, and recognising the voice of farmer Li, admitted the little group of fugitives and heard their story.

No doubt a prayer meeting was held during the small hours of the morning; but Hsi was a man of action as well as faith, and had not yet learned to leave in wiser hands the management of such affairs. "Resist not evil," and "Vengeance is mine, I will repay, saith the Lord," were teachings that had yet to come home to him in power.

It was a serious matter, as Hsi knew well, to be mixed up with such a quarrel, for there is never any telling, in China, to what a village feud may grow. But fearless of results, and confident in the righteousness of his cause, he lost no time in carrying the case before the local mandarin. Were there not treaties with Europe and America, securing protection for all who desired to embrace Christianity? Did not the Lord Himself say: "All power is given unto me, in heaven and on earth: Go ye therefore and disciple all nations?" No doubt those treaties were part of the power lodged in the hands of Christ; and so beyond question was his own ability to carry his case successfully through the law courts. Did not all his powers belong to the Lord, including this facility gained through years of practice and pains? Surely now an opportunity had come for turning his talents to account in the service of his new Master.

It was plausible reasoning enough, and many an older Christian has been misled along the same lines. The deeper teachings of Christ are hard sayings still, and hidden from many eyes.

And so, as in old days, Hsi carried the matter with a high hand, pressing his demands in such a way as to alarm the local authorities. He fumed and stormed publicly, in proper quarters, and made his grievance so serious that immediate action was taken. The mandarin sent out soldiers to the hamlets in question, and promptly restored law and order, establishing the rights of the Christians.

The entire proceedings occupied about a month, and during that time the refugees were hospitably entertained in Hsi's own home. With no sense of inconsistency, he exhorted them to trust in the Lord who had promised to be their refuge, and not to fear the wrath of man. Daily he conducted worship among his guests, instructing them carefully in the doctrines of Christian living. Thus, at his own expense, he cared for them all until the trouble was over and they could return to their village in peace.

Thankful and comforted the Yangtsun Christians went back, to find their neighbours frightened into submission. The persecution was not resumed; on the contrary everyone seemed to hold the foreign religion in wholesome fear. This encouraged timid inquirers, and when the Li brothers opened their house for public worship on Sundays, numbers of people flocked in. Hsi came over frequently, as before, and found whole families ready to burn their idols. Neighbouring villages caught the enthusiasm, and from considerable distances people came in, bringing their sick friends to be healed, and asking the Christians to go back with them and preach the Gospel. Gradually in these places too, weekly meetings were established, and Hsi found his hands full of pastoral and preaching duties. In one place six families, in another eight or nine, turned to the Lord, and as many as thirty people would assemble for regular worship.

But as time wore on Hsi was distressed to find that somehow these believers did not develop as he expected and desired. They were all right as long as everything went well, but as soon as trouble arose their faith seemed to waver and their hearts to grow cold. Nurture and care for them as he would, the little churches never really flourished, and as years went by there came sad backslidings and deterioration. This was a keen sorrow to their ardent friend, and grew into one of the deepest lessons of his life.

At first he did not see it, and only very gradually the truth became clear to his mind. Not until after repeated occurrences of the same kind did the conviction come to him that persecution and trouble are allowed as a necessary test to prove whether people are willing to suffer for Christ's sake and walk in His ways when sacrifice is involved. Then he began to value such experiences at their true worth, as sifting and strengthening processes that nothing can replace. In a word, he came to understand that God knows best how to care for His own, and that what He allows of trial, we cannot afford to be without.

It was an important development, and, like many another, grew out of painful experiences overruled of God. With so much to learn as well as unlearn, he made many mistakes at the beginning. But he was following on. And never heart responded more loyally to fuller knowledge of the divine will.

# 15

# Growing in Grace

THOSE were early days, and in spite of the reality of his love to Christ and his uncompromising devotion, Hsi was only a beginner in spiritual things. In later years he became a man of such rare illumination in the knowledge of God, that it is startling to find how long it took him at first to see some things that to us would appear self-evident.

God has His schools for training. Even among the heathen, missionaries are not the only teachers. Often indeed, if wise enough, they are the taught; awed by the manifest working of the Holy Spirit in willing hearts. We blunder in our efforts to enlighten, hindering often by our very haste to help. The Great Teacher is so wise and patient, never discouraged, never at a loss for natural, simple means of bringing home the needed lesson.

Thus Hsi developed; learning all he could from occasional intercourse with the missionaries in the city, and taught of God, often in quaint, surprising ways, through the enlightenment of His Word applied to the daily experiences of life. In the matter of ancestral worship, for example, means were used to awaken him that probably none of us would ever have thought of.

For some months after he became a Christian, Hsi still kept in his guest-hall a tablet bearing the name of his first wife, and supposed to be tenanted by one of her three spirits.[1] This occupied an honourable place among other tablets belonging to the family, and was of course his special property, though he had ceased to burn incense before it.

Apparently it had never occurred to him that to retain the tablet he had ceased to worship was to temporise with an evil. He seems not to have thought about it at all; or if he did, it was merely to conclude that though he could no longer worship the tablet, it might still remain among the others, and be treated with respect. Its removal would certainly give offence and be misunderstood.

[1] Another spirit is said to occupy the grave, and is worshipped at proper seasons. The third it is believed has already departed to the Unseen World, and must be provided for by occasional offerings of paper money, houses, clothes, etc.

Under these circumstances, what was to be done? With no one to show him the inconsistency, how was conviction to come, as come it must, if he were ever to become a strong, wise leader in the church?

Time passed, and the tablet was still there, Hsi quite unconscious of his duty regarding it; until one morning, coming into the room as usual, what was his surprise to see this almost sacred object lying with its face upon the ground. None of the other tablets had been touched; but this one had fallen over, apparently without hands, for it was prone upon its face just in front of the spot where it had always stood.

Hastening to raise it, Hsi's astonishment was increased when he saw the cause of its fall. The base of the wooden slab had been deliberately gnawed across by rats, a thing that had never happened in his experience before. Carefully he repaired the damage, and restored the tablet to its place. One lesson was not enough.

Strange to say, only a few days later the same thing occurred again. The same tablet was assailed, and tumbled over as before. This was too marked an occurrence to pass unnoticed. Raising it thoughtfully, Hsi could not but wonder why his particular tablet, belonging exclusively to himself, should have been singled out twice over and thrown down in so unusual a way.

The circumstance led to thought and earnest prayer. And then, very simply, the conviction grew upon him that the whole system of ancestral worship was idolatrous and of the devil, and that as a Christian he could have nothing to do with it any more. This settled the matter. The tablet was at once destroyed, and his testimony upon the subject became clear and uncompromising.

But he always felt that the Lord had allowed light to come to him gradually in that strange way to teach him to be gentle and patient with others under the same circumstances.

"We need to be very careful," he would say, "in putting this question before young converts and inquirers. Of course ancestral worship is idolatry. It is simply exalting human beings, dead men and women, in the place of God. And yet there is much that is tender and beautiful connected with it: memories of the past, gratitude, reverence, and natural affection. We need to discriminate. Great harm may be done by utterly condemning the best a man has known, before you make sure that he has grasped something better. Like dead leaves, wrong and questionable practices will fall off when there comes living growth."

It certainly was so in his own case, not only in the matter of ancestral worship.

One is surprised, for example, to find that during the first summer after his conversion, he continued with a clear conscience to grow and sell opium, and this although he knew so well the deadly effects of the drug. No one had suggested to him that, as a Christian, he ought not to have anything to do with the production or sale of the poison. The crop was most valuable, bringing five times the price of wheat. Of course he no longer used it himself; but if others wanted the drug . . .?

"Take heed, lest by any means this liberty of yours become a stumbling-block to them that are weak. . . . And through thy knowledge shall the weak brother perish, for whom Christ died. . . . Wherefore, if meat make my brother to offend, I will eat no flesh while the world standeth, lest I make my brother to offend. . . . We suffer all things, lest we should hinder the gospel of Christ. . . . Giving none offence, neither to the Jews, nor to the Gentiles, nor to the church of God. . . . Not seeking mine own profit, but the profit of many, that they may be saved."[1]

No wonder he came to see it, as the truth began to exercise more influence upon his life. And then he unhesitatingly made a clean sweep of the whole business, though it involved the sacrifice of a considerable portion of his income.

Not content, indeed, with banishing opium from his estate, he also abandoned the growth and use of tobacco, and would not tolerate it in his household. Nor would he continue to keep pigs on his farm. "No," he insisted, "they are filthy." Which is certainly true in China. "We must have nothing to do with that which is impure."

"Be ye clean, ye that bear the vessels of the Lord,"[2] was a command that gradually came to exercise much influence in his life. He endeavoured to apply it in every detail, including personal cleanliness and exemplary household management.

Another great truth that began to influence him early in his Christian experience, was one of the deepest yet one of the simplest of all: the necessity and privilege of sharing the sufferings of Christ, if we would follow in His footsteps. To deny self and endure hardness for Jesus' sake, and in the service of others, seemed to him only the right and natural thing. And he was very practical about it.

[1] I Cor. viii. 9, 11, 13; ix. 12; x. 32, 33.     [2] Isa. lii. 11.

On one occasion, for example, when he had been converted a little over a year, he went into the city as usual to attend the Sunday morning service. This was a walk of over thirteen miles, and he was still far from strong. But as he tramped the dusty road he "thought about the Lord Jesus carrying that heavy cross over a much more weary way; and so pressed forward, not daring to fear difficulty."

The service over, he was resting a little while before the homeward journey, when a poor man sought him out and begged him to go at once to the village of the White Mountain, to pray for a woman, dangerously ill, who wanted to hear of Jesus. The village was seventeen miles farther on. No cart or animal had been provided. The road was lonely and somewhat dangerous. And no one was going home that way with whom he could travel. But it never even occurred to him not to go.

Hour after hour, faint and solitary, he pressed on. At length evening fell, and he had only reached the rushing torrent three miles from the village. Very soon it was dark, and neither moon nor stars could be seen. Belated on that mountain road, he knew that travellers were exposed to the attack of hungry wolves grown fearless since the famine. And sure enough, as he stumbled on, he heard sounds that too plainly indicated their approach. Yes, they were on his track. Nearer and nearer came the howling, until he knew that they were all around him in the darkness. But there was a Presence nearer still.

Falling on his knees in that moment of peril, Hsi cried aloud to the Unseen Friend. He never knew what happened, or how he was delivered; but the next thing he was conscious of was silence, and that he was alone.

"Everything," he records, "grew strangely still. I know not when the wolves disappeared, or where they went. But they returned no more. Truly the Lord was my shield and my protector."

A little later he reached the village, and had the joy of telling the glad tidings to the sick woman and her friends, who probably had never seen a Christian before. What the result was in their lives we are not told. But the preacher himself never forgot that remarkable deliverance, nor the blessing that came to him in a service that involved some suffering.

In his brief chronicle of those early days some incidents are recorded that to us may seem trivial, until we understand the intense sincerity of the man, and how all life, to him, was of one piece—no difference of secular and sacred, great or small, but God in all circumstances, and some purpose of blessing in everything that affects His people. In this faith he saw deeper significance in the details of life, and took little account of second causes, tracing everything to the will, or the permission, of the Father with whom alone he had to deal.

One evening, in the gloaming, he had gone to bring the cattle home. Passing along a steep hillside, probably absorbed in thought, his foot slipped and he was thrown down an embankment of considerable height. The accident was one that might easily have proved fatal, but strange to say he was little hurt. Climbing painfully up to the road again, instead of being annoyed by what had happened, he began to think over the circumstance and wonder what lesson it was meant to teach. There must be some purpose in it. "The steps of a good man are ordered by the Lord." Why should his steps have been permitted to slide in so unexpected a way?

And then it came to him that he had not been watching the path as he walked along. He had been careless, and so fell into trouble. And how much more serious would spiritual declension be; the falls that would certainly result from carelessness in his walk with God. His heart was thoroughly awakened, and more than ever he sought to watch and pray as he travelled the heavenward road.

Again, a little later, he needed warning along similar lines, and records a humiliating occurrence. He seems to have been off his guard in some way, and even allowed himself to be drawn into a lawsuit among his heathen relatives. Mixed up in this proceeding, he acted in a way dishonouring to God.

As he left the scene of the disturbance, conscious of having done wrong, he was suddenly attacked by a powerful, ferocious dog, which threw him to the ground, and seemed as if it would tear him in pieces. In his peril it flashed upon him how much more terrible were the assaults of Satan, who as a roaring lion goes about seeking whom he may devour. Earnestly he cried to the Lord for deliverance; and the first thing was that, without any apparent reason, the dog ran away; but this was followed by very real and deep repentance, that put the great enemy to flight.

It was also not a little characteristic that when the onlookers wanted to chase and beat the dog, Hsi would not permit it, saying from a full heart:

"No, this is my Heavenly Father's chastisement. I have needed the lesson. What has the dog to do with it?"

Now all this may seem to us most elementary. But is it really so? Perhaps as we grow in grace ourselves, and walk more constantly and closely with our God, we too, though in a different way, may have more practical evidence of His presence and be more conscious of His unseen hand in our circumstances.

At any rate is there not something for the oldest Christian to learn from a testimony, such as the following, culled from those early pages:

On account of many onslaughts of Satan, my wife and I for the space of three years seldom put off our clothing to go to sleep, in order that we might be the more ready to watch and pray. Sometimes in a solitary place, I spent whole nights in prayer: and the Holy Spirit descended. Frequently my mother noticed a light in our bedroom toward midnight, by which she knew that we were still waiting before our Heavenly Father.

We had always endeavoured in our thoughts, words, and actions to be well pleasing to the Lord, but now we realised more than ever our own weakness; that we were indeed nothing; and that only in seeking to do God's will, whether in working or resting, whether in peace or peril, in abundance or in want, everywhere and at all times relying on the Holy Spirit, we might accomplish the work the Lord has appointed us to do. If we had good success, we gave all the glory to our Heavenly Father; if bad success, we took all the blame ourselves. This was the attitude of our hearts continually.

# 16

# Starving the Village Idols

PERHAPS no better evidence can be given of the genuineness of Hsi's Christian life in those early days than the changed attitude of the community in which he lived. Neighbours know pretty well how a man lives, especially in China.

Only a year or two had elapsed since the whole circle of his acquaintance had turned against him, predicting all sorts of calamities as the result of his change of faith. But the logic of facts was beginning to convince them that his mistake had not been so serious after all. At any rate, as they could see, the man himself was brighter and better than he had been for years, his family relationships were happy, and his property well cared for. And more than this, there was a strange power about him, for all his new gentleness and quiet ways, an undefinable sort of influence, that all were conscious of but no one could explain. Not a little discussion was given to the subject on summer days and winter evenings, and the result was a growing respect for the Christian scholar, if not for the religion he professed.

The time was drawing near for the local election, to fill the coveted post of village elder, or chairman of the Parish Council. Matters of considerable importance were involved, for the headman was responsible for the gathering of taxes, the maintenance of law and order, the defence of local rights, the care of temples and public buildings, and of the festivals proper to each season of the year. Energy and experience were required, and moral rectitude according to Chinese standards. In fact, the more they considered the question, the more it was evident—yet surely that was preposterous! But there was no getting out of it. And little by little, opinion became unanimous that no one was more suited to fill the post than the scholar Hsi, now that he was no longer an opium-smoker.

It was a strange conclusion to come to, but the Chinese are sensible people, and the practical value of Christian principles had not been unobserved. So the chief men of the village arranged an interview with Hsi, and laid before him the surprising request that, for the well-being of the neighbourhood, he would sacrifice himself so far as to assume the headship of the community.

"But, revered elders," exclaimed the scholar, "have you forgotten that I am now a Christian, and disqualified to serve you, much as I should value the privilege?"

"That is a private affair of the conscience," replied his neighbours, embarrassed, "and need not enter into the present question."

"You must also have noticed, honoured sires, that your younger brother is continually busy about the affairs of the Church of Jesus Christ. Day and night I have no leisure for ordinary business, nor does there remain with me any desire to enter into worldly affairs, however dignified the position."

But refusals were all unavailing. With one consent the election was made, and Hsi was informed that it was now an accomplished fact.

"If you really desire me to accept this office, honourable fathers," he replied, "there are two stipulations upon which I must insist."

"Only impose commands," they protested. "Whatever you say shall be law."

"Gentlemen, you are too courteous. My first stipulation is, that under no circumstances can I have anything to do with sacrifices in worship of the idols, or with the festivities of the temple and seasons. I will at all times pray to the living God for the prosperity of the village, and for abundant harvests. But I can do nothing that would compromise the honour of His name."

To Hsi's surprise, this condition was readily agreed with; for among themselves the village authorities had already prepared for such a contingency. They had not failed to observe that Hsi's prayers in the name of Jesus were remarkably effective, and they were quite willing that he should seek on their behalf the favour of his God.

But his second stipulation was most unexpected.

"Honourable fathers," he continued, "listen to my final word. Should I accept this office, not only will I refrain, myself, from all sacrifices to idols, but I must require that the entire village take the same position. If you will close the temple completely, and promise that no public worship of the gods be held throughout the year, then, and then only, can I consent to serve you."

Perturbed and excited, the assembly broke up crying, "Alas,

this condition is impossible! It is indeed out of the question. We cannot agree."

"Then, gentlemen," replied Hsi gravely, "neither can I agree to your proposals."

For a time the result was uncertain, but when Hsi was again called to meet his neighbours, he found them prepared to accept and enforce his proposal.

It was a strange anomaly; but all went well. Hsi did his best, and was very prayerful. At the close of the year it was found that the affairs of the village had never been more prosperous, and the headman was re-elected on his own terms.

Again he undertook the work as to the Lord, with the result that harvests were good, money matters successfully dealt with, and peace and contentment prevailed. Naturally the election went in his favour a third time with acclamation. Nothing was said about any change of basis, and again Hsi consented to serve them. For three whole years the temple was closed, and no public festivals were held in worship of the gods. And yet the village prospered.

At the close of the third year Hsi was once more unanimously chosen. But by this time his evangelistic and other labours had so increased, that he could no longer properly attend to the needs of the community. Courteously but with decision he refused the office, and when congratulated upon the service he had rendered, smilingly replied that perhaps the village had been saved some needless expense, adding:

"By this time the idols must be quite starved to death. Spare yourselves now any effort to revive them!"

It was a practical lesson, not easily forgotten.

# 17

# Under-Shepherds: A Problem

IT was indeed a problem. And plan as they might Hsi and his wife did not know how to meet it.

The work that had grown up around them was becoming increasingly complex. More and more the Christians from neighbouring villages, brought to the Lord through their efforts, looked to them for help and teaching. The mission station in the city was fully ten miles away, and though younger men walked over on Sunday for the services, thus coming into touch with the missionaries, old people, and most of the women and children found the double journey more than they could manage. This meant that they must be cared for nearer home. And in many cases the help needed was for body as well as soul.

For the converts were not only poor, they were often persecuted. Many a man who had managed to provide for his family before becoming a Christian, suddenly found himself bereft of all means of subsistence. His heathen employer, or relatives, turned him off; or the work he was doing was of such a nature that he was obliged to abandon it. Others were oppressed and defrauded, and sometimes driven out of house and home. Opium crops had to be sacrificed, with their large profit; and more honest methods in business often meant financial loss. Suffering and impoverished, many of the converts were in need of temporary succour, and Hsi's resources were taxed to the utmost.

Then again there was not a little hospitality to be exercised by one in his position. Inquirers coming from a distance frequently had to be entertained for a few days in that Christian household, that they might see in practice the truths they were being taught. Believers gathering from miles around for Sunday services were often weary, and too far from home to go back between the meetings for their mid-day meal. Some brought flour, bread, and other provisions; some had little or nothing to bring; and all needed the use of kitchen and guest-hall, not to speak of the women's apartments. Then benches for the meetings had to be provided; oil for the lamps; hot water for perpetual tea-drinking, without which nothing can be done in China, and many other hospitalities too numerous to mention.

"I thought much," Hsi recorded, "of the parable of the Good Shepherd; and pondered the words of Christ: '*They shall go in and out and find pasture!*'"

To his mind this clearly meant that the sheep must be looked after in temporal as well as spiritual things. Young believers going in and out of this fold must have their needs supplied. Coming long distances to worship on Sunday, it was his business to see that they did not go away hungry. There must be practical proof of Christian love towards the brethren. This was part of the problem.

The rest of it was—the wider issue. This message of salvation must be preached "to every creature." Clearly the missionaries, alone, could never accomplish so great a work. And then, the converts won must he helped, if they needed it, to find some suitable means of support. Of course they could not depend on the foreign missionary. Native workers, many native workers, would be needed. They must be drawn from the ranks of these very converts. And some way must be devised by which such men could earn an honest livelihood, while giving themselves to soul-saving work.

It was not that this view of the matter presented itself definitely or all at once. But little by little, as they did their best in the midst of a growing work, Hsi and his wife came to see these things, as parents the needs of their own children. And they came to realise, also, that the care of His lambs, His sheep, meant sacrifice; and that for sacrifice even under-shepherds must be prepared.

Power to help all; willingness and ability to serve the greatest number; these constitute the seal of a divine commission to lead among men. "He that will be greatest among you, let him be least of all and servant of all." Whether or not Hsi fully understood this principle, he was beginning to put it into practical effect.

As need arose, he had from the first willingly parted with his superfluous belongings, selling whatever could be spared, that he might help the brethren. He went all lengths in their service, and would just as readily boil the copper and make tea on Sunday as lead the meetings, or give money and advice to those in need. His home, time, and influence were all theirs. He shared the

burdens of the troubled; visited and prayed with the sick; pre-
scribed and gave away medicines; and received into his own care
one and another enslaved to opium-smoking, that he might the
better watch over and help them in their struggle to be free.

It must not be supposed, of course, that he did all this without
mistakes of manner and method at times. Not in one year, or
ten, can lifelong faults be conquered. He was still, often, quick-
tempered and overbearing, lapsing into the haughty manner of
the scholar, and bent upon having his own way. But the willingness to toil and suffer for the Lord he loved, and for the good of
souls committed to his charge, was very real.

Already the work entailed considerable financial burden, and
now for the first time he had come to an end of his resources.
With urgent claims in many directions, he had no money to
draw upon, and no means left of raising even a few strings of
cash. This was, for the moment, the pressing difficulty; and with
his wife he took it to the Lord in prayer. Helpers of each other's
faith they truly were, and in sharing all their burdens made them
lighter.

As they prayed, light came; Mrs. Hsi had a plan. She could not
offer much toward the permanent solution of the problem, but
she could at least give temporary aid.

Stored away in vermilion-coloured boxes were still a number
of garments and some jewellery, part of her bridal outfit. Her
husband, though disposing freely of his own belongings, had
never thought of drawing upon her supplies, and was reluctant
still to let her make the sacrifice.

"But I do not need these things," she urged. "Why should we
store them up? Gladly let us make them an offering to the Lord
to provide means for shepherding His flock."

So the boxes were investigated and a number of articles chosen.
Quickly the mules were harnessed, and Hsi set off for the city.
The joy of sacrifice was in their hearts. There must be no delay.

But difficulties were not yet at an end. Half the journey still
remained when clouds began to gather and the wind blew up,
bringing a drenching storm. Soon the cart and its occupants were
soaked, and even the important box suffered damage. But
though attributing this misfortune to "the prince of the power of
the air," Hsi cheered himself by remembering that the Heavenly
Father had allowed it to happen, and that it must be all right. Far
from vexed or troubled, he went on his way "praising the Lord

with a loud voice" for the privilege of enduring hardness for Jesus' sake. In spite of their wetting, the things obtained a good price; and in fair weather, with a glad heart, Hsi journeyed back across the plain.

Now it happened that just at this juncture a shop became vacant in the town of Tengtsun, only five miles from his home. This led to a practical suggestion. Tengtsun was a market town, frequented by crowds of people from all the surrounding villages, very few of whom had ever heard the Gospel. Why not rent the house, and employ some of the Christian men needing help, to open it as a drug-store? If well managed it would soon become self-supporting, and at the same time be a centre for missionary work throughout the neighbourhood. The more he prayed over it, the more Hsi liked the plan. As a Chinese doctor he had some knowledge of drugs, and from a business point of view was fully equal to the undertaking.

And so it came to pass that the summer days of 1881 witnessed a fresh departure of some significance. A medical mission station, on purely native lines, sustained and conducted apart altogether from foreign supervision, was a new thing in those days. The missionaries in the city were interested and sympathetic, but thought it wiser not to render any direct assistance. Alone and very prayerfully Hsi went to work, and soon the new drug-store was in running order.

The room behind the shop was fitted up as a guest-hall. High-backed chairs stood in the place of honour, ready to welcome visitors. A bright brass teapot and china cups waited invitingly on the table. Christian mottoes adorned the walls, and a good supply of books and benches suggested the evening meeting and Sunday services. The shop itself was neat and attractive, from the open window with its plentiful supply of drugs,[1] to the conventional corner within, where the doctor interviewed his patients and made out prescriptions. Over the doorway hung the characters Fu Yin Tang—Hall of the Happy Sound or Joyful News.

Hsi was very busy in those days, for he was doctor, preacher, and business manager all in one. He was, in some sense, doing the work of a medical missionary, with the advantage of being a voluntary native agent as well. It was a good combination.

[1] Probably including lumps of rhubarb, sticks of liquorice root, cubes of catechu, nux vomica beans, and the other crude drugs commonly found in a Chinese pharmacy.

Meanwhile, in his own village, responsibilities were increasing round him. His home, capacious like his heart, was filled with people needing help. As early as the summer of 1881, scarcely two years after his conversion, the missionary in charge of the district wrote as follows:

A man from Hsi's village was here at the meetings yesterday, well-dressed and healthy-looking. He prayed in beautiful Chinese, that we all might learn what it is to die with Christ, to be buried with Him, and with Him even now to rise and live the resurrection life. A few months ago that man was ragged, dirty, and miserable; a heavy opium-smoker. He used to consume nearly an ounce of poison daily. Hsi took him by the hand, had him in his own house, treated him like a brother, bought opium medicine to cure his craving, cared for him, and led him to Christ. He is now perfectly free from the opium-habit, and is Hsi's right-hand man at all the prayer meetings and services. Whether he is truly converted or not I cannot say; but as a specimen of the work our brother Hsi is carrying on, he is to my mind a most cheering case.

Hsi has also opened a medicine shop near his home. . . . The idea is to make it a basis for missionary operations in the town. . . . At present I do not go over as I intended, because there is a great deal of ill-feeling against the "foreign religion," and I think my presence would only hinder the cause. These brethren are quite competent, guided and strengthened by the Holy Spirit, to carry on the work they have undertaken. Being voluntary, unpaid agents they naturally feel a deep interest in their own work, and need less looking after than might be required by men receiving several dollars a month from us.

It was not all smooth sailing, even after the medicine shop had been opened. In China as well as at home there are people who will profess almost anything for the sake of gain; and some among the inquirers doubtless thought that by becoming Christians they would establish a claim for financial aid. Nothing could be further, however, from Hsi's point of view. Independent and resourceful himself, his ideals were high for the native church. But with the heart of a true shepherd, he always felt deep solicitude for the suffering and weak. He never could merely say "Be warmed and fed," and let a fellow-believer go away hungry and miserable. He never did. At the same time it was useless to try to impose upon him. No one could more swiftly discover a fraud, or detect insincerity wherever it existed. This penetration of character saved him from many a blunder, and balanced his large-hearted sympathy.

Then, also, he was among his own people, and understood them so well that he was not likely to be much misled. From the beginning he was too wise to suggest, or even think, that missionaries from abroad should attempt the same forms of benevolence.

Necessarily unfamiliar with Chinese character and customs, they were so much more open to imposition; besides which they occupied a different relationship to the native church. But, personally, he never saw any reason to curtail his own generous hospitality, and as long as he lived his home was open to all whom he could serve for Jesus' sake.

Occasionally he had disappointments. The men, for example, whom he first put into the medicine shop, failed him, and would not stay because of the smallness of the profits. Hsi was concerned about this, chiefly on their account; and as he feared, they never afterwards proved satisfactory. Undiscouraged, however, he filled their places with others, and carried on the work of that station for more than twenty years.

# 18

# Light on the Problem

IT was the beginning of 1883, the fourth year after Hsi's conversion. Unconsciously, he was drawing near a time of crisis. New developments were at hand, destined to throw light upon the problem and lead to his life-work.

Twenty miles north of the scholar's village, on the main road to the capital of the province, stood the city of Hungtung, guardian of a populous plain. Numerous towns and villages crowded the open country and climbed the lower spurs of the mountains, while cities of importance marked the course of the rapid river. Travelling through this beautiful region, missionaries had often been impressed with its importance as a centre for evangelistic work, but hitherto it was unreached by the Gospel.

Left so long in darkness by the Christian Church, the people sought as best they might to satisfy the hunger of the soul. They were ignorant, but far from indifferent as to spiritual things. Some fifty years before, a reformer had arisen in the north-east of the province, a thoughtful, earnest man, who gave his life to recalling his fellow-countrymen to the best they knew, with a zeal and devotion that produced remarkable results. Careless as to his own comfort, he travelled far and wide, enduring any amount of hardship, living in poverty and loneliness, always ready to give his last cash to anyone in greater need, and preaching everywhere the duty of self-denial and faithful service of the gods. With burning enthusiasm he called on men and women to repent, and turn from their selfishness and evil ways, exhorting them to cultivate virtue, care for the needs of others, practise benevolence, spend time and money in the relief of suffering, accumulate merit —in the hope of balancing the soul's account in the dread days to come.

Such exhortations appealed to the Chinese strong sense of duty and still stronger fear of death and retribution—the judgment of Heaven that none can escape; the terrors with which a guilty conscience invests the great Unknown.

How little light he had to give; how little help! Yet people flocked to him. They had nothing better. His followers were numerous, and of all ranks and conditions. Confucianists, Buddhists, and Taoists, men and women alike, they banded themselves together into well-organised societies, and did much to revive the worship of idols and the regular performance of religious rites. Even to their eyes Buddhism and Taoism were terribly corrupt in Shansi.

Specially on the Hungtung plain and in the surrounding district this influence was felt. The whole region became a stronghold of these idolatrous societies. The leader of the movement passed away. He died shortly before the first Protestant missionaries came to Shansi. But his followers carried on the work. The more zealous of them became vegetarians and even celibates, giving themselves to the practice of severe austerities. Some took to reciting their daily chants and prayers, kneeling upon the points of sharp iron nails driven through a board for the purpose, while slowly a required length of incense burned away. Others, though not torturing themselves or giving up the relationships of home life, endured much hardship in pilgrimages to distant shrines, and spent money freely in doing "good deeds," such as providing coffins for the poor, mending roads, supporting the priests and temples, and liberating birds, fish, and animals that were to be used for food.

Well known as a leader among these little bands was a bright, enthusiastic man named Fan, who lived in a village a few miles east of Hungtung. Though devoted to the "cultivation of virtue," as they understood it, he was weary and dissatisfied in heart, longing for something more, something better, he knew not what.

A friend of his from the city accosted him one day with strange information. Foreigners had appeared in the neighbourhood selling religious books, and talking about a God they called the true and living God and some plan by which sins could be forgiven. The friend was not much interested, but he thought Fan might like to hear of it; and he handed him a tract entitled *The Three Needs*.

It did not take Fan long to make up his mind. This new religion was at any rate worth looking into. The foreigners had left Hungtung, but were living, he heard, in the next important city to the south, only a day's journey away. He would go down and see them, and find out for himself all about the teachings that interested him so strangely.

But first of all he must prepare a gift. From his own experience he understood the inwardness of these things. It would never do to go down empty-handed. This caused a little delay, for the sum he felt it necessary to take was considerable. Then there was the opposition of his family and friends to overcome, and the work of the farm to provide for. But finally Fan felt himself free, and bidding good-bye to wife and children, he set out for the city of Pingyang.

The foreigners' house was easily discovered, and Fan was warmly welcomed by Sung and others, who led the way to the guest-hall and were soon interested in his story. They answered many of his questions, spoken and unspoken, and seemed to understand so well just what he felt. They told him of not a few in and around the city who had accepted the new faith, and specially of one scholarly Confucianist, named Hsi, already quite a leader among the Christians. This surprised Fan, who was not prepared to find literary men of their number, and made him eager to hear more.

Greater still was his interest when the missionaries came in. He had previously learned that they dressed and spoke as Chinese, but was astonished to find them so completely like himself in things external. They were kind and courteous, and seemed to appreciate his position as a religious leader. They spoke freely of eternal life, the danger of the unsaved, and the joy of sins forgiven. But much that they said was mysterious to their unaccustomed listener, and the missionaries had to leave before they could make everything plain.

With a feeling of disappointment Fan returned their cordial salutations, and though pressed by Sung and others to stay the evening and hear more, said that he must excuse himself, but might return another day.

This was too much for one of them, the warm-hearted soldier Chang.

"Oh, do not think of leaving," he exclaimed. "You have hardly begun to understand this wonderful teaching. Come with me to the Western Chang village. It is only a few miles across the plain, and Hsi will be so glad to see you."

To this unexpected suggestion Fan consented, and the two set out toward the mountains. As they went, Fan listened with growing satisfaction to all Chang told him of the man they were about to meet. Here, at any rate, he would be on familiar ground. Was not Hsi a Confucian scholar, and like himself a preacher of benevolence? They would soon feel as brothers. And happily Fan was well provided with the best talisman for winning an entrance into the secret mysteries of any sect.

Seated in Hsi's guest-hall, he felt quite at home. True, there were no mottoes or pictures such as he was accustomed to, in honour of the gods; no idols or incense-burners, and no ancestral tablets. In place of these were scrolls with inscriptions that he could not understand, probably quotations from their Christian classics. But this was all part of the simplicity of their religious notions, and with suspended judgment he awaited the appearance of his host.

Acquainted by Chang with the circumstances of the visit, Hsi hastened to meet the stranger kindly, and pressed him to stay the night, that they might have time for the discussion of important themes.

This pleased Fan, and was no less than he had expected. For the moment he was at a disadvantage, Hsi having given him no opportunity for presenting the money order he had brought. But evidently he was not the only man there as a learner. Quite a number were coming and going, who seemed to be members of the household. It was not likely that any of these disciples had paid as handsomely as he was prepared to, for instruction. And with a consciousness that he would soon be master of the situation, Fan bided his time.

At length, laying aside other duties, Hsi invited his guest into a quiet room, and Fan, with polite regrets as to the unworthiness of his offering, produced the fee of ten thousand cash. Grasping at once the situation, Hsi expostulated:

"What! do you regard the grace of God as something to be purchased with money? Sir, you must immediately repent, that your sins may be forgiven and your heart renewed, through faith alone in the Saviour's merit."

Greatly surprised and perplexed, Fan withdrew the money, and begged his new friend to explain how and on what footing he might enter the Christian religion. This could not be done in a moment, and Hsi detained him as his guest for several days.

Long and earnest were their conversations. Fan was an eager listener, and grasped the truth with clearness. Feeling at length that there was no need of further instruction, Hsi rose, and coming to where Fan was seated, laid his hands upon his head, praying for him in silence.

"Then," as Hsi recalled long after, "Fan was moved to the heart. He sobbed aloud, though at the same time rejoicing and praising God. All who saw it were alarmed. But I reassured them, saying, 'There is no need for fear; it is the power of the Spirit who has come upon him.'"

And so indeed it proved.

On the following morning, as soon as he awoke, Fan was again filled with wonderful joy, and declared himself a believer.

"I see it all now," he exclaimed. "Idols indeed are false and useless. Our Heavenly Father is the true and living God, and Jesus the only Saviour."

Hsi persuaded him to stay a little longer, that he might learn more about prayer and Christian living, and then let him go his way, eager to carry the glad tidings home. Full of thankfulness, Fan returned to the city, and spent a day or two with the missionaries, who supplied him with a New Testament and urged him to come again at the earliest opportunity. This he gladly promised to do, hoping that he might bring some of his followers with him. At first there would be misunderstanding, no doubt, and perhaps suspicion, but he felt so sure that they would appreciate the glad tidings before long. Alas, he little dreamed how bitter was the opposition that awaited him, and from how sad a cause.

Toward evening he approached Fantsun, and sighted the familiar homestead where he had left wife and children only a few days before. But no little ones ran out to meet him, no kindly welcome was spoken as he passed down the village street. Something evidently was wrong. There was trouble in the air. He heard sounds of wailing as for the dead. This seemed to grow louder as he neared his own dwelling. Could it have anything to do with him and his?

Dazed by the dreadful tidings, for a time he could hardly take it in. His son, his own bright bonnie little son, killed during his absence! Torn to pieces by a ferocious wolf. It seemed too terrible to be true. And then he had to suffer all the reproaches of wife and relatives, who poured upon him the bitterness of their grief and indignation.

Of course it was his fault, his son. The gods were incensed, and no wonder. Had not all gone well with them up to the time of this renegade errand? Was not the religion of his fathers good enough for him? Alas, that an innocent child must suffer for his folly, and a poor mother be heart broken! For himself, it was richly deserved. Had they not told him there would be trouble, from the first?

It did all seem inexplicable, and an older Christian than Fan might well have been staggered. But in that hour of anguish he was not left alone.

"I greatly obtained God's grace," was his testimony, "and the Holy Spirit, filling my heart, caused me to know my Heavenly Father better, and to trust Him more."

But the neighbours could not understand such calmness, and only thought his delusion the more terrible. They insisted that he must at once renounce these dangerous heresies, and bring offerings to appease the idols.

"Calamity will overtake us all," they cried. "Hitherto you alone have suffered. But drought will come, and famine. The gods will be revenged upon the whole community, and then do not expect to get off easily. We shall certainly destroy your house and all that you possess."

"See," said Fan quietly; "the God I worship now is the living God, who made heaven and earth. He can prevent the drought from coming. He is stronger than our idols. I do not fear them any longer, and will pray to Him who is above all evil spirits to protect the village from harm."

Something about his confidence seemed to impress them, and they were in the habit of looking to him as a leader in religious matters. At any rate they left off threatening, and settled down to wait and see. "But remember," was the frequent warning, "if trouble comes, you will be the first to pay the penalty."

As the summer days wore on, all eyes turned anxiously to the mountain stream. Fan by this time had taken down his idols, and was openly preaching Christ. And his wife had found a measure of comfort in her sorrow. Whether it was that his changed life appealed to her, or that she herself was coming to know the Saviour's love, the severity of her opposition ceased, and she even consented to a visit from her husband's teacher and friend.

Full of sympathy for the family, Hsi came over and spent some days in the village. Neighbours were interested and curious. Impressed by his evident culture, they thronged to hear him discourse upon the new doctrine, and even the most unwilling had to acknowledge his sincerity and power. Fan was jubilant, and the more so because all fear of drought was forgotten. The river was unusually full of water, and his confidence in prayer increased day by day. Among his former co-religionists, not a few began to show deep interest in the Gospel, and at the close of Hsi's visit, his wife and some members of the family declared themselves Christians.

Then it was the blow fell: a sorrow so overwhelming that it seemed as if it must uproot their faith. How often such mysterious assaults are experienced by converts emerging from heathenism in lands "where Satan's seat is." The great enemy does not readily relinquish his hold. But, thank God, there is a place of refuge: "He that was begotten of God keepeth him, *and the evil one toucheth him not.*"

Fan was away from home. He had gone down a second time to visit the missionaries in Pingyang. His two remaining children were playing in the village, without a thought of danger, when suddenly a hungry wolf appeared as before, and carried off the boy, a little fellow of only five years old, killing and devouring him within sight of his father's door. The villagers were horror-stricken. His second son to meet a death so terrible! The drought truly had been averted, but the offender was again singled out as a mark for the vengeance of the gods.

Heart-broken, the parents wept together—both their boys taken from them, within six months of each other, by a tragedy so mysterious. To be without a son in China is the worst of all calamities, and added to this were the cruel reproaches of neighbours and friends. But they were not left alone in their sorrow. The cry of their hearts, "Lord, I believe; help Thou mine unbelief," brought divine comfort to their aid.

Fan especially was lifted above the trial. "Let the devil harass if he will: *I know that Jesus saves,*" became his motto.

With intense fervour he now threw himself into the work of God. The enemy of souls had smitten him sore; he would in return devote every energy to snatching others from his dominion. Such earnestness, under the circumstances, was doubly impressive. He established regular Sunday services in the village, which were well attended; and the missionary came over frequently from the city to strengthen his hands.

But as the work developed and his neighbours became more interested, Fan was perplexed by a new and serious difficulty. He found that the inquirers, even the most promising, were in too many cases confirmed opium-smokers. There was not a man among them who would attempt to defend the habit. All alike were convinced that it was harmful and degrading. It never even occurred to them that they could be Christians and continue smoking opium. But they knew no way to be delivered. And the sad conclusion seemed that there could be no hope for them; they could never be reckoned among the followers of Jesus.

But this Fan would not believe. Full well he knew the difficulty. But there must be some way by which even opium-smokers could be saved. Had not the Son of God come on purpose "to seek and to save that which was lost"?

The obstacles were great and many. He could not take all these inquirers to Hsi's home or to the missionaries in the city. They had no accommodation for them. He was not himself a doctor, and would be unable to proceed with their cure, even if he had the needed medicines. And yet how could he go to these men, knowing there were medicines that would help them, and tell them they must face the awful struggle in faith alone? Most of them would give it up on the spot. No, he felt that in some way he must strengthen them to conquer. God had given him this work to do. But—how?

At length, as he prayed, the thought dawned upon him that if the patients could not go to the doctor perhaps the doctor might come to them. Mr. Drake had medicines, and knew how to use them. He had also a kind heart. His own home, a cave-dwelling, was large enough to take in a dozen or twenty people at a time. He would himself house and care for both doctor and patients, as long as might be necessary, and give everyone who wished it a chance to be free.

This novel proposal Mr. Drake received with favour. He was deeply interested in Fan and his village, and consented to go over for a month, and complete the cure of all who would put themselves under his care. This was a good beginning.

At first, however, only two men were courageous enough to go in for the treatment. The rest crowded the guest-hall and courtyard, lingering about from morning till night to watch the progress of events. The house was a simple structure, consisting of three long, tunnel-like rooms, side by side, in imitation of the cave-dwellings so common in the mountains; the front wall, built of mud bricks, having a window in each of the side rooms for ventilation, and in the central room a door. The three apartments opened into each other; the guest-hall being in the middle, the sleeping rooms to right and left. One of these was devoted to the missionary and his patients, but could not afford much privacy, as it was open to observation from without and within.

Fan was in his element, watching the medical treatment, preparing food and tea for his visitors, and preaching all day long to crowds in the courtyard and guest-hall. As the cure proceeded, the interest of onlookers became intense. They did so want to go in for it too; but could the sufferings really be endured?

At length one of the two patients, an earnest inquirer, was in agony of mind and body so great that he could bear it no longer. It was midnight; but he roused Fan, imploring him to cry to God for his relief. In a moment Fan was kneeling beside him, confident that prayer would bring the succour medicine alone could not afford. All had been done that could be done, and now they cast themselves upon the power and pity of the Saviour they believed to be so near. Again the touch of His hand brought healing. The sufferer was relieved, and could hardly wait till morning to tell how quickly his distress had been removed, and how all his fears were gone.

"Certainly the medicines are good," thought anxious observers; "and apparently prayer also helps not a little."

The result was that one and another applied for treatment, until Mr. Drake and his enthusiastic lieutenant had nineteen men on their hands for the remainder of the month.

To distract their thoughts and use the opportunity, the missionary taught them hymns and passages from Scripture, and conducted morning and evening services, with plenty of singing, which largely augmented the congregations. Between times, the verses were committed to memory in correct Chinese fashion; every man repeating his lessons by the hour together in loud, sing-song tones, accompanied by a swaying motion of the body. The babel may be better imagined than described, but the result was satisfactory to all concerned.

Slowly the days wore on, until at length the undertaking was crowned with success. All the patients were cured, and most of them went home renewed in soul as well as body. Mr. Drake returned to the city, weary but rejoicing; and Fan was left full of thankfulness, with a growing work upon his hands.

The movement thus begun, it was impossible to discontinue.

Opium-smokers all round the neighbourhood heard the story, and applied to Fan for help. Mr. Drake sent to the coast for medicines, and the Refuge was kept going throughout the year. A strong spiritual influence was encouraged by frequent visits from Hsi of the Western Chang village, who, making little of the journey across the plain, would come at any time to the assistance of his friend. By degrees the missionaries in the city were less able to give personal supervision, and Fan came to count increasingly upon Hsi, who took up the burden with him, entering into every detail with keenest interest. He would talk and pray for hours with patients and inquirers, conduct services, entertain visitors, comfort the suffering, and be ready with wise counsel in cases of difficulty. Yet neither he nor Fan had any idea to what end all this was tending.

At length, early in 1883, the emergency came that opened their eyes. The Refuge had been at work all through the previous year, and scores of men had been successfully dealt with. A number of patients were in the midst of their course of treatment, and more medicine was required. Fan sent to the city, expecting to obtain it as usual, but found to his consternation that the supply was exhausted and the missionaries were away on a long journey.

Just at this juncture Hsi was impressed with a desire to go over to the Refuge, and, knowing nothing of the circumstances, was surprised at the eagerness of his welcome.

"Oh, elder brother," Fan exclaimed, "surely the Lord has sent you to deliver us. We are like men climbing painfully out of a miry pit. And now we can go neither up nor down. Quickly, I pray you, think of some plan to save us."

It was indeed a difficult situation, and Hsi knew as little as Fan how to proceed. But he was sure of one thing.

"The work is of God," he replied. "Do not fear. Give the men what medicine you have left. I will go home and see what can be done."

It was a long twenty miles that day, and most of the time was spent in prayer. For Hsi, too, it was a life crisis, though at the moment he did not know it. These men must be helped, and helped at once—that was the burden. And God surely would give him light, for there seemed no one else to help them.

Already, in his suspense, the thought had come that possibly the Lord would use his knowledge of native drugs to enable him to compound a medicine that might take the place of the supply that had failed. It seemed a bold idea, but the more he considered it the more he felt encouraged. Thoughts passed rapidly through his mind, and by the time he reached home he was ready to make the attempt.

"With prayer and fasting," he writes, "I waited upon the Lord, and besought Him to point out to me the proper ingredients, and to strengthen and help me, that I might prepare the pills quickly and carry them to the Refuge, that those who were breaking off opium might partake thereof and be at peace."

And then, very simply, it all came to him just how those pills were to be made. The drugs were at hand in his store, and, still fasting, he took the prescription, compounded the medicine, and hastened back to the Refuge.

Then he and Fan together, assured that this remedy was of God, administered it to the patients. It proved an entire success, and with grateful hearts they gave Him all the praise.

The pills were just what was needed. Inexpensive and easily made, they could be produced in large quantities and at short notice. This entirely changed the aspect of opium refuge work. No longer dependent upon foreign supplies, why should not such effort be systematically developed and made self-supporting? And to Hsi's mind it raised the further question:

"Have we not here light upon the problem we have been pondering so long—How best to bring people everywhere under the influence of the Gospel, and provide employment for Christian men needing some means of subsistence?"

It all unfolded and developed in the most natural way. The key fitted the lock, opened the door, and gave access to a wide beyond of opportunity and promise.

# 19

# Finding His Life-Work

THE Refuge at Fantsun now became the laboratory where first experiments were worked out. Fan, in his gratitude for the relief Hsi had afforded, was more than ever grateful to his friend. Together they worked, planned, and prayed. Hsi possessed in unusual degree the power to lead, and, as he was also doctor and druggist in one, the chief responsibility tended inevitably to devolve upon him.

Before long the anti-opium medicine prepared for the Refuge became deservedly famous. Fan was in difficulty to know how to accommodate all the patients seeking treatment. Hsi came over more often, staying days at a time to help in various ways. The work was financially and spiritually successful, and developed the men whose hearts were in it for larger efforts in days to come.

As to the need for such enterprise there could be no divergence of opinion in Shansi, where, according to common report, *eleven out of every ten smoked opium*!

For almost a century the fatal habit had been gaining ground in China. Fostered by foreign merchants, it had laid hold upon that immense population with astonishing rapidity. Every effort to prohibit the trade had proved unavailing, supported as it was by the strength of European arms. Compelled against their will to admit vast quantities of imported opium, the Government, in self-defence, at last relaxed the stringent laws forbidding the cultivation of the poppy on Chinese soil; with the result that everywhere rich tracts of wheat-producing land had been given up to the growth of opium.

Shansi had suffered as much, if not more than any other part of the interior. From the cities the trouble spread to the villages, and from the men to the women—even infants being born with a craving for the poison. Few habitual smokers ever succeeded in escaping that terrible bondage, which had become so general in Hsi's day, that the people of his province might well have echoed the piteous appeal addressed by their fellow countrymen to the Confucian scholars of Canton.

"We aged artisans," wrote the village elders of that district, "are reduced to extremity in providing for our families. This bitter poverty, sadness, and pain is entirely owing to the injury of opium. We piteously beseech you, Teachers, to have compassion on the poor, and establish a law of prohibition in the villages."

But what power had Confucianism to help the sufferers in their need? Too many of the ruling class were themselves enslaved to opium-smoking. Legislation was useless, as long as foreign nations, at the point of the sword, insisted upon flooding the country with "the flowing poison." And as to any hope of rescue for the confirmed opium-smoker—could water be made to run uphill, or fire not to burn?

But from all this misery and degradation Hsi had been delivered, and into it now he was sent with hope and help for thousands.

The work of the Fantsun Refuge was full of difficulty, however, as well as encouragement, and often enough Hsi and his associates found faith and courage taxed to the utmost. Prayer was the great resource, and many were the deliverances granted in answer to their petitions.

Some among the patients, for example, unknown to them, might be suffering from serious maladies in addition to the opium-habit, and interference with the accustomed supply of the drug would give rise to alarming complications. Others had taken to opium in the first instance for the relief of acute illness, and any lessening of the dose meant a return of the original malady. It was impossible in such cases to foretell the course of events, and at any hour of the day or night symptoms might arise that threatened a fatal issue.

To have a patient die in the Refuge in those early days might easily have wrecked the whole work. But Hsi, when such troubles arose, would give himself to prayer and fasting, sometimes for days together. The power of God was very manifest on these occasions; and many of the worst sufferers were healed when human help seemed all unavailing. As the fame of these doings spread through the country-side, sick people began to come from distant places, suffering with all sorts of ailments, and present themselves at the Refuge, asking to be prayed for.

"At that time," wrote Hsi, "the Lord frequently used me in the Refuge and in neighbouring villages, to heal diseases through prayer, and to cast out devils. Between fifty and sixty men believed in the Lord Jesus, and met regularly (at Fantsun) for worship. This was during the fourth year of my Christian life."

But Hsi and his fellow-workers were not content with praying themselves only; they did all in their power to lead the patients also to pray. Everyone entering the Refuge was expected to join in morning and evening worship.

"If you are not willing," they would say, "to unite with us in prayer to the true and living God, we cannot undertake the responsibility of your case."

For Hsi had no confidence in medical treatment alone to accomplish a permanent cure. From his own experience he was sure that a power more terrible than opium lay behind the fascination of the drug. Sin was to him the grip of the devil, and the opium-habit one of the strongest chains with which he binds the soul. Men of iron will might break even those fetters, but that would not free them from the tyranny of Satan, and in nine cases out of ten they would return to the vice before long. Medicine was good; help and sympathy in the hour of need invaluable; but Hsi knew only one Deliverer, and He never failed.

So his first care was to point men to Christ, deprecating trust in himself or any medical treatment apart from the power of the living Saviour. All their own strength, and all the help that could be given, must prove unavailing when the real struggle began; a fact the poor fellows were ready enough to believe, in their hours of anguish. Then came the practical test; and the relief of suffering in answer to prayer was the miracle that first drew many of those fifty or sixty to the feet of Jesus.

It was indeed wonderful to see how immediate was the response that often followed those simple, childlike prayers. But to Hsi and his associates it seemed most natural, for—was it not prayer *in the name of Jesus*?

On one occasion, for example, three men came together from a neighbouring village, begging to be taken into the Refuge. Hsi was there at the time, as it happened, and was doubtful about receiving them on account of age. They were all advanced in years, the youngest being over sixty, and were opium-smokers of long standing. But they were so eager to be cured that, finally, they were admitted, the principles of the Refuge having been made especially plain.

For the first day or two all went well, and the old men became much interested in the Gospel. But by the third evening one of them was feeling desperate, and during the night he called the others, begging them to rouse Hsi or Fan, and get something to relieve his agony.

"Why should we wait for that?" cried his friends. "It is not medicine you need. Kneel down, and let us pray."

Only a poor room in that little village, far away in the heart of China, and three old men kneeling alone at midnight. Was He there, that wonderful Saviour? Would He respond with ready succour as of old?

Tremblingly the cry went up in the darkness: "O Jesus, help me. Save me. Save me now."

A few minutes later the sufferer was lying quietly wrapped in his wadded coverlet again. His groans ceased. His distress passed away. And in a little while he was fast asleep.

"Jesus truly is there," whispered the others. And they too slept till morning.

Then bright and early they were up, eager to tell their story, and with smiling faces accosted everyone they met:

"True? Why, of course it's true! We know all about it. Your Jesus does indeed hear and answer prayer."

They were overflowingly happy, with a joy and confidence that proved contagious. And faith in many hearts was strengthened. For such testimony cannot be gainsaid.

Among the men brought to the Lord in those early days at Fantsun, were several who afterwards developed into valued leaders in the opium refuge work. They were hard cases some of them, but prayer prevailed, and the result was worth the cost. One such was Sung, of Fan's own village, who was the means of winning hundreds to faith in Christ; another was Liu of Sopu, afterwards well known as a deacon of the Hungtung church.

Five miles north-east of the Refuge, this noted gambler lived in a little hamlet among the hills. He had long been a slave to opium, and seemed as hopelessly sunk in sin as anyone could be. His wife, a constant sufferer, was hardly able to bear the burden of existence from day to day; and they had no son to care for their advancing years. Tidings of what was taking place at Fantsun reached Liu in his miserable life, but far from being attracted, he was enraged to think that the "foreign-devil doctrine" should have found adherents in his neighbourhood and be gaining so much influence.

One day he learned that an opium-smoker friend of his named Chang had been so far deluded by the enthusiasts at Fantsun as to put himself into their hands for treatment. He had actually gone into the Refuge, and was fast being won over to the strange faith.

As if this were not enough, a few weeks later Chang himself appeared, his face radiant, his opium craving gone, and his heart full of the love of Christ. With surly indifference Liu listened to his story, but Chang exclaimed:

"Elder brother, why do not you also give up opium-smoking, and pray that your sins may be forgiven?" He angrily retorted: "What! bewitched yourself, and deceived by these foreign devils, would you have me too drawn into the snare"—and in sudden passion drove him from the house.

Undiscouraged, Chang soon paid a second visit. But this time Liu was more violent than ever, and his friend had to retire, feeling that no good had been accomplished.

After he was gone, poor Liu could no longer stifle the convictions that for some time had been troubling him. Conscience spoke, and would not be silenced. Lying awake that night his misery was so great that he cried aloud:

"Wife, what have I done? Surely my sins are overwhelming. Alas, I have driven from the house the only friend who can help us. Though I have shamefully reviled him, I would give anything to be as he is. His opium craving is cured, and his heart is at peace. How different our condition. You live a life of weakness and suffering, and I am destroyed by this opium. What was it Chang said about his God, the true and living God? Did he not speak of hope—even for us?"

"If there be a living God," responded the poor woman, "doubtless He could help us. Certainly no one else can. But you have treated Chang so badly he will never come again."

"Wife," replied Liu with conviction, "if his God is indeed willing to help us, Chang will come back. Something tells me so. And if he does, I will listen to his words."

Meanwhile Chang was praying; and after a few days he decided to try once more. Making his way slowly toward the house, he found Liu at home, and was surprised by a friendly welcome. Then, over a cup of tea,[1] came the unexpected question:

[1] Tea in Shansi often means nothing but hot water, as the people are poor and tea-leaves expensive.

"Brother Chang, how was it, after all, that you were able to break off opium?"

"Ah," he answered guardedly, "I fear it is no use repeating that story, for you seem determined not to believe. If only you would try the same plan, however, your craving too would be conquered, and your wife's illness cured."

"I am indeed ready to believe," cried Liu earnestly. "Only explain to me this wonderful religion."

"If you want to understand," replied Chang, "you must be willing to repent and put away your idols. In that case, come with me to the Fan village, and you shall find out for yourself the power of Christ to save."

To this Liu actually consented, and Chang bore him off in triumph. His fame had gone before; and when Fan took in the situation, he received the new patient cordially, overjoyed to bring so notorious a sinner into an atmosphere of love and prayer.

And now the opium-smoking gambler found himself surrounded by conditions that were new and strange indeed. He could not account for the kindness of these Christians, nor for their constant cheerfulness and joy. They seemed to be all the time either singing or praying, and this not as a religious duty, but just as naturally as he would grumble and swear. And yet, what there was to make them happy, for the life of him he could not tell. They were poor, like himself, and had to work hard. They did not drink wine, or play cards. They neither attended theatricals, nor spent money in feasting and fine clothes. He could discover no reason why they should be more satisfied than other people. But so contented were they, that they seemed never to quarrel or fight. The men did not beat their wives—unless they did it at night, when he was not there to see—and the women went about their work with good temper, so that the disturbances so common in "the inner apartments" were conspicuous by their absence.

There was a warmth too about their kindness that made his heart glow. Nothing seemed any trouble to them. They would get up at night if he were suffering, to make him food or tea; would sing to him, and comfort him with pleasant, cheery talk; and if that were not sufficient, they would go down on their knees beside his bed, and tell all his troubles to their unseen God. This was the strangest thing of all, for when they prayed for him he was sure to be relieved. Who could this new God be?

Gradually, as the days wore on, a change was noticeable in the Sopu patient. His opium craving lessened, his strength returned, and he began to take a deep interest in the Gospel. But there was a burden somewhere; and instead of growing happier, he seemed only the more troubled. Observing this, Fan said to him at length:

"Elder brother, your heart is not at rest. Why are you sad and anxious?"

"It is the illness of my wife that troubles me," responded Liu. "Under your care and treatment, I am coming back to life again, and hope revives in my heart. But she, who through my sins has suffered greatly, is sick and all alone. I do not even know, after this interval, whether she is living or dead."

"Why did you not speak of this before?" cried Fan. "Let us at once ask our Heavenly Father to make her better. And as soon as you are well enough, we will go over and see if we can help."

Daily, to Liu's astonishment, the Christians continued to remember in prayer this sufferer they had never seen; and with apparent confidence they assured him that it was just as easy for the Lord Jesus to heal people at a distance as near at hand.

"He did so when on earth," they said. "And now there is no far and near, for He is everywhere."

Meanwhile, Mrs. Liu in the mountain village was wondering what had become of her husband. In spite of his evil ways she loved him, and was lonely in his absence, as well as sick and sad. Once and again a rumour reached her that he was doing well: and whether it was this, or simply her desire to grow strong, that she might make home a little brighter for his return, she certainly did improve, much to her own surprise.

At the first opportunity, Liu and Fan set out for Sopu, to see what answer had been given to their prayers. Not expecting any great change, Liu led the way to his little courtyard, on which the cave-rooms opened.

"I am ashamed to bid you enter, Brother Fan. Pray do not laugh at our unworthy dwelling."

But as soon as he saw his wife's face, all else was forgotten in joy and wonder. The first glance told him she was better; and when she hastened to light the fire and prepare tea with her own hands, a thing he had not known her to do for years, his astonishment was complete.

This seemed indeed almost a miracle, and Liu could not tell

what to make of it. He returned with Fan to the Refuge, and heard the Christians praising God and continuing as before to plead for blessing on himself and his wife: but still he could not pray. There was a hymn they used to sing, beginning: "Alas, my heart is all darkness." That seemed just to express his case; but as he went no further than the first line, it did not help him much.

A little later, when his cure was complete, he went down with a number of inquirers from the Refuge to one of the quarterly meetings at Pingyang, and there met with Hsi for the first time. Having heard of him as a professional gambler noted for dishonesty and daring, Hsi was delighted to find him free from opium-smoking and evidently anxious about the welfare of his soul. Patiently he sought to meet his difficulties and lead him into peace; with the result that Liu went back to the Refuge when the conference was over, rejoicing in full salvation.

And now the time came for leaving his new friends. At one of the last meetings Fan took as his subject the cleansing of the lepers, of whom only the Samaritan returned to give thanks. This greatly impressed Liu, who felt as if he had been delivered from a condition at least as bad as theirs.

"Nine men out of the ten," thought he, "forgot Him who had cleansed them. I will be the one to return and give thanks for God's grace."

He hastened home at once and told his wife all that was in his heart, praising and blessing God for His wonderful goodness to them both. Soon Mrs. Liu also found the Saviour; and so much was she strengthened physically that her husband declared they were "like two people raised from the dead." From that changed home in Sopu shone a light so bright and cheering that it brought hope to many a dark heart among the mountains.

"Elder brother, what has made you so different? And is there hope for me?" became a frequent question.

A visit from Hsi and Fan, who came over as soon as they could to look after these young Christians, made an impression upon Liu that was never forgotten. It was the first time Hsi had been in their home; and he read the Scriptures and prayed with them, doing all in his power to strengthen their faith in Christ. At the close of his prayer, Liu followed; and then, to everyone's surprise, his wife prayed also, her heart overflowing with joy in the Lord. Hsi was astonished at the advance she had made in spiritual things, and exclaimed again and again: "Truly this is the grace of God!"

It was hard to bring the visit to a close; but finally Liu set out with his guests, to escort them some little distance on their journey. Before parting, they knelt together under the open sky, and Hsi once more commended these new believers to the care of God: and as he prayed he wept. This greatly puzzled Liu, who was full of gladness. But later on Hsi told him he had been moved to tears on his account; by overwhelming apprehension lest, through the wiles of the devil, he should be ensnared and led away from Christ.

A few days later, at the Refuge, Hsi preached a memorable sermon on soul-winning. Liu was present; and the conviction came to him that we are saved not for our own happiness merely, but that we may become saviours of others. This new inspiration he carried home to his wife, and together they began to think and pray about the people around them.

Feeling the need of help in bringing the Gospel to Sopu, they definitely asked the Lord to lead to Himself someone in the village who might become a fellow-worker. This petition was not long on their hearts before they were surprised by a visit from a neighbour with whom Liu had been on terms of open enmity.

It soon appeared that this man was thoroughly awakened. "You were once as heavy an opium-smoker as I am. How were you delivered? And is there hope for me?"

With joy and thankfulness Liu told him of Jesus, and took him down to the Refuge at Fantsun. There he was cured of his opium-habit, and won to faith in Christ. Returning to Sopu, he also was fired with a longing to bring others to the Saviour, and having a large guest-hall, he threw it open for regular meetings. This was just what Liu and his wife had desired, and, greatly encouraged, they commenced Sunday services.

Later on Hsi came again, and started an Opium Refuge in the village, where it was much needed. The Lius were put in charge, and blessing soon followed their labours. This led to wider opportunities, and they became valued as faithful workers in several important spheres. Liu was for many years a deacon of the church, as well as one of Hsi's most valued helpers.

His wife, when no longer able to leave home, because of asthma and other illnesses, would not hear of his remaining at home on her account.

"No," she said steadfastly, "feeble as I am, I would rather be alone for months together than hinder him in his work."

Too aged and infirm at length to leave her room, she still gathered a few of the village women about her, teaching them to read and pray, and gladly entertained the preachers who came over to keep up the Sunday services.

Such Christians are the great need of China. Rescued themselves from heathenism, living in Chinese homes, understanding Chinese hearts, and fired with love for souls for whom the Saviour died, they are among her best and most successful missionaries. One outcome, perhaps the chief outcome, of the work in which Hsi was now engaged, was the development of just such men and women.

# 20

# A Visit to the Capital

FIVE years only had elapsed since the commencement of settled missionary work in Shansi, at the end of the terrible famine. The period, though brief, had been one of encouraging progress.

In the spring of 1878, when David Hill and his fellow-workers first reached the province, there was not one Protestant Christian, and scarcely even an inquirer among all its millions of people. In the summer of 1883, the fourth year after Hsi's conversion, there were already two stations at important centres, from which varied work was being carried on; two little churches had been formed, numbering some scores of believers, and the inquirers waiting to be received were many. In the northern city of Taiyüan, the capital of the province, a strong medical mission was in progress, attracting patients from a radius of two hundred English miles. Some thousands of people were under treatment annually, and the acknowledged skill of the foreign physician, Dr. Harold Schofield, was winning friends far and near. At Pingyang, a week's journey southward, the zeal and devotion of the converts had so spread a knowledge of the Gospel that Christians were to be found in scattered hamlets fully forty miles apart.

It was a time of progress and development in missionary work all over inland China. Seven years before, in September, 1876, the signing of the Chefoo Convention had thrown open the whole interior to the Gospel. Members of the China Inland Mission, ready and waiting for this opportunity, set off at once for the far interior; travelling within three years thirty thousand miles on pioneer journeys, and preaching Christ for the first time in regions the most remote and inaccessible. Their work had been attended with blessing, and as in Shansi, settled stations were beginning to spring up and little churches to be established in provinces hitherto wholly unevangelised.

So rapid had been the growth of the work that in all the new stations thus established by the Inland Mission reinforcements were sorely needed to enter widely-open doors.

Thus, early in 1882, definite prayer was commenced throughout

the Mission for at least seventy new workers to be sent out
within the next three years. "Other seventy also." They were
needed, and they were given. And the prayer that went up from
all the stations, and was so remarkably answered, did not a little
to deepen the spiritual life of the missionaries in their isolation,
and of the converts by whom they had come to be surrounded.

This was the movement into which, at his conversion, Hsi had
been brought; and though unconscious of the wider issue, reaching out to distant provinces, he shared the spirit and the faith that
aimed at nothing less than bringing the Gospel within reach of
"every creature" throughout inland China.

Though largely independent by force of circumstances, he was
a member of the church at Pingyang, and his work was officially
connected with that station. He still went over as often as possible
on Sundays, and was never absent from the Communion services.

But the great occasion that gathered all the Christians at Pingyang was the unique "quarterly meeting" held in the old mission-
house in that city. It was a delightful institution, and did much to
mould the life of the growing church. Then Hsi would come in
from his village, bringing a band of Christians on fire with
devotion like his own; and Fan from the Refuge, with his saved
opium-smokers and fellow-workers—Liu of Sopu, Sung, Chang,
and all the rest. Singing as they tramped the long day's road
across the plain or over the mountains, little companies gathered
from many a village and hamlet, growing in numbers as they
neared the city wall. And then what greetings when the mission-
house was reached, and evening brought the last familiar faces to
complete the circle.

Too numerous to crowd into the chapel or guest-rooms of the
house, they cheerfully took possession of the open courtyards and
made themselves at home. Supplied in many cases with their own
bedding and provisions, they settled down, the men in one court
and the women in another, hospitably cared for by the missionary
household. For the meetings a large awning was stretched across
the inner courtyard on poles of strong bamboo. Stools and
benches filled this spacious auditorium, where the baptistery also
was placed; and the raised ledge or pathway all round, on which
the dwelling-rooms opened, formed a platform for the speakers
at one end and a sheltered place for women who wished to be
out of sight at the other.

To Hsi and his immediate family the quarterly meeting of

April, 1883, was of unusual interest, for on that occasion his wife
and Mrs. Liang her mother, as well as his aged stepmother, were
to be baptised. Never before had such an event taken place in the
whole province of Shansi. Among the earlier members of the
little church were a few, a very few, women. But all of them
belonged to the poorer classes, and the fact of their baptism had
not attracted much attention. The present case was very different.
For the wife and mother of a scholar, an ex-Confucian gentleman,
to leave the seclusion of their home, and be openly seen in the
city, joining in the rites of the strange foreign religion—this was
an event indeed.

To the ladies themselves it involved no little self-denial.
Accustomed to the secluded life of women of their position,
whose only contact with the outside world is through the men
to whom they belong, a journey of even ten miles to the city was
a serious undertaking. And then, there is no denying it, the ceremony of baptism by immersion is to the Chinese Christian, man
or woman, a severe ordeal. For that very reason it has an added
value. It makes confession of faith in Christ so much more real
and definite, and draws a clear line of demarcation between inquirers and members of the Church. It costs something; but "for
Jesus' sake" makes it well worth while.

Mrs. Hsi and her mother-in-law had been Christians for some
time before they could decide to take this open stand for the
Master; and it was a great comfort to them that Mrs. Fan from
the Refuge was to be baptised on the same occasion. How strange
would seem the long day's journey across the plain, ending in the
city streets, the mission-home, the welcome from their foreign
friends and introduction to so many fellow-believers whom they
had never seen. Yes, Mrs. Fan was there, and Mrs. Liu from
Sopu, and not a few beside whose hearts warmed at the sight of
the scholar's wife and mother, for among them all Hsi's name was
a household word.

"I am only a feeble old woman, over seventy years of age,"
responded Mrs. Hsi to the greetings that assailed her. "It has truly
been a difficult undertaking; but I could not stay away. At my
age, life is uncertain. And how could I be willing to depart
without having confessed my Lord Jesus before men?"

Another reason for the joy of this occasion was a recent answer
to prayer in connection with annoyances that Hsi himself had
suffered. For some time past efforts had been made by the literary

men of the district to force him to abandon his faith in Christ, or at any rate to be much more reticent about it. The persecution culminated in a successful appeal to the Chancellor of the University to degrade the Christian from his rank of "Cultured Talent," or in other words to take away his B.A. degree. This was a terrible disgrace for every member of the family, and Hsi felt it keenly, in spite of the manifest injustice of the decision. But when reasoned with the Chancellor merely replied that he could have his degree again if he wished it; naming a sum of money beyond his means to afford even had he been willing to resort to such an expedient.

There was nothing to be done, as bribery was out of the question, and Hsi would not go to law in his own interest. But it was far from easy for a man of his prominent position, and naturally imperious temper, to submit patiently to public injustice and ridicule. But prayer was made for him continually, and he was helped to bear the trial in a Christian spirit.

The missionaries did not think it wise to interfere from the point of view of treaty rights, but Mr. Drake felt free to lay the facts before the provincial Governor, who might or might not take action in the matter. As it happened, the Governor was interested, and sent instructions to the Chancellor to reverse his decree. For a time the Chanceller took no notice, and it seemed as though the illegal action would stand. Finally, however, he thought better of it, and the degree was restored with honour. This happy conclusion called forth much thanksgiving, and was felt by all who understood the working of such affairs to be a remarkable answer to prayer.

It was about this time, before the lamented death of Dr. Schofield, that Hsi went up to the capital to see something of the missionaries, tidings of whose work had reached his distant home. The visit was brief but memorable, for it was his first introduction to anything like a foreign community. Even in those days missionary operations were considerably developed in Taiyüan. Two societies were represented by quite a staff of foreigners (six or eight households) engaged in education and the production of literature, as well as in medical and evangelistic work. All this was a revelation to the Christian scholar from the south of the province, and helped to broaden his horizon.

But the members of the church were few in the provincial capital, and not accustomed to just the type of spiritual life and power with which Hsi was familiar. The experiences he spoke of were a stimulus to their faith and no small encouragement to the missionaries as well.

Among the Christians up there at the time of Hsi's visit was one old lady with whom he would feel thoroughly at home. As in the case of his own wife and mother, her baptism had been long delayed, and from a cause that must have specially appealed to him.

Converted a year or two before, her love and faith and the consistency of her Christian life were undoubted. And yet she never asked to be received into the Church, and seemed distressed when the subject of baptism was mentioned. This puzzled the missionary ladies, who could not think of any reason why Mrs. Han should hold back.

At length in a quiet talk one day the old lady unburdened her heart.

"Alas," she said wistfully, "if only I could be a true follower of Jesus, and be baptized."

"And why not?" questioned the missionary, much interested. "Is there anything to hold you back?"

"Me? Why of course there is," exclaimed the visitor sadly. "How could I be His true disciple? I could never accomplish the work."

"But what work?" said her friend kindly. "Did not Jesus do it all?"

"Oh yes! and I do love Him, and am trusting Him alone for salvation. But I know that the Lord Jesus said that His disciples were to go into all the world and preach the Gospel to every creature. Alas, I am not able to do that.

"I do love to tell of Him," she went on as her missionary friend seemed for the moment unable to reply. "I have told my son and his wife, and all our neighbours, and in the summer time I can go to several villages near at hand. Oh, I am not afraid to tell of Jesus! It is not that.

"But I am old and very feeble. I cannot read. My eyes are growing dim. And I can only walk a little way. You see it is impossible for me to go to foreign countries and preach the Gospel. If you had come earlier, when I was young—but now it is too late. I cannot be His disciple."

With a full heart the missionary explained the meaning of the Saviour's words, and spoke of His perfect sympathy and keen appreciation of every act prompted by love to Him. He knew about the widow's offering; and said of another who was not able to serve Him much, "She hath done what she could."

"*What she could.*" Was that what it meant? Oh, then, it might be after all! And the dear old lady could hardly wait till the following Sunday to be baptised. Full of joy in her new privilege, she was one of the brightest members of the little church, and her earnestness in doing what she could was a frequent incentive to others.

At the close of Hsi's stay in the capital an incident occurred that caused him much exercise of mind, and ended sadly.

While Dr. Schofield was seeing patients one day, a young woman was brought to the hospital suffering from what her husband described as "an evil spirit." The doctor went into the matter carefully, but could find no physical explanation of the distressing symptoms. She seemed wholly given up to evil; and the violence of the paroxysms into which she was thrown was so great that life itself was imperilled.

After prescribing what he hoped might help her, the doctor, who had other patients waiting to be seen, suggested that Hsi of Pingyang, who was still in the city, should be invited to visit their home.

Thankful for any ray of hope, the husband went to Hsi with his sad story, imploring him to come and do what he could to deliver the household from misery.

To Hsi the duty was most painful. If there was one thing more than another from which he naturally recoiled, it was contact with just such cases. He knew how real and terrible can be the power of evil spirits, and their conscious presence under such circumstances. The look in the eyes of the miserable victim is often enough to make one shudder, and the convulsive movements and fiendish utterances inspire a horror that can hardly be expressed. But difficult as it was he dared not shirk the duty, and with a heart that cried to God all the way, he followed the young man, who quickly led him to the house.

There was no mistaking the excitement and confusion that prevailed on their arrival. The girl was in one of her terrible seizures, and had to be held down by half-a-dozen neighbours to prevent injury to herself and those around her. Calling the family together, Hsi briefly explained that he, like themselves, could do nothing, but that the God he worshipped was the living God, who could perfectly heal and deliver. They listened with apparent interest while he told the wonderful story of the Saviour's love, and were willing to take down their idols then and there, if only he would pray for them that their trouble might be removed and their sins forgiven.

After public prayer for God's blessing, Hsi was taken to the room from which the cries and confusion proceeded. Immediately he entered, there was a lull. The girl saw him, ceased struggling, and in a quiet, respectful way asked him to take a seat.

Astonished, the onlookers cried at once that the spirits had left her.

"No," answered Hsi, who could tell from her eyes that something was wrong, "she is as yet no better. The devil is merely trying to deceive us."

The girl was still friendly, and tried to make the polite remarks usually addressed to strangers; but Hsi went over, and laying his hands on her head, simply and earnestly prayed in the name of Iesus, and commanded the evil spirits at once to come out of her.

Suddenly, while he was still praying, she sprang to her feet with a terrible cry, rushed out into the courtyard, and fell to the ground unconscious and to all appearances dying.

"Alas, she is dead! You have killed her now!" cried the startled friends.

But Hsi quietly raised her. "Do not be alarmed," he said. "The spirits are gone. She will soon be all right."

Recovering in a little while from what seemed a heavy swoon, the young woman came to herself, and was soon restored to a perfectly normal condition.

For some time the husband, full of gratitude, attended the services at the mission chapel and made a half-hearted profession of Christianity; but sad to say it was not the real thing with him or any of the family. As long as Hsi remained he went now and again to see him, carrying some little present to express indebtedness and thanks.

At last one morning he returned from such a visit bringing with him a packet of confectionery that was meant for Hsi.

"Why have you brought back the present?" cried his wife as he entered the courtyard.

"The scholar has left the city," he replied, "and is on his way home to the south of the province."

Scarcely were the words spoken when the poor girl relapsed

into the old condition. In the midst of most terrible convulsions, foul language and blasphemies streamed from her lips. She seemed possessed by a more fearful power of evil than before.

"He is gone; he is gone!" she cried. "Now I fear no one. Let them bring their Jesus. I defy them all. They will never drive us out again, never."

This continued for a few terrible days, until exhausted by the strain, she died.

# 21

# How the Work Spread

ON his return from the capital Hsi threw himself more ardently than ever into his well-loved work. All he had seen during his absence convinced him the more of the need and opportunities round him, and of the adaptability of opium refuge methods to the conditions prevailing in Southern Shansi.

Fan was still on fire with love for souls; and the Refuge, full of patients, was more than able to defray expenses. From village to village interest continued to spread, as men of all ages returned to their homes cured of the terrible craving. The number of converts too was increasing, and as at Sopu, little light-centres were beginning to shine out in the darkness, through lives transformed by the power of Jesus.

Such work could not but develop. It was too good a thing not to be wanted; and the element of self-support made extension possible. Among the converts there were already some who were quite capable of carrying on little Refuges in country places, with help and supervision; and from neighbouring towns and hamlets the call was coming for just such work and men. All that was needed was someone to organise and be responsible for the Refuges, and men, more men, of the right spirit and training, to make them a success. Hsi saw the opportunity, and was burdened with longing to turn it to the best account.

"The work the Lord has given me to do," he said, "is not so much that of a sower casting forth his seed, as that of a fisherman drawing in his net. Preaching the Gospel far and wide is like seed-sowing. Helping men, one by one, to break off opium and believe in Jesus is like catching fish." And to this enterprise with skill and patience he devoted himself.

But not all seed sown falls into good ground; not all fish that come into the net are safely landed. Hsi was beginning to find that often the inquirers who seem most hopeful, and for whose salvation one has specially laboured, disappoint one at last.

And to such trials he was peculiarly open on account of the very nature of his work, which seemed to offer financial as well as spiritual attractions. The Refuges had to be made to pay their way, and if possible yield some small margin of profit. It was only by the greatest care and good management that this could be accomplished, especially in country places. But, seeing the success of some of the older Refuges, people began to imagine that it was an easy way of turning an honest penny. They felt that the work was good and terribly needed, and concluded that in its prosecution they could enrich themselves while at the same time benefiting others. But what they did not see was all the prayer and self-sacrifice, the labour, patience, and practical organising power behind the Fantsun effort. And yet these things alone, by the blessing of God, could ensure success.

Thus, very early, men with mixed motives began to give trouble, supposing they could make a gain of godliness. But even the anxiety that came upon him in this way was secondary to the sorrow caused by backslidings and divisions among the Christians. For these things Hsi had hardly been prepared. Difficulties of all sorts from without he expected, as part of the natural opposition of the devil; but grievous failure and dissensions within were heart-breaking indeed. Already he was learning to bear, in some measure, the apostolic burden: "the care of all the churches."

Meanwhile the work grew rapidly, and inexperience might well have supposed that the Kingdom of God was about to be established in Southern Shansi. And so indeed it was. But not without the ebb and flow that always accompany a rising tide, even in movements of a spiritual nature. Fifty to sixty men meeting regularly for worship at Fan's village, and hundreds of more or less interested inquirers in other places, gave good ground for hopefulness about the future. As time went on, numbers of these men and women proved to be truly converted and taught of the Spirit; others again were found to have been influenced by purely natural causes, carried away for a time by superficial emotions. It was impossible at first to distinguish the tares among the wheat. Both had to grow together until the testing came that, sooner or later, revealed the true nature of each one's profession.

Has it not always been so, not excepting the life-experience of our Lord Himself?—at first many followers, eager attention, enthusiasm kindled by wonderful doings, bringing benefit of a material character apparent to all; a time of general ingathering: then, as the conditions of discipleship are better understood, a period of trial and elimination; "Many went back and walked no more with him": but always a precious residuum left, the gold shining more brightly for the fires; "Ye are they which have continued with me in my temptations."

This principle, so clearly taught in our Lord's own parables, if rightly apprehended, will prove of great value in missionary service; steadying the soul against overwhelming discouragement, as one and another are found to be unstable, and the suggestion comes: "Alas! this cannot have been the work of God, or it would never have ended in failure such as this."

But is it really failure, or only a necessary stage in progress? No strength of Christian character can be obtained without discipline. For every man who will really follow Jesus, there is a cross. Some of whom we have had the brightest hopes are sure to fall away under these searching tests. But "He shall not fail nor be discouraged." There is no need for disquietude and alarm.

In China, as at home, it is questionable kindness that seeks to prop up young Christians and shield them from every breath of temptation and trial, as though the Lord could not be trusted to deal with such tender plants. Far better let Him blow with His rough wind, if He sees fit. Storm and cold are needed, as well as sunshine. He knows best how to strengthen His own.

And those He has in training are sure to come out right at last. It does not really matter how ignorant and slow of heart, weak and faulty they may be, if only they are in His hand. Peter and the rest of His chosen friends, men who were to "turn the world upside down," were just as human as we are; but with all their weaknesses, they were men upon whom the Holy Ghost could come.

These lessons Hsi was learning in the Refuges and village gatherings in which the Lord was using him at this time. He did not understand at first and was almost heart-broken when quarrels and persecution arose, scattering hopeful little churches and causing the love of many to grow cold. But by degrees he came to see that "it must needs be that offences come," and learned to possess his soul in patience, leaving to God the issues of His own work.

Among the scores of inquirers around him were not a few who had the essential quality, and could be developed into soul-winners by the blessing of God. These served to comfort Hsi for sleepless nights of prayer and all the tears and anguish caused by others who disappointed his hopes. And the Lord never failed to bring blessing out of even the saddest experiences. It often seemed as if the devil overreached himself. The work grew by its very difficulties, rooted all the more firmly in faith and prayer. And Hsi himself was learning through his failures. Each fall cast him more on God, and made him more distrustful of himself, and therefore stronger.

Thus the work and workers developed together, and evil was overcome of good, as may be seen from the following circumstances that occurred about this time.

Among the many patients cured at Fantsun were several men from the little village of Tsaoseng, lying ten miles away to the north. These men while in the Refuge had learned a good deal of Christian truth, and had renounced idolatry, but without experiencing any real change of heart. On returning to their own village they were impressed by the number of opium-smokers, former acquaintances and others, who came to inquire about the wonderful treatment; evidently with the hope that something might be done for them. Instead of being moved to pity, the men, or most of them, saw in all this chiefly an opportunity for a profitable investment on their own account.

Why should they take these would-be patients to Fantsun, or send for Hsi to open a Refuge farther north? Had they not watched his methods, and learned to use the pills? They would pay Hsi well for the medicine, and start a Refuge on their own account, charging more highly than he did, and making sure of payment in advance. By selling the medicines to them direct Hsi would receive his money with far less trouble than by curing the men himself.

Thereupon seven of this little band set to work, borrowed a considerable sum of money, and went down to Fan at the Refuge to purchase supplies. But Fan was not at liberty to sell the medicine. Hsi had to be personally applied to. And somehow, face to face with him, they did not feel quite so sure of their ground. Perceiving at once the danger and their real motives, Hsi sternly replied:

"How dare I regard this medicine, that the Lord is pleased to use for saving the souls of men, as a matter of trade and money-making. Were I to do this our work would no longer be prospered. The pills are not for sale at any price."

This naturally made the impostors furious, and away they went to spread all sorts of calumnies about Hsi and his work. But not all the seven were impostors. Some, though misled, were true men, and, impressed by Hsi's exhortations, they wished to remain under his influence and learn more. These two or three Hsi kept with him, and finally, seeing they were in earnest, he sent them to one of the Refuges for training. They developed well, and became established Christians. And when Hsi himself was led to open a proper Refuge at Tsaoseng, he put them in charge, and his confidence was not misplaced.

The result was a remarkable movement in that neighbourhood. Numbers of men passed through the Refuge. Within the first year, over fifty people professed conversion, not a few of whom were received into the Church: and as from Fan's village the blessing spread to many surrounding places.

About two miles to the west lay the charming village of Pantali, from which one of the first and most promising of these inquirers came. Famous for its perennial spring, this quiet hamlet was unusually attractive. From a walled-in opening in the ground the water gushed forth in such abundance that even at its source it was almost deep enough to swim in. Clear and cool the stream flowed down the village street, bordered with drooping willows and spanned by the graceful arch of a moss-covered bridge. In this beautiful spot Chang was well known as a man of some influence, elderly and well-to-do, but—an opium-smoker.

Earlier in life he had fallen in with Romanists, and had nomin-ally become a Christian. But he went on smoking opium just the same, and succeeding years only found him more deeply sunk in sin and misery. At length he heard of the Refuge at Tsaoseng, and went over to see what was happening. And there, at last, Chang really met the Saviour he had heard about so long. His chains were broken, his life transformed, and he went back to Pantali rejoicing.

But one great trouble remained. His wife was not a Christian. At times she seemed interested, and would go over to service at the Refuge. But she was bound by a tyranny more terrible than the vice that had so long enslaved her husband. Suffering from the malady that, though common, is always mentioned with bated breath, she was known throughout the neighbourhood as a demoniac.

After her husband's conversion, this poor woman seemed to be worse than ever. The fits of frenzy were more frequent, and she would cry out as if in terror:

"I fear nothing and no one, save Pastor Hsi of the Western Chang village." And this she repeated constantly.

The circumstance was peculiar, and attracted a good deal of attention in the district. Finally, Hsi heard of it, and was not a little troubled. Already he had found considerable difficulty in preventing the Christians from speaking of him as "Our Pastor," a title he felt to be most unfortunate, and to which he had no claim. For at that time he was only an elder in the Pingyang church; and there were no ordained pastors in the province, except the missionaries. But try as he might, he could not wholly check the use of the term, and was open to a good deal of misunderstanding in consequence. And now the poor frenzied woman at Pantali would persist in crying:

"I fear nothing and no one but Pastor Hsi."

At length, distressed on her account as well as his own, Hsi went over to the village, and was warmly welcomed by the Christian husband. A crowd gathered as usual in and around the house, to see what was going to happen. After putting the truth plainly before them, and committing the whole matter to God in prayer, Hsi laid his hands on the woman, and in the name of Jesus commanded the evil spirits to leave her and return no more.

From that moment the trouble ceased. Mrs. Chang became quiet and self-possessed. All the symptoms of her strange disorder passed away, and she was soon as earnest as her husband in seeking to bring others to the Saviour. The interest aroused by this circumstance, among neighbours and friends, was so great that the Changs soon found their guest-hall too small for the people who wished to attend the meetings. At their own expense they rented a house near at hand for the purposes of a Christian church, and before long twenty or thirty believers were meeting regularly in that mountain village, from whose changed lives and fearless testimony the blessing spread to other places.

But all was not smooth sailing at Pantali even in those early days. Dissensions among the Christians arose here as elsewhere, and Hsi had to be sent for to put matters right. With the heart of a father toward his children, he always suffered keenly in their sins and failings. He felt them as his own. Instinctively the thought would come; if he had been more watchful, more prayerful, more instant in season and out of season in the care of these little churches, the trouble might never have arisen; and all the sorrow and dishonour to the Master's name would have been spared.

On one occasion he was hurriedly called to Pantali on account of a disturbance that threatened to prove serious. It was the depth of a cold northern winter, but he went at once. Wrapped in his fur-lined gown, he made the toilsome journey over those mountain roads, his heart heavy for the scenes he knew he was about to face.

Two brothers named Chang, both leaders among the Christians, had quarrelled over some trifling matter, and several of the others had become involved. As the dispute went on, neighbours and friends gathered round, until the excited crowd seemed to embrace the whole village. In the midst of this disgraceful scene, the younger Chang, transported with passion, seized a chopper that was lying close at hand and flung it at his brother's head. The instrument was sharp and heavy, and the blow, if well directed, would doubtless have proved fatal. But missing its aim, the chopper struck another man, an inquirer named Koh, wounding him severely in the knee.

It was a dreadful moment, for murder had been intended, and the assailant was a younger brother. This in Chinese eyes added to the crime tenfold. And then poor Koh was seriously injured, and all his relatives involved. After the first breathless pause the strife and altercation were more violent than ever. Nothing could be done to quiet the brothers, and the friends of the wounded man purposely aggravated the trouble. Then it was that, seriously alarmed, some of the Christians sent off a messenger to the Western Chang village.

Arrived at the scene of disturbance, Hsi found matters even worse than he had anticipated. The Changs were irreconcilable; Koh's party, perceiving their advantage, were pressing outrageous demands for compensation; and worst of all, the cause of Christ was openly dishonoured before the heathen. Satan had triumphed; and there was no telling to what proportions the trouble might grow.

All eyes were turned on Hsi. What would he say? How would he handle the affair? Everything seemed to depend, just then, upon his skill and strength. In the midst of such an outbreak the wrong word would be a spark to gunpowder; while any sign of fear or weakness must make matters worse. Hsi knew well enough the danger of the situation: old enmities and village feuds on the point of reawakening, and a lawsuit imminent, or perhaps several, with all the bribery and oppression involved. For one thing leads on to another in China, and the chain seems endless.

And more than this, he knew what lay behind it all; that such anger is, in terrible reality, giving place to the devil,[1] against whose wiles he was powerless indeed.

And so the thing he did was just what no one expected. He simply walked away without a word, and left them. To upbraid or condemn would be useless. No appeal to reason or conscience would be tolerated at that moment. So just as he was, without food or rest, he sought a place, alone, where he could pray.

A considerable time elapsed before Hsi was seen again, and curiosity as to what he could be doing grew to almost suspense. And when he did appear the surprise of the crowd only increased. For instead of addressing the angry disputants, or attempting to pacify Koh's relatives, he quietly made his way to the corner where the wounded man was sitting, neglected in the general excitement, and asked to be allowed to do something for his suffering limb.

This effectually changed the current of thought and feeling. And as Hsi dressed the wound with remedies he had provided, talking kindly with the patient meanwhile, even the onlookers could not but feel more or less in the wrong.

Then while still busy with Koh, Hsi began to express his deep sorrow for all that had happened, and the shame it was to himself and those present who called themselves Christians. By this time he had the sympathy of the crowd, and could say almost anything. Little by little he went on, still making himself one with the offenders, until he could speak more directly to the Christians, and lift the whole matter on to a different plane. Not against each other or their fellow-villagers only was this sin, but against the One who loved them best, and whom in their deepest hearts they truly loved. Then turning to the Changs he appealed to them on this ground, with humility and tenderness that would have been hard to resist. He spoke of the triumph of the great adversary, and of the sorrow of the heart of Christ whom they had crucified afresh, putting Him to an open shame. Earnestly he besought them both to acknowledge their wrong-doing, for each had been

[1] Eph. iv. 26, 27: "Be ye angry, and sin not: let not the sun go down upon your wrath: *neither give place to the devil.*"

It is noteworthy that a large proportion of alleged cases of demon-possession in China are directly traceable to such a commencement. Of those that have come under the personal observation of the writer, nearly all were said to have begun in some fit of anger or grief, lasting perhaps for days.

to blame, and ended by reminding them how much worse matters might have been had not God in His mercy intervened.

"Chang, younger brother," he exclaimed, "go thank the Lord upon your knees for saving you from untold misery and remorse. Had not He turned that blow aside, your brother's death might even now be at your door."

"And as to Koh," he continued, addressing the crowd, "he is indeed to be thanked. For, receiving in his own person the wound intended for another, he has prevented a greater injury, and probably averted the death of his friend."

This was a new point of view, and approving glances were turned upon Koh, who began to assume the role of benefactor. His relatives, in spite of themselves, were disarmed. And meanwhile the Chang brothers had an opportunity to recover themselves. Appreciative comments followed Hsi's exhortations, which appealed to Christian and heathen alike, and he was able finally to explain the true principles of the faith that had been so sadly misrepresented.

But Hsi went a step further than this. He knew that words, no matter how convincing, would never heal the breach nor mend the injured limb. Something more practical was needed. It was no use telling the Changs to make reparation, or exhorting the Kohs to be forgiving. They were not yet ready for this. Besides it is so much stronger to preach by example than precept only. "Come . . . follow me," is still the most eloquent sermon.

Practical compensation had to be made, for Koh was disabled from work, and in a good deal of suffering. The relatives must be satisfied, and onlookers convinced that Christianity is right and honourable, not in word only. And most important of all, the Changs had to be fully reconciled, and the Christians made to feel that such sin could not be lightly passed over, and though forgiven, must entail suffering and loss.

Hsi had not come prepared for financial outlay. But he was not without resource. Leaving the village for a while, that his words might take effect, he went himself to the nearest pawnshop, and came back without his fur-lined gown. The loss was immediately noticed, for in the absence of his outer garment he was poorly clad for such wintry weather. But regardless of remonstrance, he handed a generous sum to Koh and his family, not as reparation, but in token of his sympathy and sorrow as a Christian for what had taken place.

Then with tears and great freedom of heart he besought the Changs to be at peace, and all the Christians to confess their sins to God with true repentance. To see him suffering for their fault was more than they could stand. The Changs were completely broken down. Love and unity were restored. And Hsi was able to put other wrong things right, and leave the little group of Christians stronger in some ways for the sad experience that might have had so different an ending. They could not make up to him what he had sacrificed, and were distressed to let him start on that long cold journey so unprotected. But he tried to comfort them, insisting:

"It is all right, and only my duty. God has called me to bear your burdens, and care for you as my own children. I must do it, because I love you and have you in my heart, and cannot help it."

From that time the work at Pantali flourished in quite a special way. The Christians drew together, and not a few were added to their number. Before long so many opium-smokers were applying for help that Hsi had to commence a Refuge in the village. This was made a blessing, and men saved there for this life and the next, carried the glad tidings to many distant places.

And the Chang brothers never went back. They grew in usefulness as years went on. One of them, the offender on this occasion, became much valued as a deacon of the church, and the other, who was first a deacon and then an elder, subsequently laboured for some years as a missionary a thousand miles away from home, in the most anti-foreign province in China.

# 22

# How God Provided

AND now to return for a while to the Western Chang village
and the work Hsi was doing at home. Changes not a few had
come since the days of opium-smoking idleness that preceded his
conversion, and since more recent years that found him free
enough to accept the duties of headman of the village. Now his
home was a hive of industry, as full and busy as any opium refuge,
and with more varied interests.

For gradually Hsi had been drawn into a new line of service,
the complement of all he had hitherto undertaken. With every
added Refuge the circle of his influence widened, and with it his
sense of responsibility. Among the patients were many who,
though cured of opium-smoking, were far from established in the
faith. A month or two under Christian influence had convinced
them of the folly of idol-worship and made them long for better
things. They were in many cases earnest inquirers, but unfit to
face persecution or make satisfactory progress alone. To send them
back into heathen surroundings, beyond the reach of further help
and teaching, would have been to risk losing them altogether.

Many also, when the time came for leaving the Refuge, were
still far from strong. Some former ailment may have reappeared,
threatening to drive them back to opium for relief. These men
required care and watching and to be taught the unfailing power
of prayer. But often the Refuges were full and all accommodation
needed. Must they be turned out and allowed to drift for lack
of a helping hand?

Then there were always others who during their stay in the
Refuge had been truly converted to God, and a few who were
manifestly fitted to become soul-winners and helpful assistants,
if not leaders, in the future of the work. Some were ignorant and
some were poor; some needed help, having lost their means of
livelihood by becoming Christians; and all required much careful
training in view of days to come. To neglect the development of
these men would have been fatal to the best interests of the work
and to his stewardship of the talents God had given him.

And so it came to pass that all these, and many others difficult to classify, found a place in Hsi's household as well as in his heart; gathered into the old home at the Western Chang village, from whose doors none whom he could help was ever turned away.

At first especially they were a motley crew, and it was difficult to maintain order and keep them usefully employed. But method and experience worked wonders, and the results were increasingly satisfactory.

One rule Hsi insisted upon was: "If any man will not work, neither shall he eat." This saved a great deal of trouble. For if by chance impostors were taken in who did not relish honest toil, they soon made an excuse for retiring. Fortunately the little property he still possessed was sufficient to supply employment for a good number. To encourage his guests he worked with them, giving all the time he could to manual toil. And the knowledge of farming he had gained on first becoming a Christian proved invaluable, enabling him to direct as well as assist their labours.

It was a busy community, for almost all the needs of the household were supplied at home. Flour-grinding, bread-making, water-carrying, spinning, weaving, tailoring, carpentry, and the all-important medicine-making, were some of the employments that filled the flying hours. Hsi's own time was much occupied with daily classes and meetings, for the deepening of spiritual life was his first concern, and all under his roof were either souls to be won or Christians to be made into soul-winners.

As the household grew enlarged accommodation was needed, and Hsi became a skilful architect and builder. Gradually he erected near the threshing-floor a number of small houses and a kitchen, and one of the barns was adapted for use as a chapel. Details of housekeeping and domestic affairs were largely taken off his hands by Mrs. Hsi and her sister. They were his chief helpers also in the manufacture of the anti-opium pills upon which the Refuges were dependent. It is satisfactory to note that the sister, little Miss Liang, became increasingly useful, and by her marriage a few years later with one of Hsi's most valued assistants, was permanently attached to the household.

The medicine-making was no sinecure. As the Refuges increased, it came to be one of the most serious of Hsi's undertakings. And though he trained and used helpers, it was a task he never entrusted wholly to others.

The mere time and labour involved were considerable to say

nothing of the skill required with such poor appliances. But Hsi was not content with making the pills anyhow. They were for the work of God, part of the ministry he had received, and to "save the souls of men." To this end he was most particular that they should be "well made and attractive-looking." And there was nothing but a simple, corrugated basket hanging from a rope, with which to swing them into shape.

But his chief care was that the blessing of God should so rest on the operation that the pills should be successful in their mission, and be the means of bringing spiritual as well as physical healing. He had no confidence in the medicine by itself. But he was very sure that the Lord had led him into the opium refuge work and had given him that prescription in answer to prayer, and that as His blessing rested upon them, the pills could and would be a means of salvation to multitudes. So whenever it was necessary to make a fresh supply, he began with prayer and fasting. It was his habit to go without food the whole twenty-four hours of the day given to that work. Sometimes he was so exhausted towards evening that he could hardly stand. Then he would go away for a few minutes alone to wait upon God. "Lord, it is Thy work. Give me Thy strength," was his plea. And he always came back fresh and reinvigorated, as if with food and rest.

The method followed was as simple as it was ingenious. First a good day was chosen, suitable for drying the pills as fast as they were made. Then the drugs were gathered together, weighed, and examined, for all the ingredients had to be the best obtainable. After that they were thoroughly pounded with a rough pestle and mortar, mixed in the required quantities, and piled up in great heaps of reddish-brown powder. Then came the more difficult process, generally undertaken by Hsi himself. The powder had to be moistened with just sufficient water and kneaded to a particular consistency, so that it would roll off into nice, firm, little balls when properly swung in the basket. This last stage of the proceeding required dexterity as well as patience. But when the basket was kept swinging they could turn out hundreds, if not thousands, of pills in the day.

By careful management and the help of his guests in various ways, Hsi was able to make his household largely self-supporting. But there were other expenses connected with the entertainment of visitors, especially on Sundays, and with the support and extension of his Refuges. The farm produced no ready money.

And the profit derived from the pills, which were sold to his patients only, did not amount to much. Amid all these responsibilities, Hsi was beginning to prove not only the trial but the blessing of an empty treasury that casts one upon God.

One remarkable thing about him from the beginning was his freedom from the love of money, or the desire for financial returns for his own benefit. Of course he had to make his Refuges pay, as far as possible, and to take whatever profit accrued in one case to supply the lack in others. But he would never allow the money question to be made prominent, and it was perfectly clear in the long run that he was not seeking personal advantage.

For one thing, he never insisted upon payment. His charges for medicine were from seven hundred to two thousand cash (two to six shillings), according to the severity of the case. Most of the patients brought their own food. But if patients were unable to afford so much, he would return part of the money, or take them in his own home free of charge. And if they were dishonest, and though reasoned with refused to pay, he simply made it a matter of prayer, and left the results with God. Not infrequently the consequences proved serious for the delinquent.

Another way in which his conduct was unusual was that money given him for the work he would not hesitate to return, if he felt that the blessing of God did not come with it. A gift made from wrong motives, or reluctantly he found to be no help. "It must proceed out of a pure heart," he would say, "and from a willing mind, in order to have the Lord's acceptance and blessing." And without these, how could it but be harmful? Was it money they were seeking, or the blessing of God? Poverty only cast them the more upon Him, but money without His blessing would soon bring trouble.

An occasion of this sort occurred in connection with a man named Tsui, who was a professing Christian. A stone-mason by trade, he had done well in business, and was known to have hoarded up more than one hundred thousand cash, quite a fortune in that part of the world. But not a fraction would be spare for the Lord's work. No appeals moved him. And this, naturally, was a stumbling-block to poorer Christians, who had to make up in their contributions for his parsimony.

At length Tsui was taken seriously ill and seemed in danger of death. He immediately sent for Hsi and besought him to pray for his recovery.

"I am willing, Brother Hsi," he groaned, "to contribute forty thousand cash, if only you will get me out of this trouble."

"What have you been doing," exclaimed Hsi, "to have fallen into such a condition? Do you suppose you can bribe the Lord, and purchase your life with money? Sincerely confess your sins, and I will pray for you. This is no time to talk of gifts."

Apparently the man did cry to God for mercy. Hsi prayed for him, and he was speedily better. But, as might be expected, he said nothing further about the money. The contribution he had been so eager to make was quite forgotten.

Not long afterwards the same illness returned with still more serious symptoms. In great alarm Tsui sent again for Hsi, and this time putting a bank draft for a large sum into his hands, begged him to pray at once for his relief. But Hsi returned the money, saying sadly:

"Alas, I fear it is too late. Yet it may be that God will have pity on your soul. Cry to Him in the name of Jesus for pardon. I cannot take the money."

A day or two later Tsui passed away. Within a few months his widow married again—a terrible disgrace to the memory of the dead man—and his hoarded wealth was scattered.

But though Hsi was independent in these ways for the honour of his Master's name, and though he managed his farm and opium refuges with economy, using every cash as carefully as possible, it was far from easy to make both ends meet. It was all very well to speak about following the Lord's example in feeding the multitudes, but as a matter of fact it meant either bankruptcy or drawing upon divine resources.

Toward the close of the year, when Hsi came to balance his accounts, he found to his dismay that there was a threatened deficit of over eighty thousand cash: just what the foreign shepherd had feared, and what the heathen around him were always prophesying. He could see his way to making up about a third of this sum, but that would still leave him nearly fifty thousand in arrears. He could not borrow money, for that was against the clear injunction "Owe no man anything." And rack his brains as he might, no plan presented itself by which so large a sum could be raised. His heathen relatives angrily declared that he would bring them all into trouble. His wife and fellow-workers were silent and anxious. But Hsi gave himself to waiting upon God.

And just then the unexpected happened. From the capital of

the province a remarkable paper made its way down to Hsi's neighbourhood and came into his hands. It contained a list of a number of subjects connected with the Christian religion, upon which literary men were invited to write theses to compete for valuable prizes. The essays were to contain about five thousand characters, and might be written either in verse or prose, but the highest prize was for poetical compositions, and consisted of fifty ounces of silver. The offer was from the Taiyüan missionaries, and open to all the *literats* of the province.

"This," cried Hsi with enthusiasm, "is the Lord's answer to our petitions. The first prize shall assuredly be mine."

With faith and courage he set to work. It was already the tenth month of the year, and there was no time to spare. The first prize was for poetry only, and so to that line of things he confined himself.

Little though he realised it at the time, there was a deeper purpose in that versifying than the one he had in view. The growing church of his own hills and valleys needed a new hymnology, something of their own, expressing in local language the experiences of the heart. Hsi was dimly conscious of the need. He knew the hymns they used did not appeal much to the people. But it had never occurred to him that he might be enabled to write others that would. Now as he pondered, pen in hand, thoughts came to him and the verses flowed, until one after another poems were written that discovered a gift never again lost sight of.

A little later the missionary paid a visit to the Western Chang village, to confer upon the winner of the first prize a *shoe* of silver worth seventy thousand cash—amply sufficient to close the year with a balance on the right side. This was to Hsi a memorable experience, quite a milestone on life's journey.

From that time he continued, like the Psalmist, to weave all vicissitudes into songs of praise and prayer. Lessons learned amid joy or trial, defeat or deliverance, flowed from his pen in simple, often beautiful verse. And the Christians of Shansi took up these hymns with delight. Sixty or more of them passed into the life of the people, and so live on, though his loved voice is silent.

But times of financial difficulty were not the only occasions for proving the power and faithfulness of God. Others, of a more painful nature, arose from the character of the men with whom Hsi had to deal. Some were satisfactory from the first, and soon became useful members of that busy household. Others, though amenable in the long run to wise and patient influence, needed time to free themselves from the trammels of the past; and living with them during the process was not easy. But there remained a few so depraved and unresponsive that to attempt to reclaim them at all seemed hopeless. To be under the same roof with such men, month after month, and responsible for them, was a serious trial, but one from which Hsi had no escape. He was increasingly cautious as time went on about those whom he received into his home; but once he had undertaken a case, nothing would induce him to abandon it.

"No," he would say, "I dare not begin a task and then quickly give it up because of difficulties in the way. If it is not of God, one should not begin at all. If it is, it would be sin to drop it. Were I to do so He might also drop me, as far as usefulness in His service is concerned."

It was his rule, therefore, never to send a man away. He believed that the power of God could save even the most hopeless, but that if in the end any were irreclaimable, they would go of their own accord to their own place. It might involve long-continued suffering for those who sought to save them, but is it not God Himself who suffers most? So he prayed over these men, and was patient with them long after others had given up hope. Sometimes even in the worst cases his faith prevailed; sometimes it all seemed wasted. But sooner or later those who would not yield were sure to be removed without Hsi's intervention, sometimes in very solemn ways.

One secret of the power he undoubtedly possessed was the love that made it possible for him to hold on to these men with such wonderful patience. He always saw good in them, and hoped the best. But when they sinned he suffered as love only can. And as they were inmates of his home night and day, this meant frequent pain of heart, and constituted one of the keenest trials he had to bear.

One case recorded by a missionary who witnessed it may give some idea of the difficulty of such circumstances.

In the early years at Tsaoseng a woman named Kuo came to Hsi in great trouble about her only son. The young man was thirty years of age, but far from being a comfort to his widowed mother, he was, as she said, "an opium-fiend," and thoroughly dissipated and unfilial. With many tears the poor woman besought Hsi to undertake his case. Involved in gambling debts, and thoroughly frightened at the result of recent excesses, he was himself anxious to turn over a new leaf and be taken under the wing of the Christian scholar.

After considerable hesitation Hsi consented. There was something prepossessing about the poor fellow, and he seemed more than willing to work on the farm for his living, and conform to all the regulations of the household. On this understanding he was received; Hsi paying no wages, but providing for him as his own son.

At first he behaved pretty well, and in spite of great suffering and difficulty was cured of his opium-habit. He rapidly acquired the outward form of Christianity, and became familiar with the Bible and its teachings. But before many months were over he grew impatient of restraint, and set all his ingenuity to work to make trouble. Quick-witted and unscrupulous, he generally managed to keep up appearances, and make other people suffer for his wrong-doing. Patiently Hsi bore the annoyance, trying in every way to bring him to reason, but without avail. Year after year this went on, and still Kuo did not wish to leave the household, and the Lord did not interfere to remove him.

At length, at the end of four years, there came a change. Suddenly the young man seemed to wake up to a realisation of what it all meant. The grace of God laid hold upon his heart, and to all appearances he was truly converted. Full of joy, Hsi more than forgave the past, and welcomed him to a son's place in his affections. And time seemed only to prove Kuo's sincerity. His ability and brightness were increasingly a comfort, and he became one of the most useful members of the household.

And then, just as he seemed indispensable, the missionary in charge of the district came over and asked for this very man to work under his supervision in an adjacent province. It was a great sacrifice to Hsi, but as he prayed about it he felt:

"This is the command of the foreign pastor. I dare not refuse. The Lord will give me another helper."

Kuo went, and for some years did well. His preaching was popular, and his manner attractive. The missionary trusted him completely.

But a time came when he was left alone in charge of the station with considerable sums of money passing through his hands. The work flourished, and numbers of people thronged the chapel.

And then, lifted up with pride, Kuo began to go wrong. He yielded to dishonesty. The love of money got hold of him. And after that he rapidly made shipwreck. The missionary hastened back and found himself embarked upon a sea of troubles. Kuo was not so easy to get rid of as he had been to secure. He defied all authority, and carried many of the converts with him. In the end, however, he was dismissed from his position, and had to leave the province.

Then, mad with rage and disappointment, his character and opportunities gone, he made his way back to the Western Chang village to pour upon Hsi the vials of his wrath. His friends there had heard the story, and were prepared to give the erring man another chance. But they little knew what awaited them. Kuo was furious. His fall seemed to rouse all the old evil of his nature, extinguishing the life of the Spirit, if ever there had been any.

To be revenged on Hsi, whom he chose to regard as the cause of all his troubles, seemed now his chief desire. With the skill of a clever reprobate he devised any number of lying accusations, going back to things long since forgotten, and finally demanded an outrageous sum of money in payment for work done on the farm from the time he was first taken in hand by his benefactor.

Distress and consternation filled the household, and Hsi had all he could do to prevent a disturbance. Kuo took delight in making the affair as public as possible, shouting his accusations at the top of his voice, and rehearsing his grievances to all who would listen. In his distress Hsi had no resource but prayer. All attempts at pacification failed. He would not resort to legal proceedings, and seemed hopelessly in the hands of this unscrupulous enemy. To buy him off with money was most inexpedient. And yet what could be done?

But as he prayed light came. New Year's Day was close at hand, the one time when every Chinaman feels it imperative to be on good terms with all around him. Why not suggest that the whole matter be deferred until after the auspicious celebrations? This would certainly commend itself to the public conscience, and if agreed upon, would give time for further thought and prayer.

And so, with a heart that cried to God, Hsi rejoined the excited crowd and waited an opportunity to speak. Then he skilfully drew the thoughts of his neighbours to the duties of the season, dwelling especially on the preparations that must be pending at home in honour of Kuo's arrival,

"If you will return, brother," he added, "when the feast of the New Year is over, we shall all be more at leisure, and will carefully consider these matters, to try and remedy what is wrong."

The suggestion was received with approval that Kuo could not afford to disregard; and knowing the sincerity of the man who made it, he had no fear of double-dealing. So, for the moment, the situation was relieved. Kuo went home to find like-minded men who would return with him to make trouble. And Hsi gave himself to prayer and fasting.

Then it was the end came. Hsi had borne long enough, hoping to save this soul. "He that being often reproved, hardeneth his neck, shall suddenly be cut off, and that without mercy."

It was most unexpected and solemn. Kuo, who left the Western Chang village with implacable enmity that day, never returned again. Before the New Year dawned, tidings came that he and two others of the family had suddenly passed away.

"What—dead!" cried the wondering neighbours. "The God of the Christians is angry. It is better to let them alone."

# 23

# A Fresh Advance

WITH increasing responsibilities Hsi felt increasingly the need for prayer. From the first he had been prayerful. But now the customary hour, morning and evening, and daily seasons of public worship, he found to be insufficient. Longer, more quiet times were needed for waiting upon God, that His mind might be made known and His fulness received. Instead, therefore, of allowing his work to drive him, and absorb his time and thoughts, he deliberately set everything aside for hours and sometimes days or nights of prayer—often with fasting. At these times it was he usually obtained new thoughts and plans for the work, and fresh visions of God's faithfulness, as well as a deeper consciousness of his own insufficiency.

On one of these occasions, early in 1884, he was surprised to find the city of Chaocheng laid as a burden on his heart. The more he prayed the more he was distressed about its people, living and dying without any knowledge of the way of salvation.

But what could *he* do to meet their need? So far he had made no attempt to commence work inside a city. His sphere seemed more among the rural population, and all his Refuges were established in country places. It was quite another matter to make headway in the governing centres of the province, among people with city-bred ways and notions, and much more prejudice against the Christian faith.

Besides, what was the use of thinking of extension anywhere just then? He had no means in hand even for travelling expenses, much less to open a new Refuge. The idea was impracticable, surely. It could not be of God. And yet, the more he prayed, the more his heart was burdened for the city.

Vainly he told the Lord that he could do nothing; he had no money; it was impossible. Chaocheng, with its strategic position, its great opportunities, its notoriously wicked, opium-loving population—souls for whom no man cared—seemed to stretch appealing hands in the darkness. And the Master who knew all, waited, expectantly waited, his response. "All power is given unto me," He seemed to say, "and I am with you alway."

It was strange how difficulties vanished one by one, and all his wise objections seemed to melt away. Money? Was it money that would open the hearts of the people and win souls? If the Lord wanted that work done, could not He provide whatever would be needful? A city; and so far away? Yes, but the walls of Jericho fell, without hands. And was it after all so distant? As he began to think, he saw that, though the place was two days' journey from his village, it was not really beyond easy reach. For it lay on the main road to the capital, and, strangely enough, the already opened Refuges formed a complete chain from Fantsun to within five miles of its southern wall. Whose hand had planned it so, preparing those stepping-stones all the way?

But there were practical details to be considered: who, for example, would undertake the work? Hsi could not go himself. And if any of his helpers were suitable and willing, how could he send them without money even for the journey?

"What has thou in thine hand?" seemed the question.

"Why, Lord, nothing but a little medicine! Only these anti-opium pills."

"Well, is not that sufficient, with My blessing?"

And as he thought again, he saw that perhaps it was. If the men were forthcoming who would go in faith, taking what pills he could give them, just to travel on foot from Refuge to Refuge until they reached the village near the city, and there wait for the Lord to lead them in—why should it not be done?

Convinced at length that the thing was feasible, Hsi called his household together for prayer, and told them how he had been led. He made it very plain that the work would be difficult; for the people were turbulent, and strongly prejudiced against what they considered a foreign faith; and also that he had nothing to offer toward starting the new Refuge, except a first instalment of three thousand pills, and the promise of faithful co-operation in prayer. But he believed the thing was of God, and that He would supply all that was needed, and make the work a blessing. Was it strange that among that little company there were others who believed it too?

After that, it did not take long to decide on the new enterprise, and in a day or two Brothers Sï and Cheng completed their simple preparations and set out upon the journey. Carrying their books and bedding, the medicine, and a small supply of food, they made their way thirty miles northward to Fan's village, where they were welcomed at the Refuge, and told their story.

"What!" exclaimed their hearers in astonishment. "You have no premises in the city, and no money to rent. No capital to start upon. Nothing but three thousand pills. What can you do at Chaocheng except land yourselves in embarrassment?"

But when the circumstances were explained, it all looked very different. Fan and the rest were full of sympathy, and promised to remember the brethren in prayer. They also supplied them with provisions for the next stage of the journey, and sent them forward to Sopu.

Thus encouraged, Sï and Cheng went on, staying a night or two at Pantali and other Refuges by the way, until they came within sight of the city. Beyond the last Refuge, in a village near the southern suburb, lived an inquirer whose name had been given them, and all they could do was to make their way to his dwelling and tell their errand.

To him it seemed a hopeless proposition. But he invited them to stay a few days, and was careful to give no encouragement.

"The people of the city are rough and ignorant," he explained. "A Refuge, no doubt, is needed. But knowing you to be connected with the foreign religion, they might foolishly object to your settling among them."

This seemed more than likely, and the brethren decided to spend a day or two in prayer before attempting to make friends inside the city.

Meanwhile the Lord was working for them. News travels fast; and in the streets and tea-shops of Chaocheng people were already talking of their coming. Unknown to them, the fame of Hsi's Refuges had reached the city; and in spite of prejudice, not a few of its opium-smoking inhabitants were ready to welcome so hopeful a project of deliverance.

Thus Sï and Cheng received an unexpected visit. While they were still praying, their host called them to the door, where two gentlemen were waiting who craved the privilege of an interview. These visitors seemed eager and friendly. They were evidently men of the city, and had brought money with them, several thousands of cash being laid in strings at their feet.

After exchanging elaborate salutations, Si intimated that they were overwhelmed by the honour conferred upon them.

"We have learned with satisfaction," replied the strangers,

"that you, sirs, have come among us with benevolent intentions, and are about to open a virtuous establishment for the cure of victims of the foreign smoke."

With suitable modesty, Sï answered that it was their desire to be of service, if the worthy citizens would grant them residence within their walls.

"As to that," exclaimed the visitors, "pray give yourselves no concern. We, your younger brothers, desire to rent and furnish premises for the honourable Refuge immediately, and beg that we may be privileged to enjoy the benefits of your far-famed cure."

Money was now produced to pay for the medicine in advance, and it appeared that the strangers were ready, then and there, to undertake all necessary arrangements. The capital invested was to be returned, or interest paid, as the Refuge became self-supporting.

With wondering hearts, Sï and Cheng looked on, as difficulties were removed and their prayers answered beyond all they had asked or thought. Nothing could have been more propitious; and soon as honoured guests they were escorted through the streets of the city in which they might so easily have found themselves unwelcome intruders.

It seemed like a dream at first, too wonderful to be true, as they saw the house rented, furniture sent in, and lamps, crockery, kitchen utensils, flour, oil, tea, and other necessaries abundantly provided. As quickly as possible they set to work, for their new friends were anxious not to lose a day in beginning the treatment. In a word, there was scarcely time to send home the good news to those who were praying for them, before the Refuge at Chaocheng was an established fact.

From the first the blessing of God rested in a special way upon that enterprise. It soon grew to be the largest of all the Refuges for which Hsi was responsible. The cure of the earliest inmates was so satisfactory that scores of others followed, and within six months a hundred patients had been successfully treated. Many of these men turned from idolatry and became earnest Christians. As in other places, regular Sunday services had to be established, and ultimately a church was organised, which to-day numbers over three hundred members.[1]

This fresh advance introduced a time of encouragement and

[1] September, 1903.

blessing all round. With greater freedom in the matter of funds, Hsi opened several new Refuges. And in each place souls were saved and little churches gathered. At Tengtsun, in connection with his medicine shop, he also commenced a Refuge; and in his own home he arranged for the treatment of both men and women patients. This added considerably to the work carried on in his household; but helpers were springing up around him, and as opportunities multiplied they learned increasingly to draw upon divine resources.

Thus at the close of 1884, little more than five years from the time of his conversion, Hsi was the leader of already quite an extended work. Eight or ten Refuges had been established: from Tengtsun south of his own home, to Chaocheng city forty miles to the north; and in villages and hamlets all along the line, little companies of believers were meeting regularly for worship.

But Hsi was not yet satisfied. A beginning only had been made. Constrained by the love of Christ and the need of perishing souls on every hand, he was more than ever eager to press forward, carrying the Light far into surrounding darkness.

Still northward from Chaocheng, a day's journey nearer the capital, lay another important city, about which he was much exercised at this time. Beautifully situated, populous, and accessible, Hochow was practically still without the Gospel. Passing missionaries had called there on their journeys, but any seed thus sown did not appear to have borne fruit. For months Hsi had wished to open a Refuge in this city, but his hands were full of other work and his funds taxed to the utmost.

Still he prayed for Hochow, not less burdened about its needs because for the time being he could do nothing else to help. Every morning at family worship he remembered the city, definitely asking that God would send workers there.

At length Mrs. Hsi full of sympathy, came to him and said:

"We have prayed a long while for Hochow. Is it not time to *do* something? Why not send men and open a Refuge there as at Chaocheng and other places?"

"Gladly would I," replied her husband. "But such work is costly, and we have no money in hand."

"How much would be needed?" inquired the little lady. "Thirty thousand cash? That is indeed a large sum." And she forthwith went her way.

But Mrs. Hsi could not forget the needs of Hochow, and all

day long she kept wondering if there were not something she could do to send the glad tidings to that city. But thirty strings of cash! At one time she might have managed it. But now she had so little of any value remaining. And yet she did long that those people might hear of Jesus.

Next morning Hsi prayed again for Hochow, pleading its needs before the Lord, and asking that soon it might be possible to open a Refuge there. The little service ended, Mrs. Hsi instead of leaving the room as usual, walked up to the table, and laying a little package before her husband, said quietly:

"I think perhaps the Lord has answered our prayers."

Wondering what she could mean, Hsi lifted the parcel. It was heavy, and folded in several wrappings. At length, inside a coloured handkerchief, he found to his surprise a complete set of all the jewellery a Chinese woman values most—the gold and silver rings and bracelets, the handsome hairpins, ear-rings, and other ornaments that form her husband's wedding-gift.

With tear-dimmed eyes he looked at his wife, understanding now the change in her appearance. The adornments of a married woman in her position were all gone. No rings were on her fingers, no silver hairpins showed below the dark braids of her hair, which was simply tied with cord and fastened with a strip of bamboo.

"It is all right," she answered gladly, to his half remonstrance. "*I can do without these. Let Hochow have the Gospel.*"

Hsi took the gift that meant so much, and with it a Refuge was opened that soon became a centre of light and blessing in the city. Numbers of patients were successfully treated, and before long a work was established that grew into a regular mission station which continues to this day.

Thus opportunities for usefulness multiplied, and Hsi was more than ever prayerful and busy. The city Refuges called for special supervision, both the spiritual and the financial side of the work. The very stress of circumstances kept him much cast upon God; and difficulties of which there were many, served but to strengthen faith.

Yet it must not be supposed that he was perfect, or without the defects of his valuable qualities. On the contrary, with all his faith and devotion, he was intensely human. Though the Divine Spirit was manifestly working in his heart, there had not yet been time for him even to recognise all his failings, much less to overcome them. And those failings, as with most strongly marked characters, were very apparent.

For one thing, Hsi was a born leader, and could not but feel it. Others felt it also, and in spite of his tendency to be too masterful at times, were ready to follow him anywhere. This weakness, however, gave rise to a good deal of friction that might have been avoided. But he deeply felt his need of more humility, the meekness and gentleness of Christ, and prayed for it accordingly.

Then too he was very independent. This showed itself in his attitude about money matters. He never accepted a salary of any kind, or looked for financial help even to the mission with which his work was connected. But it showed itself also in ways that could not but cause anxiety. He was none too teachable, and his faith and devotion led him to go ahead at a rate that was sometimes alarming. His preaching lacked balance and sobriety, and his enthusiasm needed to be tempered by experience. But he was not easy to advise in early days, much less control.

Indeed it is an open secret that herein lies one of the most serious problems of missionary work: how wisely to develop the native leader, giving him plenty of room and the responsibility that alone can draw out the best that is in him, and yet temper his inexperience and save him from injurious extremes. A great deal of loving forbearance is needed; and it is well to remember that it is needed on both sides. It takes just as much grace for a man like Hsi to work well with the foreign missionary, as for the missionary to work well with him. This aspect of the question is in danger of being overlooked.

With the best intentions, for example, Hsi was put in a predicament, about this time, that called for more real humility than many of us would have possessed.

One of his Refuges through which a number of converts had been gathered, was a little out of the line of his other operations, in a village nearer the city of Pingyang. The missionary of that city, who was also in charge of the district, feeling that Hsi had all he could manage without going out of his way to visit this particular village, appointed another man, his own paid evangelist, to live there and take pastoral charge of the work. On the occasion of their next meeting, he informed Hsi of this arrangement, adding:

"You need not trouble to go over for the services any more.

The work in and around your own home, and in the Refuges, is as much as you can properly attend to."

No doubt there was a good deal to be said for such an arrangement, from the missionary's point of view. But practically, however burdened a father or mother may be, it is not easy to relieve them of the care of their own children, especially when the ties between them are unusually tender and the change is not desired.

Hsi felt it keenly, but did not dispute the point. He tried to conform to the arrangement, and support the poor evangelist, who was finding his position far from desirable.

But when it dawned upon the villagers that they had lost their spiritual father, that he would come to lead the services no more, nor be available to give the loving sympathy and help in all their needs that they had counted on so long, the result was open rebellion. Hsi did his best to keep the peace, and induce them to submit, as he had done. But to them it meant too much. They could not bear it. So the evangelist, good man though he was, was left to empty benches and a forlorn cause. No one would attend the chapel; and those who could, walked miles to reach the nearest place where they could meet and hear the man they loved.

While it went on the matter was most painful and Hsi found it difficult to steer between Scylla and Charybdis. But in this case it was not long before the trial was removed. This missionary, after years of faithful service, was obliged to go home on furlough, and for a time no one could be sent to replace him. The mission-house in Pingyang was left desolate, and the Christians without a pastor. Elder Sung did the best he could to look after things in the city, and Hsi had to take general oversight of the work both there and throughout the district. The evangelist wisely sought other employment, and the little church in question returned to its former relationships.

It was wonderful how the people followed Hsi and loved him, even when they felt his faults the most. God had made him a blessing to them in the best of ways. Many owed him life and health, as well as all that made life worth living. And then they knew, even when he was most impatient or dogmatic, that he would willingly sacrifice all he had for their well-being, and was daily pouring out his very soul in their service.

A brief passage from his manuscript referring to this period shows something of what lay below the surface.

"The devil," he writes, "seeing that God was using me during these three or four years by the power of the Holy Spirit, sought to involve me in pride and self-consciousness. He caused ignorant men to address me as 'Pastor,' and I could not stop them. Some even behind my back went so far as to speak of me as the 'Living Jesus.' I knew that all this was just the devil's scheme to get me to take glory to myself and forsake the cross of Christ.

"Therefore I humbled myself still more, and sought to have in all things *the heart of a bond-slave*, exerting my whole strength to lead men to repent and forsake sin, and thus yield no place to the devil. Not that I was able of myself to do this; it was all and only through the grace of God."

# 24

# Reinforcements

IT was the summer of 1885, just before wheat harvest, when news reached the Western Chang village that made Hsi's heart rejoice. For months the mission-house in the city had been forsaken, and the Christians of Southern Shansi deprived of foreign supervision. Hsi Sung, and the others had done their best; but it was hard work, and they had sadly missed the encouragement of more experienced leaders. And now reinforcements were on the way. Four young men, accompanied by one of the older members of the mission, were expected shortly, to take up residence at Pingyang.

Hsi had loved David Hill, and it was with thankful expectancy he looked forward to welcoming the new missionaries.

They also were specially interested in the prospect of meeting him. Drawn from English universities and the ranks of popular professions, the young missionaries had left wide opportunities for usefulness at home.[1] The work to which they had devoted their lives was toilsome and often discouraging, and especially at first there was a good deal that was uncongenial in the new surroundings. Dressed in the loosely-fitting garments of the country, hampered by long gown and flowing queue, unfamiliar with the strangely-sounding language, restricted by formal customs and conservative ideas, and burdened above all with a new realisation of the sin and suffering of heathenism, the young men were beginning to understand something of the cost of the enterprise for which they had forsaken all the world holds dear. But to help in saving men like Hsi, and for the love of Jesus, that He might see of the travail of His soul and be satisfied, they counted it all joy. Tidings of the work in Southern Shansi and of its native

[1] The party consisted of F. W. Baller, one of the senior members of the China Inland Mission, and four of "The Cambridge Seven," whose departure for China in February, 1885, did so much to arouse missionary interest on both sides of the Atlantic, especially in the student world. The four then on their way to Pingyang were—Stanley P. Smith, B.A., of Trinity College, Cambridge; the Rev. W. W. Cassels of St. John's, later Bishop of Western China; Montague Beauchamp, B.A., also of Trinity College; and D. E. Hoste of the Royal Artillery, later General Director of the China Inland Mission.

leader had reached them, welcome proofs of the power of the Gospel they had come to bring. And now, Western civilisation left far behind, they were traversing the central uplands of that very province on their way to the scene of his unwearied labours.

It was a beautiful journey from the capital through that summer land. Amid the gold of ripening harvests, rich fields of opium poppy were in flower. Surrounded by trees and greenery, countless villages dotted the plain, while here and there a city of importance reared its ancient wall. Still travelling southward, the populous plain was left behind, until a double range of mountains closed in upon the road and river, and rock-hewn passes had to be surmounted, where the torrent raged in foamy whiteness far below.

The evening of the sixth day's journey brought the travellers to Hochow, where the Refuge made possible by Mrs. Hsi's gift had recently been opened. Resting there over Sunday, they had good opportunities for preaching, as also at Chaocheng the next evening, in spite of the crowding and intense curiosity of the people. The day following saw them at Hungtung, five miles only from Fan's village, in the midst of a district that was to become familiar to some of them ere long.

Already good progress had been made by the new arrivals. They were fairly proficient in the use of chopsticks, and were learning, among other things, that time and patience are commodities of which one must possess a full supply. If in a mudhole, for example, or on some specially bad bit of road, the heavy, springless carts were overturned, the drivers would sit down and smoke a pipe or two before attempting to get things straight again and continue their day's journey. Or in a narrow gully, when they chanced to meet a north-bound caravan, the respective carters, after a friendly smoke, would probably proceed to clean the clogged wheels of their vehicles before coming to the important question as to which should back out and concede the right of way.

South of Hungtung indications were not lacking of the activity of Hsi and his fellow-workers. There on the last morning of their journey, Mr. Stanley Smith, walking on ahead of the party, was met by a Chinese who grasped his hand in Western fashion, greeting him most cordially.

The young missionary at once concluded that this must be a

Christian, and mustering the little Chinese at his command, said inquiringly, "*Je-su-tih men-t'u?*" A disciple of Jesus?

To which his new friend with the shining face replied, "*Je-su-tih men-t'u,*" in a tone that meant volumes.

Then shaking hands all round, he led the travellers to a little rice-shop by the wayside, and insisted on providing bread and millet-gruel, the only refreshment obtainable. After this he carried them off to his home for their mid-day meal, saying that they were expected, for he had been watching for their coming and knew they must be near.

"How could you know that?" inquired Mr. Baller. "Our journey has only recently been planned."

"Oh, we were sure of it," was the smiling reply, "because we have been asking the Lord so earnestly to send us missionaries without delay.

"All the people in this valley," he continued, as they neared his village, "are giving up their idols. There is a great deal of work for you to do."

While dinner was preparing, friendly neighbours dropped in, and an impromptu service was held which greatly encouraged the new arrivals. It was their first meeting with Christian brethren in South Shansi; and though they understood but little of what was said, they were fully able to appreciate the loving spirit and heartiness of it all.

But it was not until they reached Pingyang that Hsi himself was met with. Then, hardly had they settled in, before, leaving the claims of home and harvest season, he hastened across the plain to bid them welcome. It was a meeting to do one's heart good; the beginning of lifelong friendships.

To Hsi it was a new experience, for he had never met young missionaries before who could not speak the language, nor an older worker quite so familiar with its use as Mr. Baller. Already they were the objects of no little curiosity in the city, and their visitors were numbered by the hundred. It almost amounted to a levée, those summer evenings, when scholars, merchants, and farmers, young men and old, thronged the courtyards to watch the new arrivals and listen to Mr. Baller's eloquent Chinese.

"When it grows dark," they exclaimed with astonishment, "not one in a hundred would suppose that he is a foreigner."

It was an excellent opportunity for preaching, and Hsi was delighted with the spirit in which the young missionaries put themselves at the disposal of the people. He was a good judge of character, and quick to prize indications of this sort. And yet, with such limitations, how little he could really understand and appreciate his new friends. Still less could they see in him all that was to draw out their love and admiration in years to come.

For Hsi was not impressive at first sight. To the young missionaries he was just a quiet, scholarly man of medium height and slender figure, dressed in a simple blue cotton or white muslin grown. The only thing that might have attracted attention was the power of his glance; for his eyes were keen and commanding, in spite of a slight cast that disfigured one of them.

A little later they met again, this time in Hsi's own home, where he was seen to better advantage. It was no small matter, even for him, to entertain so large a party of foreigners, and the excitement in the Western Chang village was intense. Men, women, and children thronged the narrow streets and ran on ahead of the strangers; so that when they rounded the last corner, and came in sight of Hsi's gateway in a high blank wall, the crowd had announced their coming, and they received a royal welcome.

But the interest their visit occasioned was hardly greater than that of the young men themselves in this first experience of life in a Chinese home. The patriarchal household; the love and joy that seemed to overflow all hearts; the past from which these men had come, and their present occupations and prospects; the genial hospitality of their host, and his quiet but unquestioned authority, all combined in making an impression not easily forgotten.

But best of all was the evening hour of worship under the shining stars; the songs, the prayers, the earnestness with which Hsi led the meeting, and the Unseen Presence so consciously in their midst.

Next day was Sunday, and very early the visitors were awakened by pleasant commotion, as from all the neighbourhood inquirers and Christians began to gather for the services. Dressed in clean summer garments, carrying hymn-books and Testaments wrapped in gay-coloured handkerchiefs, group after group came in. And then, what eager interest in the new arrivals, and what delight in Mr. Baller's preaching, and all the tidings he brought from other parts of China!

Meeting succeeded meeting, until the young men could appreciate as never before the intelligence and capacity of a Chinese audience. But the climax was reached in Hsi's address during the afternoon, delivered with animation and graphic power that made the scenes he spoke of live before his hearers. Thanks to notes taken at the time, the divisions of the sermon can still be recalled, giving some idea of the character of his discourses.

He rarely took a text, preferring as on this occasion a whole passage from which to draw his lessons. The subject was Paul's shipwreck, and the points he made were as follows:

1. *The indifference of the unsaved:* They pay no heed to the message of God through His servants; just as the centurion and the captain of that ship turned a deaf ear to the warnings of Paul.

2. *The prosperous beginning of a course of sin:* The south wind blowing softly.

3. *The short-lived character of the sinner's happiness:* The wind and tempest soon arose.

4. *The sinner's futile efforts to save himself:* Undergirding the ship and casting away the tackling.

5. *The despair of the soul:* Neither moon nor stars for many days appearing; all hope of rescue gone.

6. *The need of perseverance on the part of God's servants:* Paul's advice at length prevailed.

7. *The final salvation of all who obey God, and trust His promises:* The whole ship's company brought safely to land.

It was tantalising for the new arrivals that they could understand so little, and especially that they could not converse with their host between the meetings. But Hsi thought of a plan. Seeing them occupied in the evening over their Bibles, he quickly brought his own, and turned to passages expressing something of what was in his heart to say, to which the young men responded through the English rendering—so holding quite a conversation.

When springtide came again great progress had been made, and the new missionaries fully justified the surprise sometimes expressed by intelligent Chinese, that a few months in their country should so wonderfully develop the silent foreigner. They had learned to talk and to walk, as well as to dress and feed themselves properly,[1] and already displayed a *savoir faire* surprising even to their most cordial well-wishers.

All through the winter steady work at the language had made a wonderful difference; and by constantly living among the people they had become familiar with their usages.

Mr. Baller, finding the whole district friendly and open to missionary work, had rented premises in three of the neighbouring cities, and wisely scattered the young men, visiting them from time to time. Native Christians of experience were left with them, so that the crowds that came to see the foreigner might not go away without hearing the Gospel. Thus three new mission stations had been opened; one south of the *Fu* city,[2] and two beyond the river, among the Western mountains. Blessing followed the winter's work in each place, and in the opening months of 1886 new converts were ready to come up with their beloved missionaries to the great gathering in the mother station at Pingyang.

It was a glad reunion; and every heart beat high with thankfulness and hope. Scattered over a region as large as Wales, four mission stations, ten or a dozen refuges, and many village gatherings sent up their representatives. Hsi and his wife were there, and all the leaders of the older work; while full of joyous enthusiasm came the young men from the new stations, eager to introduce to the assembled Christians their brethren in the faith.

To Hsi it was intensely interesting to meet the new missionaries again, and see such fruit of their labours. Mr. Stanley Smith seemed specially to impress him. Something about his sunny temper, and the way he had of cheering and helping people, greatly attracted Hsi, and made him long for his co-operation in the refuge work. They were all men after his own heart, and the appreciation was mutual.

"Hsi is a man raised up of God," wrote Mr. Hoste, "to shepherd the flock in this district. The Lord has given him authority in the sight of the people."

With the missionary in charge, he and other elders of the church made all arrangements for the conference, and baptised over seventy inquirers from the outlying stations. There was unusual power in the meetings, which had to be held out of doors in

[1] To learn to walk in the approved manner for a scholar is not so easy as one might suppose; and there is quite an art in putting on Chinese garments neatly, and behaving at table as becomes a gentleman.

[2] Pingyang was the *Fu* or chief governing city of the prefecture.

spite of heavy rain, because no room was large enough for the assembly. After a seven months' drought, the rain was sorely needed, and the Christians did not like to pray that it might cease. Sunday was drawing near, and threatenings of a heavier downpour suggested that the company might have to be divided and the services held indoors.

"Let us not be concerned about that matter," said Hsi quietly. "I have been asking the Lord to take away the rain for two days, while the conference continues. I feel sure we shall have a fine Sunday."

And so it proved. The day was perfect. The meetings were held in the open courtyard as usual. And one hundred and twenty believers gathered around the table of the Lord.

New ideas and impressions were crowding fast upon the minds of the young missionaries, to whom all this was an inspiration.

"The conference was grand," wrote one of their number. "To be permitted to see, so soon after one's arrival in China, that which many holy and devoted men of God have toiled and prayed for all their lives but never witnessed—a living church in the heart of this poor, dark land—is a great responsibility as well as privilege."

# 25

# Not against Flesh and Blood

DARK indeed was the heathenism by which they were surrounded, as the young missionaries had opportunity of proving, even during the progress of the conference. For whether they had realised these things before or not, they were now made painfully conscious of the facts connected with so-called demon-possession and the people's experiences and ideas upon the subject. But though in this and other ways the power of the enemy was becoming better known, they were more deeply proving, also, the fullness of their resources in the living God.

"What strong consolation we find," wrote Stanley Smith, "in the three little words, 'He is able.' It is grand to change the unbelieving question 'Can God?'[1] into a triumphant 'God can,' and so lay hold on His might. Strong thus in the Lord, we are ready for the conflict: able to stand against all the wiles of the devil; able to withstand in the evil day; able to quench all the fiery darts of the wicked one."

Among the inquirers attending the conference was a young man from the Chaocheng Refuge who was supposed to be under the power of evil spirits. He was often seemingly quite well for weeks together, though at other times thrown into a condition so terrible that it resembled the worst sufferings of demoniacs described in the Gospels.

During the first days of the conference this poor fellow was quiet and harmless enough, but as the meetings proceeded he was seized with a violent access of frenzy, dangerous to himself and others. Hsi was out of the way at the time, and returned to find the trouble at its height. He was immediately made aware of what was going on, and hastened into the presence of the raving demoniac.

Strangely enough, as soon as Hsi appeared, Kung became suddenly quiet. His cries and struggles ceased, and the men who were holding him relaxed their efforts.

"He is well, he is well!" they cried. "The spirit has departed."

Not satisfied with this, however, Hsi laid his hand upon the

[1] Ps. lxxviii. 19, 20.

young man's head and prayed for him earnestly in the name of
Jesus. The result was immediate and complete relief, and there
seemed every reason to hope that the trouble was permanently
conquered.

One of the missionaries present was much impressed with all
that had taken place, and especially with the power attending
Hsi's coming and his prayers. Having a sum of fifty dollars at his
disposal, he brought it to him, saying:

"The expenses of your work must be considerable, please
accept this contribution to be used as you think best."

Surprised and hardly realising how much it was, Hsi took the
silver, but had scarcely done so before he began to feel troubled.
Fifty dollars seemed so large a sum, and it had come so suddenly.
He had accepted it, too, without waiting to ask counsel of the
Lord. Was it cupidity that had moved him? Had he fallen into a
trap cunningly devised by the devil? The more he thought about
it the more he felt uneasy. So, leaving the money with Mrs. Hsi
for safe keeping, he went away alone to pray.

Hardly had he found a quiet place, however, before a messenger
came hurriedly to seek him.

"Come quickly; the matter is serious," he cried. "Kung is
worse than ever. And we can do nothing."

Much distressed, Hsi returned to the scene of trouble; and the
moment he entered the room Kung pointed straight at him,
shouting with fiendish triumph:

"You may come, but I fear you no longer! At first you seemed
high as heaven, but now you are low, low down and small. You
have no power to control me any more."

And the worst of it was Hsi knew his words were true. He
had no grip of faith or power in prayer, and felt distinctly that
the money had robbed him of his strength. With shame and
sorrow he turned away and went for the silver, followed by the
mocking cries of the unhappy demoniac. Then, finding the donor,
he openly returned the gift, confessing that the sudden possession
of so large a sum had come between his soul and God.

With empty hands but lightened heart he now went back to the
excited crowd. Kung was still raving wildly, defying any power
on earth to restrain him. But Hsi was in touch once more with his
Master. Quietly, in the name of Jesus, he commanded the tor-
mentor to be silent and leave his miserable victim. Immediately,
with a fearful cry, Kung was thrown into convulsions, from

which, however, he presently emerged, quiet and self-possessed though much weakened for the time being.

This was to Hsi a deeply painful lesson, emphasising afresh the all-important truth that, as he expressed it, "the ungrieved presence of the Holy Spirit is more to be desired than abundance of gold and silver."

Sad to say, poor Kung, the chief sufferer, was not permanently healed. He never became a real believer, and as time went on drifted away and was lost to Christian influences.

His case was typical of many in China, not to speak of other heathen lands where the devil is deliberately worshipped both in his own name and under varying forms of idolatry. That such manifestations should follow the open invocation of demons is perfectly natural, and should excite neither incredulity nor surprise. It calls for careful consideration, however, for it discloses the true nature of the power behind the idols, and therefore the heart of the difficulty with which the missionary has to deal.

That idolatry and demon-worship are thus closely connected, the word of God itself assures us. "What say I then?" writes the missionary apostle, "that the idol is anything, or that which is offered in sacrifice to idols is anything? *But I say, that the things which the Gentiles sacrifice, they sacrifice to devils,* and not to God: and I would not that ye should have fellowship with devils."[1]

This mysterious linking of the power of evil spirits with material idols is a terrible force to be reckoned on, and shows itself in many ways. One wholly natural outcome is the belief in and practice of spiritualism, so prevalent among heathen peoples in some form or other. Specially in North China is this common, where Taoist and Buddhist priests alike obtain great influence and financial profit from communications, real or pretended, with the unseen world. These practices are regarded with abhorrence by a certain section of the people, but they are generally resorted to notwithstanding.

Men and women who in Western lands would be described as spirit-mediums abound. Some calamity befalls a family—illness or disaster. Send for the medium at once. She comes, and is respectfully welcomed. Incense is offered before the idols, for the medium always plays into the hands of the priests. She sits down, usually in the seat of honour in the guest-hall, and soon relapses into a curious trance. This is done by yielding the whole being,

[1] I Cor. x. 19, 20. See also Ps. cvi. 36–38; Deut. xxxii. 16, 17.

absolutely, to the familiar spirit. The medium just waits, like an empty vessel, for the advent of the influence desired. Suddenly:

"*Shen lai-liao, shen lai-liao!*" "The spirit has come."

The medium is now possessed, filled, transported. She speaks in a new voice, with great authority, and declares what the trouble is and how it may be remedied. More paper money and incense are burned, and more prostrations made before the idols; while gradually, with horrible contortions, she comes out of the trance again.[1]

A striking feature in these cases is the apparent inability of the mediums to shake off the control of the terrible power to which they have yielded. Unsought, and contrary to their own desire, the overmastering influence comes back, no matter how they may struggle against it. One case of the kind occurred near Pingyang about this time, and is recorded by the missionary who witnessed it.

A well-known medium, who for many years had made his living by the practice, finding his health and nervous system greatly impaired, decided to give it up. Though only sixty years of age, he was so worn and haggard that he looked at least twenty years older. The struggle was long and terrible. In spite of all his efforts, the old tyranny reasserted itself again and again, until deliverance seemed impossible. He was about to give up in despair, when providentially he came in contact with some Pingyang Christians. Just how much he understood and received of the Gospel is not known, but through prayer and a measure of faith in Christ he obtained considerable relief.

But a night came when he was returning from the city by himself, and had to pass a sacred tree in a lonely spot, believed to to be the dwelling-place of demons. As he drew near, an overwhelming impulse came upon him to fall down and worship, as in former times. Desperately he resisted, but the inward urging was too strong. He stopped, fell on his knees, and bowed his forehead repeatedly to the ground. Immediately the old possession came back in redoubled force, and the misery he suffered was appalling.

Those about him sent for the Christians, and later on for the missionary, from whose memory the despairing look in those poor hunted eyes will never be effaced. He was nearing the end

[1] The above is an exact description of one scene of this sort witnessed by the writer in the women's apartments of a home in North China.

then, for the physical and the mental anguish of his condition were more than the shattered powers could withstand. But prayer again prevailed. The distressed soul turned to Christ for deliverance, and shortly afterwards, in peace that was not of this world, he died.

Whatever theory may be adopted to account for these phenomena, experience shows the deep, practical necessity for a life in touch with God, if such sufferers are to be afforded permanent relief. Nor does this view at all conflict with a scientific recognition of physical and mental conditions often present in these cases that can to some extent be controlled. But where medical skill stops short, and all human power is unavailing, there yet remain, among the heathen at any rate, very many otherwise hopeless sufferers to whom deliverance may be brought through faith in Christ alone.

But faith that prevails is not always found either in individual believers or in churches. Its secret is a close walk with God, and the real fullness of the Holy Spirit. And for this, effectual, fervent prayer is needed on behalf of all missionaries and native Christians, that they may be strong to overcome in the conditions by which they are surrounded. Shortly before the coming of Mr. Baller's party to Pingyang, a sad occurrence took place that showed lack of power in the little church in that city. Was it due to lack of prayer at home?

From a neighbouring village a promising inquirer had for some months been attending the services. He appeared really anxious to become a Christian. But all the time his household was so tormented by what they believed to be the malicious agency of evil spirits, that life was made intolerable.

At length he came to the missionary and said: "It is no use. I must give it all up. We cannot endure such misery any longer."

The missionary endeavoured to help him, but without success, painfully conscious all the while that there was not sufficient spiritual power in the church to conquer the difficulty.

The man, in desperation, ceased his connection with the Christians, and immediately his home was left in peace; the mysterious annoyances were not resumed, nor, sad to say, was his interest in the Gospel.

These are strange stories. Yes, but they are true. Much that lies behind the facts may be mysterious, but the facts have to be dealt with. And it is still the case that when prayer ascends from the mountain top, the battle goes right in the valley. No need is more urgent in connection with missionary work than the need for more real waiting upon God for those in the forefront of the fight. For "this shall turn to my salvation *through your prayer* and the supply of the Spirit of Jesus Christ."[1]

Hsi's own view of the subject was that all unregenerate men are more or less under the power of the devil, just as all Christians are more or less influenced by the Spirit of God. Many truly converted people, indwelt by the Holy Ghost, are far from wholly yielded to His control. And in something the same way, "the spirit that now worketh in the children of disobedience"[2] has not in all cases the same supremacy. But of his actual presence in those who do not belong to Christ, Hsi had no doubt; nor that he possesses in ever fuller measure the lives of those who follow his promptings and consent to his sway.[3] He recognised also that though Satan personally is restricted within finite limitations, he is the head of almost innumerable hosts.[4] A whole legion of devils, expelled from one man, were concerned in the destruction of a herd of swine. And in his experience, evidences were not lacking of the presence of many such malignant spirits still.

In earlier years, as a Confucianist, he had been drilled in the regulation attitude of contempt for all this line of things. With other scholars of his acquaintance, he called Taoism and its accompanying devil-worship a *sie-kiao*, a vile or unclean cult. But when it came to the point he, like all the rest, would send for the medium at once and act on the directions received. Fire and water can never blend. True, but put the kettle on the hob and it boils. The Confucianist could not have explained his spiritualism, and did not theoretically believe in it. But anyone could see that it worked.

To the young missionaries so recently arrived from home, the whole question was naturally perplexing. As yet they had no experience or settled theories of their own, but they could not help appreciating the genuineness of Hsi's convictions, and the faith that made his new name as a Christian no empty boast. His devotion and prayerfulness inspired them with confidence, and they were prepared to welcome the change that was about to bring them into closer contact with the man and his work.

[1] Phil. i. 19.        [2] Eph. ii. 2.
[3] Note the progression in John xiii. 2, 27, 30.        [4] Eph. vi. 11, 12.

For some time past Hsi had been much in prayer about commencing an Opium Refuge in the city of Hungtung, a few miles west of Fan's village. During the conference he felt the time had come, and it was his great desire that Stanley Smith should join him in the new undertaking. The city was busy, populous, and important. Hsi's idea was that a combination might be effected with the happiest results. He would open and carry on the Refuge, if Stanley Smith would live in it, and develop the spiritual side of the work. This offered a sphere just suited to the young missionary's evangelistic gifts; and to Hsi's satisfaction, as well as his own, the consent of the Mission was obtained.

Feeling the need of caution in approaching so influential a place, Stanley Smith followed Hsi's advice, and was content to live for some weeks in a village near at hand, while making friends and inquiring about houses in the city. Patience was soon rewarded, for suitable and commodious premises were found in a busy street, and quietly taken possession of, no objection being raised to the presence of a foreigner. The front courtyard Hsi took over as an Opium Refuge, Stanley Smith occupying the second. And the large guest-hall was set apart for a chapel, which was soon in requisition.

Here, then, in the month of May, 1886, a new centre was established, initiating a new order of things. Hoste came over later to join his friend, and Hsi paid frequent visits, giving special attention to the Opium Refuge and public meetings. It was an admirable combination: Hsi, *plus* young, devoted, foreign workers; and a combination destined to result in blessing.

# 26

# For the Work of the Ministry

THE long summer day was drawing to a close as a solitary traveller neared the city of Pingyang. Tall and strongly built, he was no native of the province, though wearing his Chinese dress as one accustomed to it, and evidently familiar with the country and language. Through long practice the courteous manners of the people had become his own, and he seemed quite at home with other travellers on the great road, though in answer to their questions it appeared he was a stranger in Shansi.

Three months' journey lay behind him, since early in the spring he started from Shanghai for the far interior. And now, returning toward the coast, the last stage had brought him into the regions of our story, from the nearest mission-station westward, more than three hundred miles away. Since leaving that little group of workers on the Han River, he had seen no Christian and found no missionary on all his four weeks' journey across the plains and mountains of Shensi.[1] Passing its famous capital, the ancient city of Sian, he had stayed to visit the tablet and ruins outside its western wall that mark the site of a once flourishing Christian church. But that old Nestorian faith had long since passed away. No missionary was found there now, nor anywhere else in all the province except at the one isolated station left behind him.[2]

A Scot can bear solitude and does not object to roughing it, but after such a journey even he is glad of a change. And it was with satisfaction the Deputy Director of the China Inland Mission looked forward to reaching Pingyang, where he hoped to meet with friends and rest a while.

But on arrival at the mission-house he found the courtyards empty and deserted. Elder Sung was there to bid him welcome, but Mr. Baller and the younger missionaries were far away, and Hsi was busy elsewhere in his extensive parish. The traveller had half expected this, knowing that Mr. Hudson Taylor was on his

[1] Except one traveller like himself, an agent of the American Bible Society.
[2] Hanchung city, on the River Han, opened as a station of the China Inland Mission in 1879. J. W. Stevenson had just come from the conference held there in May, 1885, long to be remembered as a time of unusual blessing.

way inland for special conference with the Shansi workers, and that all who could arrange to do so would hasten to the capital to meet him. Yes, they were gone: Stanley Smith from Hungtung and the others from the newly opened stations west of the river; eager to welcome the beloved General Director of the Mission, and to bring him back with them when the conference at Taiyüan was over.

It was too late to follow, for summer heat and rains had commenced already. So, thankful for the opportunity, Mr. Stevenson settled down to wait their arrival and see something of his surroundings at Pingyang. Gathering the Christians of the city daily, he devoted himself to helping them in spiritual things. At morning prayers they studied through the Gospel of St. John, and night by night the chapel was crowded for evangelistic meetings.

But chief among the interests of that quiet month was the friendship formed with one man Mr. Stevenson had long desired to meet. Twenty years of missionary life in China had prepared him to appreciate Hsi and value the work that had grown up around him. To make of both a careful study with a view to future developments was now his object.

As soon as the news of Mr. Stevenson's arrival reached him, Hsi hastened to the city. It was just a year since the coming of Mr. Baller's party had led to closer relations with missionary brethren, and he was more than ready to welcome this opportunity of intercourse with one of the Directors of the Mission. They met, and the attraction was mutual. Hsi, finding he was understood, soon opened his heart. Long hours were spent in consultation and prayer over all aspects of the work, as well as in spiritual fellowship, and fully as much help was given as received. Too quickly sped the days, so full of varied interest; but they were long enough to establish a friendship that was to last unbroken to the end.

Years later, in a conversation with the writer, Mr. Stevenson recalled the deep impressions made in contact with Hsi during those summer days at Pingyang.

"No, he was not much to look at. But one could not be in his presence an hour without knowing that he was a man with a purpose, a message, living for eternity. Something about his eyes made you feel—here is clearness of conviction and tremendous intensity.

"There was nothing dull or slow-going about him. He was

bright in manner; always busy; seeing everything; and punctilious in his courtesy. But there was no trifling in his presence, no wasting time on side questions. He was a man of one idea, and that the greatest that can absorb the soul. To him God was a reality. In everything and always, he dealt with God. The passion of his life was—saving souls."

"*Did you see much of him?*"

"Yes, although it was wheat harvest. He came over several times, and stayed for days together at Pingyang. We had many long conversations. I heard him preach also, repeatedly, for we had meetings every night, as well as daily Bible study with the Christians. Where he was there was no letting the grass grow under one's feet. I watched him too in the management of practical affairs, and the more I saw of him the more I was impressed by his grace, wisdom, and ability."

"*And you had prayer together?*"

"It was impossible to be with Hsi without having prayer. His first instinct in everything was to turn to God. Long before daylight, those summer mornings, I used to hear him in his room across the courtyard, praying and singing by the hour together. Prayer seemed the very atmosphere of his life, and he expected and received the most evident answers.

"Travelling with him on one occasion, we reached a little inn, and I remember a poor woman coming to him with a child in her arms who was ill and in great suffering. The people used to come to him like that everywhere. They knew he was a man of God and could help them. It was most remarkable how naturally they gathered round him with their troubles, taking it for granted that his time and sympathy were at their disposal. This mother, for example, came in great distress, as soon as she knew that he was in the inn.

"Hsi rose at once to meet her. 'It is all right,' he said, 'don't be troubled. The little one will be better directly.' There and then he took the child in his arms and prayed for his recovery. The woman, greatly comforted, went away. And a few hours later I saw the little fellow running about, apparently quite well and happy. One got accustomed to such things, with Hsi.

"One scene I shall never forget. It was after the conference at Pingyang. Hsi was still there, and a number of Christians. Late at night, Mr. Cassels called me out to see what was going on. I went with him, quietly, to the front courtyard. As we drew near we heard sounds of weeping, and voices pleading in low tones. There they were, dear fellows, a whole lot of them, down upon their knees, with Hsi in the midst, crying to God for the conversion of loved ones, relatives and friends at home. Many were weeping. And the earnestness and simplicity of those prayers in the power of the Holy Spirit was most remarkable and touching.

"They believed in prayer, intercessory prayer. It would have been very little use to try and convince them that such prayer was only a sort of spiritual athletics, the benefit of which was purely subjective. They knew too well its power in the lives of those for whom they prayed, as well as in their own."

*"And how were you impressed with Hsi's work in those days? Did it seem extensive?"*

"Surprisingly so. The Refuges even then were numerous, well organised, and successful. Hsi had unusual business ability, and was so thorough in all he undertook. His large household was arranged for, and all their occupations planned, in the most orderly manner. And the medicine-making for the Refuges was a sight to see."

*"Did he not make several different kinds of pills?"*

"Certainly, for the cure of various ailments; and for them all he had characteristic names. One was *Lo-yüan Wan-tzu*, or Paradise Pill; a favourite prescription, I remember. But for the regular treatment of opium patients there were three kinds, used successively. The first was called *Seng-ming Wan*, or Life-imparting Pill. Next came the *Ku-ming Wan*, or Life-establishing Pill. While third and last was the *Fu-yüan Wan*, or Health-restoring Pill, that patients were allowed to use after leaving the Refuges.

"The whole thing was most interesting. I saw myself numbers of men saved through his Refuges. And later on, as the work grew, he kept me in touch with everything by full and regular correspondence. He wrote well and quickly, and used often to send me letters a yard or more in length!"

*"As a preacher, what were his chief characteristics?"*

"He was fearless and convincing, preaching even on the streets with great boldness. His style was cultured, and most interesting. He always used plenty of good Chinese illustrations; but even in addressing heathen audiences, he rarely referred to the classics. His one weapon was the Word of God. The people loved to hear him, heathen as well as Christians; he could hold them for hours. His sermons were chiefly expository, and I was often surprised at the way he unfolded the truth, bringing new meanings to light. I heard him give one address on temptation that was most remarkable—the temptations of Christ. The solemn impression remains with me to this day.

"But it was as a pastor he excelled, he was so naturally the shepherd. People opened their hearts to him; and he was so vigilant in his solicitude for their spiritual welfare. I was specially struck with this. He had everybody's burdens to bear."

*"Through suffering and temptation of his own, I suppose, he had learned the secret of helping others?"*

"Yes; he had lived through much himself, and was still in the midst of the conflict.

"He knew well what temptation meant. He dealt with God; and if one may say so, dealt with Satan too. For he had strange experiences at times, that used to remind one of Luther in the Wartburg. But in all such conflicts he had learned to overcome upon his knees. With prayer and fasting he fought the tempter. Indeed, whatever the trouble was, he seemed to resort at once to this scriptural practice."

*"Did not such constant fasting weaken him a good deal?"*

"No, strange to say, he appeared none the worse for it. He was of so spiritual a nature that it seemed natural. Even when travelling, I have known him fast entirely for two or three days, while pondering and praying over some difficulty in the work. As far as I remember, he did not even drink tea at such times. He used to be very silent; absorbed in thought or prayer. But he was wonderfully sustained by divine strength. And if any reference were made to his being without food, he would smile so brightly and say: *Tien-Fu-ti entien,* 'the Heavenly Father's grace.' He did not fast from an ascetic motive. It was not to mortify the body, but simply to help him in prayer. He found, practically, that he could pray better so. At such times there was something about his presence that was indescribable; a solemnity without any sadness, and a realisation of divine things that used to make me feel as if I were talking with someone from another world."

*"I can well understand that you would almost lose sight of the faults and failings of his character. Yet you must have noticed a tendency to be dogmatic and even overbearing at times?"*

"Yes, he was very positive. But you could not mistake his attitude for pride or self-will in the ordinary sense of the word. One of his most frequent expressions when I knew him was:

*T'ien-Fu-ti chih-i*, 'the will of God,' or of the Heavenly Father. And it was chiefly this—his certainty of the mind of God—that made him confident and determined. He did wait so much on the Lord, to know His will. And when once he felt that this had been revealed, he was immovable. No doubt there was danger in such a position; and he was apt to be too strong, not giving sufficient consideration to the judgment of others. But what he meant to insist upon was God's way, not his own.

"Then he was so fearless. He did not hesitate to pray definitely about things, and then commit God, so to speak, to His own promises. 'Now that is settled,' he would say; 'we have left it with the Heavenly Father. He will do it for us. Here is the promise.' Or if he believed he had been guided about a thing, he had no hesitation in saying just what the Lord had told him. People did not understand, and thought him boastful or irreverent. But it was rather David's spirit—'and now, Lord, do as Thou hast said'; and a faith that was not afraid to let everybody know—'He will do it, for He has said so.' Sometimes he was wrong, but far more often it proved that he was right."

"*Did you notice about him any special aptitude for leading and influencing others?*"

"His power in that direction was remarkable; he carried so much weight. Without any effort, apparently, he seemed to sway everybody. Instinctively, people followed and trusted him. Then, too, he possessed great power of initiative, and an energy and enterprise that were extraordinary.

"But the most remarkable thing of all was his spirituality of mind and intense devotion. To him there was nothing at all in life, nothing in the world, but that one thing—love for Christ and for the souls of men. All he had was on the altar: time, money, home, friends, life itself. One could not be with him, as I was privileged to be that summer, without gaining a wholly new ideal of Christian life and service."

.   .   .   .   .

Thus the days passed quickly, and by the time Mr. Stevenson had been a month at Pingyang he had come to know the work and its leaders in no ordinary way. Many thoughts were in his mind about the condition and needs of Southern Shansi. The time seemed to have come for more thorough organisation, with a view to future developments; and with thankfulness he

anticipated the arrival of the General Director of the Mission
for conference over these important matters.

But if Mr. Stevenson looked forward to his visit, what shall
be said of Hsi, Fan, Liu, and scores of others, to whom the name
of Hudson Taylor had so long been dear? Never in this life had
they expected to see him. But he was really coming—the "Venerable Chief Pastor," founder and head of the Mission to which
they owed so much. Even now, after a journey of ten thousand
miles from the other side of the world, he was on his way to the
province, to visit their own Opium Refuges and mission stations.
They soon would see him face to face, and have his blessing—
who had prayed for them so long.

Carried to the remotest villages by joint letters from Mr.
Stevenson and Hsi, the news called forth general rejoicing, and
Christians and inquirers everywhere began to prepare for the conference. The new station at Hungtung was chosen; for though
open only three months, it had already become the chief centre
of the Refuge work. Near Fan's village, and right in the heart of
Hsi's district, it had focussed, from the first, the life of the little
churches by which it was surrounded.

And so in the last days of July Mr. Stevenson bade farewell to
the old mission-house at Pingyang, and travelled up with Hsi
and his fellow-workers to Hungtung city. Many arrangements
had to be made in view of the entertainment of so large a company; and it was not long before Mr. Stanley Smith arrived from
the capital, to see that all was in readiness. The conference up
there had been a time of unusual blessing, and the tidings he
brought kindled fresh hope and thankfulness in every heart. Mr.
Taylor and his party, including five or six other missionaries, were
following on behind, and might be expected in a few days' time.
The news spread like wildfire; and forsaking their harvest-fields
and gleaning, the village Christians hurried in.

"The Venerable Chief Pastor has come. Let us hasten to pay
our respects, and lovingly greet him."

And so, dressed in clean summer garments and carrying little
but hymn-books, Testaments, and fans—for it was the hottest
part of the season—groups of eager pilgrims were soon wending
their way to the city. Before long the new premises were filled to
overflowing, a hundred or more cheerful villagers having
possessed themselves of every nook and corner, crowding the
Refuge, camping out in the courtyards, and appropriating even

the chapel and guest-hall of Mr. Stanley Smith's own quarters. Happily it was fine weather for picnicking. Not a shade or shower damped the ardour of the assembly.

Meanwhile Mr. Taylor and his party were in a sorry plight. Several weeks of rain, just ended, had left the roads in an indescribable condition. But the welcome that greeted their arrival at Hungtung more than made up for the discomforts of the way. Through long years Hudson Taylor had toiled unceasingly for the evangelisation of Inland China. The task had often seemed hopeless; the obstacles in the way insurmountable. But God's time at length had come. The impenetrable Rock opened. And here, in the far interior, he could look at last into the faces of men and women filled with the love of Christ, saved themselves, and living to save others.

Deeply interesting it was to be among them all, and made the acquaintance of many whose names and stories had been long familiar. How often he had prayed for them, and rejoiced in the blessing that followed their labours. And now from Hsi and his wife, Sung, Chang, and many another, he could hear for himself of the way in which those prayers had been answered beyond all he asked or thought.

And scarcely less encouraging were long hours of conference with Mr. Stevenson, and the hopefulness of his impressions after weeks of close acquaintance with the work. From his suggestions Mr. Taylor gathered much that confirmed his own opinion, previously arrived at, that the time had come for a forward movement in the organisation of the church throughout Southern Shansi. Hitherto there had been only one chief centre, the mother-station at Pingyang, to which as offshoots all the village gatherings belonged. But now around Hungtung an independent, rapidly growing work had sprung up; and west of the Fen River an entirely separate district had been added, with two new mission stations. Evidently the hand of God was in these movements; and following the line of His working, regular churches must be organised in both localities, into which could be gathered the Christians living at a distance from Pingyang.

Nor was this all. Churches must be cared for. From among the men whom God had raised up and gifted in various ways for this ministry, some must be recognised as deacons, elders, and pastors, for carrying on the work. Up to that time, no native Christians had been ordained as ministers in Shansi. But there were men whom God was evidently using in that capacity, and whose faithful labours had endeared them to the people. In the city of Pingyang, Elder Sung occupied this position; and across the river, in the new Taning district, an ex-Confucianist named Chü was undoubtedly the shepherd of the little flock. These and other appointments were talked over; and finally, in consultation with the native leaders, twenty men were chosen to be set apart during the conference for various offices in the church.

But the question still remained of the appointment of a pastor for Hungtung and the surrounding district. No one of course was thought of but the man whom God had used to found and carry on the work. But though only an elder, nominally, of the Pingyang church, Hsi was already occupying a far wider sphere. To ordain him pastor of Hungtung only, would have been to curtail his influence rather than increase it. For, as a matter of fact, he was serving the Christians in very much that relation, all over both districts, and to some extent west of the river as well. He occupied quite a unique position: "Our Shepherd," as the people loved to call him. After prayer and consideration, therefore, it was decided to recognise this, and appoint him officially as Superintending Pastor of the three districts, that all the churches might have the benefit of his ministry and supervision. This would leave him free to go where he was needed, and allow the widest scope for future developments.

But no sooner was this decided on, than an unexpected difficulty arose. For Hsi himself, when informed of the appointment, drew back, and repeatedly declined to accept the position.

"Full of weakness and failings myself," he persisted, "how should I assume oversight of all the churches? Better leave to experienced foreign teachers duties so responsible as this."

Requested to consider the matter, he gave himself, as usual in time of perplexity, to prayer and fasting. But still he could not get beyond the thought of his unfitness for the post. At length Mr. Stevenson came to him and said:

"Brother Hsi, how can you decline this position? God Himself has called you to it, and used you already for years in the very work you shrink from now. It is not a question of a new departure, but simply the open recognition of what He is doing, and has already done."

This way of putting it carried conviction. "Why," thought Hsi, "what the Senior Pastor says is certainly true. The Lord has enabled me to care for these little churches from the very beginning. If He is pleased to work through me still, and more widely, how dare I refuse?"

Thus the difficulty was conquered; and throwing himself upon divine enablement, Hsi accepted the position that he knew must involve so much. Experience had already taught him that true leadership in the Church of God means eminence in cross-bearing, in service, in self-denial. "The signs of an Apostle" repeatedly adduced by Paul in proof of his call to the ministry,[1] had acquired for him too not a little reality and meaning. But to the heart cry, "Who is sufficient for these things?" he was learning the answer, "Our sufficiency is of God."

Rapidly sped the hours of helpful intercourse so long looked forward to, and Sunday morning dawned—the great day of the feast. At seven o'clock the services commenced: and none too soon. For all over the premises, from the first flush of daylight, early risers by the score had been engaged in private devotions; singing with might and main, each one a different hymn and tune, or praying and reading aloud with the energy Shansi Christians love to put into their devotions.

At noon the chapel courtyard was crowded; no fewer than three hundred men and women, including outsiders, having assembled for public worship. It was a wonderful sight in that heathen city, until a few months before unreached by the Gospel. And scarcely less interesting was the group in native dress upon the platform, including Mr. Hudson Taylor and Hsi, who together conducted the service.

But the gatherings of the following day were even more significant; for then was held the first ordination service in Shansi.

The sun was high that summer morning as Hsi joined the assembled throng. The whole front of the chapel was thrown open by the removal of lattice windows and doors; and both it and the courtyard were crowded—all faces turned to the group in the centre of the building on the dais, where a carpet had been spread. The enthusiasm of former meetings was tempered to a deeper earnestness as Mr. Hudson Taylor opened the service, surrounded by all the foreign missionaries and well-known leaders of the local work. His words were brief but heart-moving; and

[1] I Cor. iv. 9-13; I Cor. ix., the whole chapter; 2 Cor. iv., the whole chapter; 2 Cor. xi. 5 to xii. 15.

in the silence after, Hsi was first called forward, and knelt to receive the ordination that set him apart "to watch over and feed the Church of God."[1]

It was an intensely solemn moment, and one in which Hsi was conscious of a new call and consecration to the work of coming years. The memory of those prayers, and of the hands then laid upon his head in covenant and blessing, brought ever after a sense of divine appointment that no difficulty or discouragement could avail to efface.

Then followed the ordination of Sung as pastor of the Pingyang church; and the appointment of Elder Sï, and Elder Chang, and sixteen deacons for the village districts. Very impressively, in the final charge, Mr. Stevenson dwelt upon the duties, dangers, responsibilities, and infinite reward of the service for which these brethren had been chosen.

The closing meetings of the conference came all too soon, and before evening the Hungtung church was inaugurated by the first communion service ever held in that city. Hsi as newly ordained pastor conducted the meeting, with help from Mr. Stanley Smith; and seventy men and women of the district, saved from demon-worship, opium-smoking, and degrading heathenism, gathered around the table of the Lord. It was an hour long to be remembered, and left a touch of tenderness upon the parting that followed—"Until He come."

[1] "Hsi was ordained pastor of no one particular locality. He had done such an extensive work, and had been so owned of God, that it was thought best that he should be considered free to go anywhere for the work of God in these parts, knowing well how he would be welcomed by all the churches."—From Mr. Stanley Smith's account of the ordination service, August 2, 1886. See *Days of Blessing in Inland China*, p. 141.

# 27

# West of the River

SOUTHWARD to Pingyang the travellers journeyed, while the blessing of those days was carried by the returning Christians to many a village homestead far and near. Mr. Taylor's visit was drawing to a close; but there was one place he felt that he must see before leaving the province, and to Hsi's delight he accepted an urgent invitation to spend a Sunday in his home.

But first another conference had to be held in the southern city, to meet the Christians of that neighbourhood and from across the river. Gathered in the old mission-house, numbers of them were already waiting, and soon the "Venerable Chief Pastor" was welcomed to the mother-station at Pingyang with loving enthusiasm. The earliest of all the Shansi converts were there—men who had known David Hill; and with them a group of the most recent inquirers from the mountainous country west of the river.

Full of interest were the stories unfolded in the testimony meeting that evening when, amongst many others Chü, the beloved "Greatheart" of the Taning Christians, told how he had been won to faith in Christ.

In a Buddhist temple, strange to say, he had met with Jesus. His old friend Chang, the priest, had returned to Taning after a brief absence, and with hearty welcome Chü called to see him. In a quiet room on one of the temple courts they sat long in friendly conversation. By and by the quick eye of the scholar detected a book of unusual appearance lying on a dusty shelf.

"What have you there, elder brother?" he inquired, crossing the room to fetch it.

"Ah, that is a strange book I picked up on my journey; a foreign classic. You will not think much of it."

But Chü was interested. A student by nature as well as by training, he had early mastered all the books in common use, and after taking his degree still went on studying. There was not much to read up there among the mountains. They were off the beaten track, and intellectually the life of the little city was somewhat stagnant. But here was something new; and he scanned the pages with avidity. Old Chang smoked his pipe in peace, and went off to attend to the incense and candles he had to keep burning before the idols; but Chü was lost to all else for the rest of the visit, absorbed for the first time in that wonderful Story.

It was a copy of Mark's Gospel. And as he read—that Life, so simple, so sublime, laid hold upon his heart. Again and again he came to the temple to see his friend and study the little book, until its contents from cover to cover were riveted in his mind. But not Chang, the priest, nor anyone else he had ever heard of, could tell him anything more, much as he longed to know.

Jesus the Nazarene, King of the Jews, Son of God, Friend of publicans and sinners—who could this wonderful Teacher be? What power, wisdom, love! No wonder the people cried "He hath done all things well." But how strangely the thing ended. He died, in darkness: and at the rising of the sun, lo—He was risen. Could that be true? And if true, when did it all happen? Where is He now? What is the Gospel? How can one "believe"? And those preachers, where can they be found?

That was the trouble. None of them seemed to have come to the western mountains. Try as he might, he could hear of no one who could explain the little book. And yet the book was there! Who had brought it? Were there any others like it? Did any society exist for the practice and propagation of its teachings? If so, he wanted to belong to it. But no clue could be found.

At length, after about a year, rumours reached him that a foreigner, an Englishman, had come to the south of the province, and was teaching in Pingyang a religion that he called "the glad tidings about Jesus." His name was David Hill, and he was selling books something like the little *Ma-ko* Chang had in the temple. How Chü longed to go and see him! But Pingyang was three days' journey away over the mountains, and busy with his farm and school, he could not possibly go so far.

Some months later one of his pupils had to go down for a great examination, and on returning from the city he brought with him two more foreign books that he thought would interest his teacher. Chü received them eagerly, and questioned the young man as to all that he had seen and heard. But he learned nothing further about the new religion, except indeed the address at which the foreigners lived.

A year later the student went again, and this time he brought back a whole New Testament.

"I was always reading it," said Chü, "though I understood but little. One thing that impressed me was that Jesus said the way to eternal life is strait and the gate narrow, and few there be that find it. 'Alas,' I thought, 'time is going on. The end is coming soon. I am not in the way, and perhaps shall never be able to discover it.'"

Two more years passed slowly on, and at last Chü could stand it no longer. Leaving everything, he made his way down to Pingyang, and inquired for the house of the foreigner. David Hill was gone, but Mr. Drake, seeing his visitor's exercise of mind, urged him to stay several days and go into matters quietly. This Chü gladly did. And during his visit who should come over from the Western Chang village but Hsi the Christian scholar. His help and sympathy, added to that of the missionary, soon made everything clear. And what a revelation it was.

Time fails to tell how he hastened back then over the mountains, and sought out his old friend once more; of the long talks in the Buddhist temple, and how he led Chang, the priest, to the feet of the world Saviour; or of the zeal and love with which together they set to work to make the Good News widely known. They suffered much persecution. But the fire in their hearts only burned the more brightly, and others began to long for the blessing that had so changed their lives.

On one occasion Chü took his brother down to a quarterly meeting at Pingyang, the young man having also learned to know the Lord. Returning, they found the household in great trouble. Chü's only child was dangerously ill, and within a few hours after their reaching home it died. The brother sickened also. But in his brief illness, and up to the moment of his departure to be with the Lord, he said over and over with triumphant joy:

"Thank God, thank God! Jesus is indeed the Saviour of men."

"They asked me the other day," concluded Chü, referring to more recent troubles, "whether I would recant and worship idols or no? 'Never,' I replied, 'God helping me.' Thereupon the mandarin had me beaten most severely. He now intends to take away my degree. But I count it all as nothing. Jesus has greater glory in store for us than that. Truly this salvation is like being alive from the dead. We who trust in Jesus have peace that nothing can destroy."

No wonder the Christians loved him—that warm-hearted, fearless man—and welcomed his appointment as pastor of the

Taning church, of which his old friend Chang was now an elder. The ordination took place at the closing meeting of the conference, when five more deacons also were appointed.

Much as they desired to carry Mr. Taylor back with them to the western mountains, time was inexorable, and a long farewell had to be said at the gates of Pingyang as he set out with Hsi for the Western Chang village. But although the "Venerable Chief Pastor" could not accompany them, the Taning Christians were the bearers of good tidings; for had not Mr. Stevenson promised to come over shortly with Pastor Hsi—whose name they all knew and loved.

In the cool twilight of that summer evening Mr. Taylor and his party were welcomed to Hsi's dwelling, made beautiful for their entertainment. *Ta-hsi-nien* in large characters on a red ground decorated the guest-hall: "Year of great happiness," or "The acceptable year of the Lord." And the lintels and side-posts of all the doorways were bright with appropriate texts and mottoes on broad strips of scarlet paper.

"Everything was most attractive, and we were treated like princes," said Mr. Stevenson, recalling the occasion. And as to Hsi, his happiness in having the directors of the Mission under his roof was unbounded.

Many matters had to be discussed during those busy days: questions of self-support for the church, with its newly ordained pastors; of the financial basis and the extension of the Refuge work; and of the best way of spreading far and wide a knowledge of the Gospel. Uppermost in Hsi's mind was a desire he now expressed to Mr. Taylor for a new development in one important direction. At the capital he had seen on his recent visit a phase of missionary work that interested him deeply. For there, not only the wives of missionaries were labouring among the women and children of the city, but also young unmarried ladies, free to devote all their time to schools and evangelistic work. This was just what was needed; and ever since, he had longed and prayed for such workers in his own district. But so far none had been forthcoming.

"They are so badly needed. Now at Hochow for example——"

"Ah, tell me all about Hochow," interposed Mr. Taylor. "Was not that station opened by a special gift in answer to prayer?"

"Yes," responded Hsi. "Did the circumstance come to your knowledge, so far away?"

"Assuredly it did. And I praised God for the love that prompted the offering."

Then turning to his gentle hostess, "Did you not find it difficult," he added, "to part with all your jewellery, even the things that had been a marriage dower?"

"Oh no, not difficult," was the immediate answer; "it was for Jesus' sake."

"And the work at that station," continued her husband, "has been most encouraging. Already there are twenty men converted there. But alas, no women. Our hearts are often sad as we think of the suffering and darkness of homes all around us, and we long for missionary ladies to reach the women there, and in every city, with the love of Jesus."

"But how can this be done?" asked Mr. Taylor. "The married missionaries are few, and all occupied in other stations."

"Yes, we have thought of that. We could not ask that they should leave their labours. But if you, honoured sir, would trust us with the care of two or more single ladies, the problem for Hochow would be solved in the happiest manner."

"We would love them and look after them," interposed Mrs. Hsi. "And among the women of that district they would have such an opportunity for telling of the Saviour!"

"But it is hard for young, unmarried women to leave home, and the love of parents and friends, to live alone in a Chinese city like that—contrary to the prejudices of your people as well as our own."

"Our women would soon understand," eagerly replied Mrs. Hsi. "Of course it would be difficult; more perhaps than we realise. But do you not think there might be found one, or even two, who for the love of Jesus would be willing; that the women of Hochow might have the Gospel?"

Much moved, Mr. Taylor promised to see what could be done; and special prayer was made that the Lord would Himself choose and send before long at least two missionary ladies for that city. This prayer was graciously answered in the closing months of the year.

There was something specially hallowed about the intercourse of those hours, with their consciousness of coming separation. They were the last talks, the last prayers, the last meetings before he was to leave them—the loved friend who might never again come to Shansi. But there was a brightness too, and enthusiasm,

rarely equalled even in Hsi's household; for Mr. Stevenson and
and Mr. Stanley Smith were there, and Dr. Edwards from the
capital,[1] as well as Pastors Sung of Pingyang and Chü from across
the river.

When Sunday came, no room was large enough to hold the
Christians; and the small courtyard, nicely covered with an
awning, had to do duty for a chapel. Chü led the morning meeting, in his own cheery way; and from that time onward, the day
was crowded with interest; until as evening shadows fell, a
testimony meeting drew the services to a close, with many a
touching recital of the wonder-working grace of God. Oh, those
stories, told with such joyous faith, such shining faces, how they
moved the heart of the man who for twenty years had prayed
and laboured that Inland China might have the Gospel.

But still more touching and memorable was the quiet hour of
the following morning, when for the first time in the Western
Chang village was commemorated the dying, never-dying love
of Him who said: "This do in remembrance of me." Summer
sunshine stole into the chamber and fell upon loved heads in
tender silence, as the friends so soon to be parted gathered around
the table of the Lord.

Then came final preparations for the long journey, ten weeks
or more, back to the coast. It was late in the afternoon when
Mr. Taylor and his party set out, choosing to travel at night rather
than in the dust and heat of day. Quite a company left the village
with them, reluctant to say farewell. And it was not until the
"Venerable Chief Pastor" would let them go no further, that they
could be persuaded to turn back. But even then Hsi would not
leave him. Many thoughts were in his heart; many questions;
many longings: and together, mile after mile over the silent
plain, they went on.

.          .          .          .          .

The parting came at last. And slowly the distance widened
between that solitary figure and the loved friends going from
him to other scenes.

As Hsi returned alone that evening, in the twilight, he was
thinking of the life God had so used and made a blessing; and
thinking of his own. What changes in and around him since that

[1] Dr. Edwards had succeeded the late Dr. Schofield in charge of the medical
work in Taiyüan.

other parting seven years before, when David Hill, through whom he had been led to Christ, had left him bereft indeed, at the gate of Pingyang. Then he was the only Christian in his family and neighbourhood. Now—and his heart went out to all the Refuges and churches, the village gatherings and scattered Christians in the three wide districts over which he had been appointed to so sacred a charge. And that was only the beginning. What were coming days to bring?

As the moon rose over the mountains he could see village after village, wrapt in silence, where men and women were living, dying, in the dark. And just out of sight lay scores of towns and cities, and beyond them hundreds more, full of suffering and sin. Never had he felt so much before, the need, the opportunities. Never had he been so conscious of his own need—of God.

"Remember them that had the rule over you (or *that are the guides*) which spake unto you the word of God; and considering the issue of their life, *imitate their faith*. Jesus Christ is the same; yesterday, to-day, and for ever."

"Jesus Christ is the same." The same for us as for them. They pass: but He remains. What matter then the unutterable need; the loneliness; the longing? Launch out into the deep. "*Jesus Christ is the same.*"

. . . . .

Three weeks later Hsi entered upon a new phase of his life-service, when he started with Mr. Stevenson for a visitation of his wider parish; to organise the little churches and baptise fresh converts in Chü's district west of the river.

What living power there is in the Word of God, applied by the Spirit to a heart prepared for its reception. Eight years before in that Buddhist temple, a single copy of Mark's Gospel found a reader ready for the message. Five long years succeeded, in which the truth was germinating slowly in that one life. All alone amid profound spiritual darkness he accepted what he knew, the little that had come to him, and was led gradually into fuller light. No Christian or inquirer beside himself was to be found at that time within several days' journey. And he had never met anyone in all his life who knew or loved the Lord. But at length came the moment when, brought into touch with other believing hearts, "God's great sunrise found him out."

Three years only had gone by since then; but how quickly

harvests appear from long-buried seed, under the warm touch of spring.

The Book had lain for years in that little temple, but only to one soul had it spoken the life-giving message. But as soon as there was a living, loving heart, overflowing with the joy of His great salvation, through which the Saviour could reveal Himself, that bit of concrete Gospel began to tell. For "I, if I be lifted up . . . will draw all men unto me." Yes, they were drawn to Him: Chang the priest, and Chü's own brother, his aged mother too, and many more, made hungry by the blessing they could see in a life just like their own. And the more these Christians lived the teachings of their Lord, rejoicing to share His cross and in spite of persecution and suffering to confess His dear name, the more that uplifted Saviour drew other hearts into His peace and joy.

And then the missionaries came. Finding a living work of God, they set themselves to nurture and develop it. And so the blessing spread; until Mr. Stevenson and Hsi had to journey over the mountains, to establish settled churches and baptise many believers who had never been able to travel as far as to Pingyang.

How the Truth had found its way to many a heart in these remote cities and hamlets we must not now attempt to trace; nor how the travellers, fording streams and climbing mountain passes, journeyed from day to day through that lovely, lonely region, rejoicing in the manifest working of God. At Taning, the first city reached after three days' climb over the watershed, they found a deeply interesting work in progress, and stayed in the mission-house where Mr. Cassels had so endeared himself to the people that strong men wept like children when he left them for a more needy sphere. Gathering up the Christians and applicants for baptism, they went on westward to Chü's home in a steep narrow valley, through which the mountain torrent, swollen by recent rains, foamed its way, a racing cataract, down to the Yellow River.

There a welcome awaited them such as only Christians who meet once in a lifetime, amid the dense darkness of heathenism, know how to give. It was the first time Hsi had visited the district, and was he not their own "Shepherd" in a special sense? It was the first gathering in which Chü was present as their newly appointed pastor; and their first introduction to missionaries well known by name and loved for their work's sake. And then those days were to witness the inauguration of the Taning church and the first baptisms west of the Fen River. They were days of persecution too; and a solemn sense rested on all hearts of the possibility and privilege of fellowship with the Lord Jesus in His sufferings, even unto death.

So the blessing and solemnity of those hours in Chü's home among the mountains cannot be expressed. Such experiences are among the rich compensations of the missionary's lot and have to be purchased, it may be at no little cost, before they can be known. Wonderful was it to feel the love and joy that made all hearts one; to hear the testimonies of those simple, earnest men and women who had really been delivered from the power of Satan and brought into the glorious liberty of the children of God; and to join in the prayers and praises that made that crowded cave-room, dug out of a loess cliff, far in the heart of China, seem like a gate of heaven. The flickering lamps burned dim, and the hours sped one by one, till midnight gave place to early dawn, and yet the meetings could hardly be drawn to a close.

But even more heart-rejoicing were the scenes of the next day when, amid a crowd of heathen villagers awed to silence, nineteen men and women confessed their faith in Christ by baptism, while the encompassing hills resounded with praise to God; and again in Chü's home at eventide, when that little company of believers united for the first time around the table of the Lord, and He was known to them, as long ago in the breaking of bread.

It was hard to leave such opportunities, and to part from those who responded so eagerly to spiritual help and teaching. But Chü was remaining with them; and the work begun by the Holy Spirit would not lack His constant care. How much there will be to talk over in the home with many mansions, when they all meet again to tell of His faithfulness who led them safely to the end, even through the dark hours in which some of the Taning Christians won the martyr's crown.

Up and up the travellers journeyed, following the course of a mountain stream through green and lovely valleys that took them three days' journey northward from Chü's village to another district visited by divine blessing through his instrumentality.

It was a lonely hamlet. And evening shadows had fallen, when, after a long climb, the strangers drew near. But they were not unannounced. For the first signs of their approach had roused the

village watch-dogs in all directions; and before they could reach
the homes of the Christians, doors were thrown open and friendly
voices called them in from the gathering gloom. And what a
welcome it was! A large cave-room was put at their disposal;
hot water and "tea" were soon provided; and while they were
making friends with the neighbours who crowded in, supper was
quickly prepared, the Christians vying with each other in con-
tributing such simple luxuries as their homes could afford.

Next day was Sunday, a red-letter day indeed. Never had such
meetings been known in Taohsiang, where the Christians had
only once seen a missionary, and he a new arrival who could not
speak much of the language. Now there were three foreign and
two native pastors. Hardly had they realised the Church of Christ
to be so august an assembly before.

And in that lonely hamlet the missionaries were deeply touched
to find such faith and love. Many of the inquirers were anxious
to be baptised, and their answers to the questions put by Mr.
Stevenson were most interesting. When it was pointed out to
them that faithfulness to Christ would surely involve persecution,
and might even mean laying down life itself, one and another
eagerly responded, "Rather would we die than part with Jesus."
And, as time was to prove, it was no empty boast.

That afternoon a quiet place was found where the mountain
stream ran still and deep, and there, on a little stretch of green
sward, they knelt together under the open sky. It was the first
baptismal service the villagers had ever witnessed; and six
women were among the number who professed their faith in
Christ.

But there were no onlookers in the last sacred hour. Then,
shut in together by the quiet night as in some Upper Room, they
held their first Communion to remember Him whom not having
seen they loved. Hsi and Chü led the meeting; and some present
who had been in many services numbering thousands, thought
they had never witnessed one more impressive and heart-
moving.

And there next day the travellers parted: Mr. Stevenson to go
northward to the capital of the province and thence to the coast,
Chü to remain among his scattered flock in the mountains, and
Hsi to return with Mr. Stanley Smith across the river to their
own work in the south and east of the province.

Autumn was coming on, and much remained to be done in

preparation for the winter. They were going back to new conditions full of promise.

Mr. Hoste was already at Hungtung waiting their arrival; and two lady missionaries were on their way from the coast, to settle among the women of Hochow. All over the district work seemed to be opening up. Scores of people, influenced through the Refuges, were asking for baptism. Hsi's helpers in all departments were becoming more experienced and dependable. And the conferences of the summer had left the Christians eager for coming blessing.

# 28

# A Winter's Work at Hungtung

"*THOSE were days of heaven upon earth: nothing seemed difficult.*"
It was a great deal to say. But who that has known the real
fullness of the Holy Spirit, overflowing heart and life with a peace
and power not of this world, will doubt the reality of the experience? This joyous testimony from a missionary who had just left
the province, might well have described that winter also at
Hungtung for those who remained behind.

There was much in outward circumstances to encourage.
Everything opened brightly. Full of hope and enthusiasm, Mr.
Stanley Smith and Mr. Hoste threw themselves into the work of
their new station, ably reinforced by the native Christians. It was
no question of "employment"; so much work for so much pay.
There were no salaries. People who loved the Lord preached the
Gospel just because they could not help it. And the earnestness and
devotion of the young missionaries did much to encourage this
spirit.

The sphere in which they found themselves was of unusual
interest. Years of seed-sowing had prepared the way. Over a
range of country more than fifty miles in length, from Hochow
in the north to some distance south of the Western Chang village,
Hsi's Refuges were scattered—all of them more or less centres of
spiritual blessing. The first journey round the district was sufficient
to reveal great possibilities, if only the inquirers could be given
help and teaching. At Chaocheng, for example, Mr. Stanley
Smith found more than fifty professing Christians, only seventeen
of whom had been baptised; and in a busy town farther south there
was a nice little chapel with twenty or thirty regular worshippers,
but no one to lead the meetings except the local Christians. The
young converts in these and other places were doing the best
they could, and the Holy Spirit was blessing their efforts. But
most of them were country people with little or no education.
The majority could not read. And even the leaders were not far
enough advanced to deepen the spiritual life of those whom they
had been used to gather in.

Someone was needed to take up the work and carry it forward;

to follow the Spirit's leading, seeking to strengthen and develop the workers He was using and deepen in all the life He had begun to impart. Hsi had keenly felt this need, and rejoiced in the coming of missionary colleagues able to supply his lack of service. And the people most cordially joined in the welcome.

"Oh, foreign shepherds, do come and live with us," was everywhere the cry. "Stay in our village and teach us. We need you more than they do in the city."

But the district was large: they could not stay everywhere. So in consultation with Hsi, a double plan was decided on. They would gather all who could come to the city for a Bible school or conference to open the winter's work, and follow that by regular, frequent visitation of a number of centres during the next six months. Mr. Bagnall, the new missionary superintendent of the province, was coming to live at Pingyang and would be present. And as his bride was with him, he was sure of an extra welcome, for no foreign lady had ever yet visited Hungtung.

They came in the end of October. And for the first few days it was a problem how to satisfy the curiosity of the city people, who flocked to the mission-house in crowds to see the English lady. Preparations for the conference also were in progress, so that it was indeed a busy scene. But many hands make light work. Three kitchens and nine stoves kept going for a week, managed to supply enough bread and other provisions for a couple of hundred guests. And Mrs. Bagnall's courage and patience were equal to the occasion.

It was the largest church-gathering ever held up to that time in South Shansi, and gave the missionaries the opportunity they needed for coming into touch with every part of their wide field. Among the inquirers not a few seemed ready for baptism, and their cases were carefully considered, with Mr. Bagnall's and Pastor Hsi's help. Meanwhile Mrs. Bagnall was making friends with the women, who implored her to stay in the district, and could only be comforted, when they found she must go on to Pingyang, by the promise of a visit shortly from Mrs. Hsi. The meetings were full of power, and fired all hearts with the expectation of greater things to come. A large new baptistery had been built into the chapel courtyard, and was used for the first time when, at the close of the conference, fifty-four men and two women were received into the Church.

Then came the winter's work. Dividing the district into

sections, Messrs. Stanley Smith and Hoste arranged to visit
fifteen or twenty centres regularly, at which the Christians from
surrounding villages could meet them. Little intervals between
these journeys they gave to rest and study. Not much progress
could be made, however, with classical Chinese during those busy
months, though they got on famously with the spoken language.
Of course it was strenuous work, entailing constant hardship on
cold, rough journeys and in the simple homes of the people. But
they accustomed themselves to such conditions by living entirely
in Chinese style in the city. They always ate with chopsticks, slept
on heated brick beds like their neighbours, and wore the dress of
the ordinary Shansi scholar. So that when they started out month
by month on their long circuits the necessary inconveniences were
not unbearable.

Dressed in wadded cotton garments, with fur-lined caps and
wadded shoes, they were proof against the inclemency of the
northern winter; and not being accustomed to stoves at home,
they were ready to fight the cold in the Chinese way. Their
rounds were made on foot, through winter sunshine, over snow-
covered mountain roads, or across the frozen valley and ice-bound
river, where towns and villages lay thickest under their veil of
white. Accompanied by willing helpers, they spent many an
hour singing and talking as they tramped, making good use of
opportunities by the way, as well as at various stopping-places,
where so warm a welcome met them.

The Christians of the district were intensely fond of singing, a
happy proclivity that the young missionaries turned to good
account. In their own quarters at Hungtung, on their journeys in
all directions, and in homes wherever they went, they kept the
people singing. Hsi had done a good deal on these lines already,
and his hymns were deservedly popular. To the best of these
Mr. Stanley Smith added others from various sources, with songs
and choruses of his own. The collection grew into a nice little
volume, and met a long-felt need. So much was it appreciated
that fully a thousand copies were purchased that winter, and the
hymns were sung everywhere with enthusiasm, until outside
heathen people began to pick them up.

So the life of the Hungtung Christians was set to song. The
outcome was not always musical, but it was full of blessing. A
good hymn is a reservoir of truth, and through constant use much
sweetness is extracted by even the dullest saint. Singing was thus

found to be a most important means of grace, as well as practically
helpful in other ways. Nothing cheered the patients in the
Refuges so much or was so speedy a cure for anxious care. Often
in the coldest weather, the missionaries would be amused to see
the Christians with whom they were staying, or the more
vigorous of the opium-patients, drive away chilliness of soul and
body by singing over their work, or as they walked up and down
for exercise, until the ardour of their efforts was attested by the
perspiration that ran down their faces. By that time despondency
and depression were pretty sure to have taken flight.

The tunes were in many cases as original as the hymns. Pastor
Hsi was himself always singing. Many of the airs he adopted
were of native origin; and others, European by extraction, "had
their heads shaved like the missionaries and were put in Chinese
dress." These naturalised melodies took wonderfully with the
people. Hsi had also his own way of leading. He loved to pitch
the tunes as high as possible, and keep them up to a good, swinging pace. There was nothing dull or drowsy about the Hungtung
services when he was present. And the same tone of cheerfulness
pervaded the meetings in the Refuges and elsewhere.

It was a wonderful winter. The Word of God was widely
disseminated; backsliders were restored; and young converts filled
with love and fire. Sometimes when Mr. Stanley Smith was
preaching at Hungtung, the place seemed filled with the power
of the Holy Spirit. And Hsi was no less used, there and throughout
the district.

Some mistakes, of course, were made, and friction caused by
difference of opinion. The young missionaries had much to learn,
and Hsi was far from perfect. Full of enterprise, they went ahead
a good deal in their devoted way. And he, not always approving,
rather grimly looked on. But he loved them far too well to mis-
understand. And by prayer and patience on both sides, anything
like serious difficulty was avoided.

And even when most conscious of his failings, they could not
but see how manifestly he was blessed and used of God. All that
winter he was so under the power of the Spirit, that he seemed
even to impart the Divine Presence to others. When he found
among his helpers faithful brethren tried by special temptation, he
would give himself to prayer and fasting and then lay his hands
upon them; with the result that repeatedly such men were filled
with the Holy Spirit. This had always been his practice to a

certain extent; but now he found increasing blessing to result from it. And not only in these cases were his prayers answered. Frequently in the Refuges and among the Christians he was asked to lay his hands on people and pray for them, that they might receive comfort and uplifting: a result that often followed, but only when he himself was in close touch with God.

Hsi's work at this time was constant and varied. In addition to the pastoral care of the district, he had all his Refuges to visit, in several of which enlarged accommodation had to be provided. He went down also during the winter to a conference at Ping-yang, and helped Mr. Bagnall in the baptism of new members and the appointment of additional church officers. And at Hung-tung special building operations had to be put through, for the Refuge was popular, and often fifty men at a time were under treatment. All this involved frequent absences from home, and would have been impossible but for the help of Elder Sī, who was married during the winter to Mrs. Hsi's younger sister, and was able to take charge of affairs at the Western Chang village.

Saved from the depths himself, Sī had the keenest sympathy with all the work that Hsi was carrying on. His experience in the Chaocheng Refuge and elsewhere fitted him to be helpful in training others; and his gracious, humble spirit endeared him to his fellow-workers. With a great heart and unbounded sympathies, he was filled with a solicitude for the sinful and suffering that amounted to a passion for souls. And yet this man only a few years before had been so hopelessly sunk in sin that for months he had been refused admission to the Fantsun Refuge.[1] His story is interesting as showing the kind of men with whom Hsi had to deal and the secret of his influence over them.

It was in Fan's village, near Hungtung, that young Sī had grown up. His father, a well-to-do man, was a confirmed opium-smoker, day and night under the influence of the drug. With such an example before him, the lad early began to go astray. At sixteen he commenced the fatal habit, and ten years

[1] This was the man who started the work at Chaocheng with nothing but three thousand pills. After his appointment as one of the first elders in the Hungtung district, he laboured faithfully at the Western Chang village for many years. And when Hsi was taken, it was he who was chosen by the sorrowing church to succeed their beloved leader as head of all the Refuge work. During the Boxer persecution of 1900, he was the first in Shansi to be attacked. He was stabbed in the abdomen, and though he survived for some time, he never regained his health, and died in 1902.

later was well known as an "opium-fiend." Health and character suffered, until morally and physically he was little better than a wreck. Friends who at one time were earnest in exhorting him to reform, abandoned the useless effort, and young Sï rapidly drifted from bad to worse.

Still, he was not particularly concerned. He was well provided for, and cared little about his reputation as long as he had money to spend and plenty of opium. Fan, who was a religious man though not at that time a Christian, repeatedly did his best to rouse young Sï to a sense of his danger. But he was only laughed at for his pains, and finally desisted.

Then came the drought and famine—three long, dreadful years. Riches took flight; the comforts of life quickly disappeared· and ere long actual want, if not starvation, stared the family in the face. How they came through that terrible time, and managed still to secure enough opium to satisfy father and son, was a mystery. But it left them financially ruined, and the younger man eager, at last, to get rid of his vicious habits. But for long years he struggled in vain.

At length a change came in the village. Fan the Buddhist had become a Christian, and was full of a new joy and hope. His house became a centre to which numbers of people were attracted to hear the "glad tidings," as he called his new religion. Finally, moved with pity for his opium-smoking neighbours, Fan persuaded the foreign teacher to come over from Pingyang and undertake the cure of any who were willing to give up the habit. The attempt was remarkably successful, and led to the establishment of a permanent Refuge, by means of which numbers of men from all the countryside were finding their way back to life and health.

But for poor Sï the opportunity seemed to have come too late. Strange to say, he was so bad a case that Fan would not receive him. "No," he said, "our hands are full with men who can be cured. You are hopeless." But at the same time he invited him to attend the services.

This Sï continued to do. But all he heard at the meetings only deepened his concern. At length a sermon preached by Mr. Drake roused him to such an extent that he applied again to be taken into the Refuge. But still Fan was unwilling.

His only hope now lay in Hsi, and taking advantage of his next visit to the Refuge, Sï made a final appeal. Hsi was deeply moved, and pleaded his cause with Fan. "Why did the Lord Jesus come into the world at all?" he said. "Was it not to save sinners? Do not let us consider whether his life is good or bad. It may be the Lord will have mercy, and save him." And so, in the end, he was admitted.

With special care the principles of the Refuge were explained to the new patient, and he was made to understand that nothing but prayer and the power of God could save him. That night, in his earnestness to be brought through, the poor fellow spent hours in trying to pray. He supposed that in such matters one could only be heard for much speaking; and on and on until early morning he repeated the same cry for help, hoping to move the heart of the Christians' God. And heard he assuredly was, for the rapidity with which his cure was effected was remarkable.

Within a week he was well enough to begin to hope even for his poor old father. Obtaining leave of absence from the Refuge, he sought him out, and pleaded long and earnestly that he would break off his evil habits before it was too late. But no; it seemed impossible. The old man was glad enough to see his son reform, but he himself had been an opium-smoker for over forty years. There could be no changing now.

The son had to go back disappointed. But not for long. Sickness came; and in terror of death the old man determined to break off his opium as a last chance. It was a risky business; but much prayer was made on his behalf, and "God helped him also," as his son so simply said.

It was very touching, when both were cured, to see them start out together on a new life. While still in the Refuge they had agreed to take down all their idols; and the first thing on reaching home was to carry this resolve into effect. The father had been a zealous idolater, but now he was eager to burn every vestige of their former gods. The change in that home was so great that many a heart began to long for the same blessing; and the old man soon had the joy of taking his brother, also a confirmed opium-smoker, to the Refuge, where he too found deliverance.

After this the younger Sï went down to the Western Chang village. Deeply interested in his welfare, Hsi did all he could to establish him in the faith. Gradually Sï came out into full light and blessing. He and his father were baptised together, and under Hsi's influence the younger man became a successful soul-winner, and later on one of the leaders of the Refuge work.

Hsi had such a way of inspiring and developing these men. He knew how to bring out the best that was in them. No wonder his influence over them was almost unbounded. And yet his manner tried them too, at times. He had not fully learned the secret of ruling by love, and leading without appearing to lead.

It was evident, even during that first winter, that the prominent position to which he had been appointed might become a source of danger, if any of his fellow workers drifted away in heart from the Lord. Fan, for example, had declined somewhat in spiritual life; and his work no longer prospering, he had been glad to accept a position in one of Hsi's newer Refuges. But though outwardly friendly, he was envious and dissatisfied, and even then was beginning to prejudice others. If Hsi had been more humble in his dealings with these men, and more watchful against the temptations of his new position, much trouble might have been avoided. But he had to learn by sad experience, and meanwhile roots of bitterness were springing up, in spite of all the blessing of that wonderful time.

Perhaps no better idea can be gained of his character during these months, than from Mr. Stanley Smith's own recollections, embodied in a recent letter:

"Socially," he writes, "Hsi was a thorough gentleman, and a most interesting companion. Intellectually he had mental gifts of a high order. His powers of imagination, organisation, oratory, memory, and judgment were uncommon. In temperament he was enthusiastic, bold, and decided. In his spiritual character, when I first knew him, amid much that was lovable and attractive, there were some points in which he was decidedly weak. Since first believing in the Lord, he had not had the advantage of any spiritually minded man, taught in the Word, who could be a help to him in this respect, consequently his exegesis of Scripture was often at fault and fanciful. In those days, too, there was a want of subjection to the Word of God, and a tendency to exalt ideas Chinese, as well as not a little under-estimation of the foreign missionary. His prayer life, however, was full and intensely real. All matters were with him subjects for prayer, and as time went on he became a powerful exponent of the Bible, giving addresses marked by great originality and much spiritual insight.

"He had strong temptations, which were sometimes yielded to, in a direction which was a weak spot in his character—the love of

power; though it would be very unfair to put this down as
ambitious pride, pure and simple. He believed that God had given
him a position like Moses, that of leader; and in expecting the
subjection of others to his authority, he thought he was carrying
out the Divine Will. He had, however, some humbling experiences, and in the two years I was with him his progress in humility
was marked, and afterwards deepened as time went on. His love
for the Master and for souls was characterised by constant labour
and self-denial.

"He was a true member of the church *militant*, and with him
fighting the adversary by prayer, or by prayer and fasting, was a
frequent exercise. And the name he chose when he became a
Christian was no vain boast—for he would only wish it to be
understood in the sense of his receiving divine enablement—
*Hsi Sheng-mo*, Demon Overcomer."

.        .        .        .        .

Thus the spring of 1887 drew on. Six months of steady work
and prayer had told upon the district. As the snow melted from
the mountains, and all grew green again with coming harvests,
evidences were not wanting of a spiritual quickening that
promised large ingatherings. Among the inquirers, as the young
missionaries went their rounds, numbers were asking for baptism.
Family worship was regularly established in many homes. And
even the houses of the Christians had taken on a brighter look,
and could often be distinguished from those around them by
favourite hymns and passages from Scripture written on sheets of
coloured paper and pasted up outside the doors. A missionary
spirit also was gaining ground in the church. Mr. Stanley Smith
hardly ever gave an address without dwelling upon the duty and
privilege of soul-winning. This led to more definite prayer and
effort on behalf of others, and brought to decision many who
might have long remained indifferent.

Meanwhile up at Hochow a new influence for good was at
work. The ladies who had arrived during the winter were already
much beloved, and the blessing of their prayerful, devoted lives
was felt in many a place they had not yet visited. Living simply
in native style, wearing the local dress, and conforming to the
manners of the people, they had disarmed prejudice, and were
finding hearts and homes open to them in all directions.

The work of the winter had deepened love and confidence,

also, between Hsi and his missionary colleagues in both stations. So much was this the case that, at Hungtung, Mr. Stanley Smith felt it would be a great strength to the work if the pastor and his wife would both make their home in the city, and assume direct oversight of all that was going on.

"I am thinking of putting myself under Mr. Hsi," he wrote at this time. "He has been much used of God, and the work is directly or indirectly chiefly his. I am far from believing in the 'divine right' of missionaries; that simply because one has come out as a missionary, the native Christians ought all to bow to one's opinion and accept one as a guide. There is one Guide for the Church. Oh, that we all may increasingly look to Him."

These elements, and many others, combined to bring about the "great gathering" of April, 1887, which came as a climax to the winter's work and prayer.

That conference was to all present an occasion never to be forgotten. There had been not a few assemblies of the same nature before, but never one so full of power and promise. Both in numbers and enthusiasm it exceeded even the meetings of the previous year, when the "Venerable Chief Pastor" had visited the province. Then scores of Christians gathered. Now, with the inquirers, they numbered hundreds. Then, there were but few women present. Now, a woman's courtyard had been added to the premises; and Mrs. Hsi, with her newly married sister, were busy caring for country and city women from all parts of the district, over fifty of whom were about to be baptised. Then, the Hungtung church was inaugurated; and seventy believers, transferred from the mother-station, broke bread together at the first communion service. Now, over three times that number were to be received by baptism in a single day.[1]

The facts tell but little. One has to live through all the previous years, and know what it is for such a work to grow up slowly in the love and prayers of one's deepest life, to understand what such an occasion means. One soul is precious, won with great difficulty from heathen darkness. What shall be said of hundreds?

Outside the chapel, in the open courtyard, most of the services were held. The organisation was admirable, from the preparations

---

[1] Pastor Hsi subsequently proved that in such mass movements many had failed to grasp the spiritual significance of their act, but, when all due allowance is made for cases of failure, after events have revealed how much real blessing was granted.

for entertaining so large a company, down to a simple method for introducing new hymns and choruses. Two prominent pillars, supporting the eaves in front of the chapel, were made use of, and large sheets of calico on which the verses were written in clear characters, were raised or lowered as occasion required. The singing itself was an inspiration. Never before had such a volume of praise ascended to God from the far interior of China.

A whole day had to be set apart for the baptisms, for two hundred and fourteen inquirers were about to be received, of whom fifty-two were women. Pastor Hsi, who had been fasting for two days previously, spoke with great power on the Atonement, imparting a most impressive earnestness to the occasion. Early in the morning the services had to begin, and all the missionaries present took part. But it was not until the sun was going down that Hsi came up out of the water, having baptised the last group of fifty men.

The Communion that followed was a fitting close to a day long to be remembered, when nearly four hundred believers in that heathen city united in commemorating the love that gave Jesus to die: "One of the most moving scenes I ever witnessed," wrote Mr. Stanley Smith.

Little though he realised it then, Mr. Smith's work in Hungtung was almost finished. Summer was beginning, when regular itinerations would have to be suspended on account of the harvest season. And sudden, unexpected changes were at hand—a crisis that was to shake to its very foundations the Church he loved so well.

Was it in view of this he was led to plead in the last meeting for whole-hearted surrender to the Lord Jesus; and to press home the marvellous possibilities, for each one, of a life in the Holy Ghost? Some were, then and there, filled with the Spirit as never before. And the closing moments of the conference were memorable, as, "literally aglow with prayer," Hsi led in thanksgiving for coming blessing.

# 29

# Through Fire and Through Water

"ABOVE all that ye ask or think." Yes, but not always just as we expect it. The blessing comes for which the Holy Spirit inspired prayer. But sometimes only through travail of soul little dreamed of when we prayed. "We went through fire and through water: but thou broughtest us out into a wealthy place."

The conference was over. And the Hungtung mission-house, crowded only a few days before with glad multitudes, seemed silent and deserted. The Refuge patients were there, and Pastor and Mrs. Hsi, who, according to Mr. Stanley Smith's proposal, were now fully in charge of the station. But the missionaries had left, and their places were sadly empty. Feeling the need of quiet for further study impossible in their own district, they had engaged a teacher at the capital, and were there for the summer months. So Hsi was left alone as he had not been for more than a year, since Mr. Stanley Smith first joined him.

Then it was the storm broke: a change so startling as to be almost incredible had one not known something of the disaffection that for months had been leading up to it. It came as a sudden outbreak, followed by years of trouble, in which it seemed at times as if Hsi and all his work must be engulfed. But in the end evil was overcome of good.

Far from anticipating anything of this sort, Hsi was enjoying a new experience that promised a little lessening of the toil and weariness of previous years. Instead of being away somewhere on the outskirts of his orbit, or even in his busy home at the Western Chang village, he was resting, comparatively, at the centre of things, superintending all the work from Mr. Stanley Smith's own quarters at Hungtung. This was just what the missionaries had wished and planned. He could keep in touch with all the Refuges better so, and have more quiet time for thought and prayer, leaving to Elder Sï many of his former duties.

But this very change, desirable though it was in many ways, precipitated the crisis, stirring into flame the jealousy and discontent that smouldered in some hearts. This was partly due to

Hsi's own attitude; partly to circumstances over which he had no control. As indicated already, the public recognition of his gifts and unusual service by the heads of the Mission had excited dissatisfaction among a few of his fellow workers. As long as he was on their own level, they were content to follow him; but the moment he was placed above them, though it was a change only in name, they were filled with envy and suspicion. The break must have come sooner or later. For some of these men, not content with Hsi's more spiritual aims, were bent on money-making and personal advancement. But the opportunity he gave them at this time, by lack of tact and humility, no doubt made matters worse.

On Mr. Stanley Smith's leaving the station, for example, when Hsi moved into his rooms and took charge of everything, he gave out in perfect good faith that this change was of the nature of compensation for much that had gone before—part of the hundredfold reward "in this present time." He went so far as to preach one Sunday from the text, "Now is the Son of Man glorified," expounding it primarily in its right connection, but showing also how the principle works out in human experience and instancing his own. Possibly there was a measure of truth in the conception; and Hsi's idea, no doubt, was mainly spiritual, to magnify the grace and faithfulness of God. But the Chinese mind is ready to jump to conclusions, and soon slips out of metaphor into actual fact. It did not take Fan and the others long to materialise that sermon, and conclude that Hsi was glorying over them on account of his comfortable quarters rent free, the confidence of the missionaries, and the honour of his position. They judged him by themselves, and were furious accordingly.

Already they had drifted away from the Lord in heart. Fan especially had gone back in spiritual things. As an elder he had considerable influence in the church, and, supported by Elder Chang and one of the Pingyang deacons, had succeeded in drawing together a strong party composed of all the ambitious or discontented spirits in any way connected with Hsi's work. Magnifying every real or fancied grievance, they were covertly opposing his influence throughout the district; poisoning the minds of many who, left to themselves, would never have had a thought against the man to whom they owed so much. Familiar with every detail of the Refuge work, they planned to break with Hsi, carrying with them as many of his trained men as possible, and open opposition establishments on their own account, in which religious matters should have a secondary place. By underselling Hsi with medicines made from his far-famed prescriptions, they hoped to bring about a crash in his financial affairs and ultimately supplant him on his own ground.

It took some time to raise sufficient capital and foster enough bitterness of feeling to carry through the undertaking. But circumstances were not wanting that could be misrepresented to Hsi's detriment. Their anger grew to hatred as they nursed it. And finally the absence of the missionaries and the unfortunate sermon supplied the occasion and stimulus required. By that time Fan and his associates seem to have determined not only to ruin Hsi's work and reputation among outsiders, but to destroy, if possible, his influence with the missionaries as well, and drive him from his position in the church.

The plan was well worked up, and culminated in an open attack on the Hungtung Refuge. It was a tempestuous scene. Led on by Fan, Chang, and the deacon, an angry crowd took possession of the premises, hoping to intimidate Hsi, whom they knew to be practically alone, and get him into their power. Abuse and calumnies fell thick and fast. Fan, armed with a sword, was the most frenzied. He had always been a man of violent passions, and now was beyond control. Above all the noise and confusion his bitter accusations could be heard:

"You were thick enough with us in the old days, all to attain your own ends. You used me as a ladder to rise upon. You kept us all away from the foreigners while working yourself into favour. Now they come along and make you a great man. You lord it over us! You are better than we are! You grow rich on their favour, and want to dish us all out of our places. Very well then! Settle up accounts. Pay us off for all our services in the past. Stand alone if you can. But we will make it hot for you."

Quietly Hsi faced the storm, knowing well that his life was in danger. He could not escape. He could not make himself heard. But for the restraint of more sober men, Fan would have attacked him on the spot with his formidable weapon. He was practically their prisoner.

At last, seeing there was nothing more to gain at Hungtung in the absence of the missionaries, the whole crowd fell upon him and drove him out of the Refuge, crying:

"Down to Pingyang. Down to Pingyang. We will see what the

Foreign Superintendent has to say. The case shall be put into his hands."

Off they hurried to the southern city; and some hours later rushed into the mission-house, hot and dusty from the journey, and even more excited than at the beginning. Mr. Bagnall, taken by surprise, could not think what had happened until he found himself surrounded by a mob of Hsi's accusers, almost ready to take the life of their hapless prisoner. Try as he might he could not quiet them, and for a long time could not even arrive at their demands. In the midst of it all, the fact that chiefly impressed him was Hsi's perfect calmness and self-control.

"The grace he showed was wonderful," Mr. Bagnall wrote afterwards. "But while those men were raving round us, I felt as if in hell."

At length, with courage and patience, the missionary succeeded in quieting the uproar, and demanded of Fan and his company an explanation. This called forth all their accusations, which were carefully gone into. The discussion went on for hours, until Mr. Bagnall thought a temporary settlement had been reached. He was anxious to get Hsi out of their hands, and had a horse waiting to carry him to a place of safety. But no sooner was a move made to terminate the proceedings than Fan, with his sword drawn, rushed at Hsi, and the turmoil began all over again.

Seeing then that it was no use talking any longer, Mr. Bagnall beckoned Hsi to escape, and himself seized Fan, who, with his sword drawn, would have pursued him. It was a dangerous moment. But the attention of the crowd was held by the missionary's courageous action, until the horse had time to gallop away.

Thus commenced the sad breach that divided the Hungtung church. There was no further attempt at personal violence, for Fan and his party soon saw that nothing could be gained by such tactics. But they continued the fiercest opposition; accusing Hsi of every evil for which they could find the slightest pretext; openly defying his authority in his own Refuges; and seeking to make trouble for him on every hand.

With money borrowed for the purpose, they rented houses as near as possible to Hsi's Refuges in more than twenty places, and opened opposition establishments on lines they knew he disapproved. They used his medicines and his methods, underselling his prices even at the risk of their own financial position.

And, worst of all, they employed men of disreputable character, anybody and everybody who would come to them, dragging the fair reputation of the Refuge work in the mire. These agents they sent out far and wide to sell Hsi's well-known medicines everywhere. This they knew would touch him in a tender spot, for, regardless of profit, he had always refused to supply the medicine to those who were not willing to come into the Refuges, and so place themselves under Christian influence.

And for a time Hsi's enemies flourished. Fan and Chang especially were men of weight, and had local knowledge. Their Refuges succeeded, and their medicines went like wildfire. Outsiders who had been wanting to get hold of Hsi's prescription for years, now made the most of the opportunity. It seemed as though the work of the original Refuges was hopelessly undermined throughout the district. Among the church members, too, they worked hardly less havoc. The evident success of their enterprise was a great perplexity to many. Those who remained true to Hsi had expected immediate judgment to fall on the offenders. And when, on the contrary, they grew bolder and more prosperous, their plausible reasonings seemed to gain in weight.

Slowly that painful summer wore away. Poor Hsi suffered more than words can tell. Most of his helpers stood by him bravely, and it was no little compensation to discover the love and loyalty of many a true man. But they and he together had to go through the furnace. And at times it seemed as though the protecting hand of God were withdrawn, and the devil permitted to do his utmost to wreck the work.

For in the midst of the Fan troubles terrible complications arose in other directions also, and from the strangest variety of causes. Disasters occurred in all the leading Refuges, any one of which would have been serious alone. While his enemies prospered, he was compassed with distresses, "weighed down exceedingly," with a succession of trials such as he had never known before. But as the sufferings abounded, so also the consolation. In those dark days Hsi was brought to an end of himself and all human resources, and learned the deeper meaning of that "sentence of death in ourselves" that drives us to trust "not in ourselves, but in God which raiseth the dead."

"Who delivered us from so great a death," he was enabled to say, "and doth deliver: in whom we trust that he will yet deliver us."

It was really wonderful how, in answer to prayer, he was sustained through all that difficult time. Over and over again the adversary seemed permitted to do his worst; and then, at the critical moment, the Lord interfered to succour His servant.

The Chinese have a proverb full of significance, that indicates one way in which Hsi suffered at this time:

> Living, a blade of grass:
> Dying, a mine of wealth.

An ominous saying, indicating the frequency with which it happens that a man who during his lifetime was insignificant as a blade of grass, by his death becomes a source of enrichment to unscrupulous relatives.

There being no registration of deaths in China, and no post-mortem examinations, the people have a rough-and-ready method of their own for checking foul play, especially in the treatment of disease by so-called physicians. All over the country there is an unwritten law, strengthened by avarice and suspicion, that those persons are responsible for a death, on whose premises or in whose neighbourhood it occurs, and they have to meet all expenses accordingly. This affords an opportunity for levying blackmail to almost any extent; the rapacity of the relatives being only limited by the resources of the family or individual at their mercy. Hsi, through the very character of his work, was always liable to troubles of his kind. But so remarkably was he prospered, that only seven or eight deaths occurred in his Refuges during all the years he was responsible for them. Each marked a crisis of a serious nature. And strange to say, several happened at this particular time.

One of the most painful took place at the Hungtung Refuge, in the case of an old gentleman patriarch of a large and influential clan. His cure, up to that point, had been making satisfactory progress, watched with no little interest by relatives who visited him from time to time. As the accustomed supply of opium was diminished, an old malady began to reassert itself, causing the patient a good deal of discomfort. No serious consequences, however, were anticipated, or would have supervened.

But one day a young fellow of some wealth and position in the neighbourhood, strolled into the Refuge and found his way un-noticed to the old gentleman's room. The young man was a back-slider, and had no friendly feeling for Hsi or his work. In course of conversation he found that the patient was not particularly comfortable, and began to recommend some medicine of his own, warranted to cure just such disorders at his.

Unsuspectingly the old man took the pills, which apparently were poisonous, for in a short time he was writhing in agony. The Refuge-keeper was sent for, and only after much anxiety was the sufferer gradually relieved.

In the course of the evening, however, the young man slipped in again and, unaccountable as it may seem, persuaded his victim to take another dose.

"You can see," he said, "how strong and effectual this remedy must be. A small quanity has set up radical action at the seat of trouble. How much more would be accomplished by a larger supply!"

This reasoning seemed unanswerable. The old gentleman actually took a double portion of the pills. And before morning, in great suffering, he died.

It was a serious catastrophe, and almost overwhelmed poor Hsi, who was then in the mission-house. What was to be done? The news would be all over the town in no time. And who would credit facts so strange, against the plausible story his enemies could easily trump up? Word must be sent at once to the relatives. Transported with grief and rage, the whole clan would probably come down upon the Refuge—and there was no telling what might be the result. Public opinion would only justify them if they beat the Refuge-keeper within an inch of his life, and exacted an enormous sum of money, in lieu of destroying the premises. And how about the other patients? What attitude would they take in the matter? And meanwhile, as to practical arrangements, what was to be done? The Refuge was full. He did not dare to move, or even touch the body of the dead man until the relatives appeared. It would be necessary to find other accommodation; unless, indeed, all the patients went off in a body.

The complications could hardly have been more threatening. Crying to God for help and deliverance, Hsi sent off a messenger to the family of the deceased, and went over to the Refuge to see what could be done. To his surprise, no outburst of indignation greeted him. On the contrary, the patients seemed friendly and unperturbed. And on Hsi's suggesting their removal to other quarters, they said there was no need to trouble, they did not mind particularly, and would just stay where they were.

This was most encouraging; and with renewed faith, Hsi gave himself to prayer and fasting. All that day and all the next he waited upon God for the help that He alone could give. Meanwhile no word came from the relatives, which was exceedingly ominous. It looked as if they must be gathering together in force to make an attack upon the Refuge. Never had Hsi experienced quite such anxious suspense as when a third day followed and still there was no sign. And all the while the dead man was lying there uncoffined and alone.

At length the long anxiety culminated in the arrival of some of the sons. Hsi went out to meet them; and was almost taken aback to find them quiet and reasonable. Gradually it appeared that they had been detained by consultation with various members of the clan, and had now come in a conciliatory spirit to dispose of the matter quietly. This was a wonderful answer to prayer, and astonished the Christians almost as much as onlookers. The young fellow who had caused all the trouble was still in the Refuge, not having been allowed to escape. He undertook to pay half the funeral expenses, Hsi bearing the other half, and was delighted to get off so easily. Hsi sent for a suitable coffin, and arrangements were made for removing the remains at once.

It all happened so quietly that, but for the local policeman, the neighbours would hardly have noticed that anything was going on. This official, however, was furious. He had been expecting a big affair that would bring him several strings of cash. Greatly put out at this unlooked-for termination, he went to work at once and paraded the streets of the city, crying at the top of his voice that iniquitous proceedings were on foot; he would be no party to foul play in the district; the funeral must be stopped at once.

But shout as he might, no one paid much attention. It was harvest time, and people were busy with their own affairs. The coffin was brought, and the body removed. No crowd collected. And the cart passed safely out of the city. It just seemed as though the Lord Himself shut the lions' mouths. How often He has done it: praise be to His name.

It was just such evidences as these that he was not forsaken, that helped Hsi on through all that difficult time. Circumstances around him were often black as night. But he grasped a strong Hand in the darkness, and learned to trust the voice that said, "Look not around thee: for I am thy God."

Another experience of a similar nature took place in the Hochow Refuge about this time.

From a village in the neighbourhood, a poor opium-smoker had been brought, whose sad, dark life seemed drawing to a close. He was very ill, and in no condition to undergo the treatment. But his relatives, more concerned about making a little money, if possible, than about his wishes in the matter, insisted on taking him to the Refuge. If the Christians could cure him, so much the better, and if not, he would die on their hands and the expenses of a funeral would be spared.

So the poor fellow was carried to the city, too ill to care what became of him. Hsi was not in Hochow at the time, and the refuge-keepers, over-persuaded, took him in. It seemed such a pitiful case. The journey had been made with great difficulty; and the friends were so anxious to have him under Christian influence,

For some days they did their best, but the patient did not improve, and they soon saw that the end was drawing near. Filled with distress and consternation, they were about to send for Hsi when he unexpectedly arrived at the Refuge. The news was a heavy blow, coming at a time when he was sore pressed with other trouble. But the patient was still living; and without stopping to take food, Hsi went at once to the room to fight out the battle upon his knees. He was deeply moved with pity for the sufferer, as well as with anxiety on account of the difficulties his death might involve. But still more he was burdened by this fresh evidence of the long-continued and terrible opposition of Satan, whose power lay behind it all.

Hour after hour he prayed on, doing what he could medically as well. By degrees, to his unspeakable relief, a change became evident, and hope revived in the hearts of those who were watching.

"He is better. He is certainly recovering," they whispered. "All will be well."

Just then, as Hsi was beginning to feel reassured, a messenger arrived in haste, begging that he would go at once to the other side of the city to save a woman who had become suddenly possessed by evil spirits.

"She is dying! No one can do anything to relieve her. For pity's sake, implore the teacher Hsi to come quickly."

Hsi's first impulse was to start immediately. Then his thoughts reverted to the sick man. How could he leave that bedside? He looked up for guidance. And as he prayed a strong sense came over him that trouble was near.

"Is it just a device of the devil," he questioned, "to get me away from this room? As long as I am praying here, in the name of Jesus, he can do nothing. And yet, if I do not go, that woman may die, and the Lord's name may be dishonoured."

It was a sharp struggle. But it ended in his committing his patient to the care of God; and for the honour of his Master's name responding to the call of what seemed a greater need.

The woman was raving wildly as he drew near the house. A crowd had collected, and the excitement seemed greater than usual. The people knew that Hsi had been sent for, and were eager to see what would happen. As he entered the room, a strange thing took place. The woman's cries and struggles ceased. She straightened herself, and sat up, saying hurriedly:

"I know I have to go. It is all right. I know who you are, and will not make trouble." Then, as he came nearer, "I am going. I am going. Only grant me one request."

"What do you desire?" said Hsi, surprised.

"Oh, nothing," she answered quickly, "as long as you do not mind my following you."

Taken off his guard, Hsi made no objection. In the excitement of the moment, he hardly even realised what had been said. Thankful only that matters seemed to promise well, he cried to God to have mercy on the woman; and in the Name that is above every name, commanded the devil to leave her.

With a long deep shudder the woman came to herself, and looked about her, wondering. When Hsi saw that normal consciousness had returned, he earnestly besought her to turn from sin and become a believer in Jesus. Then hastened on his homeward way.

Not until he had gone some distance was he conscious of what had happened. Then a terrible oppression crept over him, and he became aware of a closely attending presence that filled him with horror. Never before had he known such an experience. He dreaded to arrive at the Refuge, and yet was most anxious to return to his patient. At the door they told him that the sick man was doing well. This encouraged him to enter. Hardly had he done so, however, before the patient became uneasy, and took a decided turn for the worse. He continued to sink rapidly, and in a few hours died.

Sorely distressed, Hsi cast himself on God, while a messenger went out to the village. Gradually a strange calmness filled his heart; and though he still continued fasting, he was able to praise as well as pray for deliverance. At nightfall the friends of the young man appeared, and word was brought that his father was with them. The wailing and commotion in the Refuge were not reassuring. But hoping for the best, Hsi went out.

What was his surprise, on entering the front courtyard, when the old father tottered feebly up to him, and falling on his knees began to protest that he knew nothing of the affair, and was no party to the wrong-doing of his family.

"They are all bad sons," he cried, "everyone of them. They will surely kill me with trouble. I was away from home, sir, when they brought their brother to your honourable Refuge. I pray you pity an old man, and be not too hard upon their offences."

With astonishment Hsi raised him from the ground, and listened to their story. Then, finding they were really poor, he offered to help with the funeral expenses. The old man was more than grateful; and the sons, who seemed thoroughly frightened, undertook to have the remains removed before morning. This was done. In the early twilight Hsi saw them depart, and returned to give thanks with the Refuge-keepers, and to trust more implicitly than ever "the God that worketh for him that waiteth for Him."

And all the while that same strong Hand was working deliverance in the greater troubles. The Lord had not forgotten his tried servant, and before autumn gave place to winter the way began to clear.

The first real lightening of the burden was when Mr. Hoste came back to Hungtung. Up at the capital the absent missionaries had heard of the attack made by Fan and his party and something of the trials that followed. But Mr. Stanley Smith was kept away by unavoidable circumstances; and not until some months had passed, could Mr. Hoste return to the station.

His coming, early in the fall, was the signal for a fresh outbreak, for the opposition was still at its height. Gathering his followers in strong force, Fan repaired to the Hungtung Refuge, and when Mr. Hoste arrived he found them in possession, intent upon gaining his countenance and sympathy for themselves and their work. To go in amongst them all was like venturing among a pack of wolves. And yet they could not but be listened to, reasoned with, and if possible won back from their misguided course. But it was anxious work; and by that time many of them had gone too far to be reclaimed. Nothing could be done with Fan, or with the deacon, who had been guilty of serious dishonesty which had already come to light. And with them went a number of others. But happily, in time, the remainder were reclaimed.

One of the questions that came up on Mr. Hoste's return was as to whether drastic action should be taken or not, with a view to purifying and safeguarding the church. In the trials of that summer the spiritual condition of professed believers all over the district had been severely tested, and not a few had gone back. Most of these followed Fan. And among the large number who were really Christians, the danger was still grave. But after prayer and consideration both Mr. Hoste and Pastor Hsi came to feel that any attempt summarily to dispose of the difficulty would be a mistake. It could only draw out sympathy for Fan and his followers, and justify those who already accused the leaders of the church of an arbitrary spirit. God alone could make it manifest who were in the right; and He would surely do so as time went on.

The event proved the wisdom of this decision. Fan, as was to be expected, gradually alienated his followers by misconduct and incapacity; while Hsi's patient and prayerful spirit effectually established him in the confidence of all right-minded men.

As months passed on signs of dissolution became apparent in the opposing party, and Hsi, after one of his customary seasons of prayer and fasting, was impressed with the conviction that the final collapse of their enterprise was near at hand. His thoughts were specially directed to John xv. 6: "If a man abide not in me, he is cast forth as a branch, and is withered." The inevitableness of this solemn judgment came to him as a message straight from God. And in all the leading centres he called the attention of the Christians to what he believed was about to happen.

"Rest quietly and wait," he said. "We do not need to fight in this battle. *Within three months* you will see the last of these spurious Refuges brought to an end."

It was a bold statement; but his words were not allowed to fall to the ground. It soon became evident that Fan was involved in hopeless complications. One by one his Refuges failed, and the whole movement sank into disrepute. Sincere men who had become involved in it, saw their mistake and withdrew. Chang, already half repentant, broke all connection with Fan, and started a work of his own on wiser lines, in another district. Deserted thus by his followers, Fan gave up the whole thing; and as a matter of fact, before three months were over, the last of his Refuges disappeared.

This was a solemn warning; and did more than any church action could have done to recall backsliders, strengthen the Christians, and safeguard Hsi's position in days to come.

Thus blessing grew out of the trouble. The church needed cleansing: and the Lord used this means for drawing off the worst elements, and deepening the mutual love and confidence of those who stood the test. Much pruning and training were required, especially in Hsi's own case, that lives the Holy Spirit was using might be more fruitful in days to come. There were dangers to be avoided and graces to develop. And it was all in wise and tender hands: "*My Father* is the husbandman."

One beautiful result of the long strain and pressure was the way in which Pastor Hsi was drawn to Mr. Hoste, and learned to value at its true worth the help of the foreign missionary. Independent as he was by nature, it had been irksome to him at times to bear with the restraints of even such co-operation. As his undertakings grew and prospered, he might easily have been tempted to swing off from the Mission altogether, and establish a purely native organisation that would have lacked important elements of permanence and strength. This the Fan outbreak finally prevented. At a critical time in his experience it threw him back upon the Mission for support, and discovered rich treasures of sympathy and friendship he might otherwise have continued to ignore. And of all fellow-labourers, Mr. Hoste was surely the most fitted to win his confidence in such a crisis. With the deepest appreciation of Hsi's character and work, he was not blind to his faults. Yet he stood by him as few others could have done: always at hand when needed, but letting him bear his own burdens; wise in counsel; steadfast in purpose and in prayer. This association was long continued, and resulted in a friendship of rare depth. Until the end they lived and worked together, in fellowship that had not a little to do with the deepening and mellowing of Hsi's character, that so markedly began in the dark days of 1887.

But it was long before the painful results of this opposition

passed away. More or less for years Hsi was involved in difficulties of which it was the fruitful source. Sad to say, the disaffection
spread to Chaocheng, and it was in the Refuge opened there
by Elder Sï that one of the most distressing experiences took
place.

At the height of the Fan troubles, quite a number of the
Chaocheng Christians sided with the opposing party. Some were
already backsliders, and others were carried away with the prospect of financial gain. They followed Fan's example, and opened
a Refuge, hoping to supersede the original work to their own
enrichment. The Chaocheng Refuge had always paid well, and
was at this time more than self-supporting. But its enemies did
not flourish. For a while they reaped a harvest, just as Fan had
done, by the indiscriminate sale of Hsi's medicine. But this was
only temporary. And the final failure of the enterprise left them
in considerable embarrassment.

A dear old man named Sung was at this time in charge of
Hsi's Refuge, and pastor of the church. Unfailing sympathy and
devotion endeared him to the Christians, and went far to explain
the success of his work. But full of unreasoning jealousy, the little
clique that had broken off determined to wreck his undertakings.
Guided by Fan's example, they planned an attack upon the
Refuge, with the purpose of driving out its occupants and
obtaining possession of the premises. They of course expected
that, this being done, Hsi would come up to look after his
property; in which case they would hold him to ransom, or force
him to buy them off with a considerable sum.

One Sunday morning, therefore, a group of these men well
known as former Christians, though they had gone back to
opium-smoking, turned up at the Refuge. They were cordially
welcomed, for Sung had the kindest heart and bore malice toward
none. It was Communion Sunday, and at the close of the first
service Sung invited all the members of the church to remain,
suggesting that other friends might retire to the guest-hall. Suddenly the little gang who had been waiting this opportunity,
sprang to their feet, crying:

"No, we will not withdraw. There shall be no Communion.
If we cannot join, you shall not have it at all."

Confusion and panic ensued. Outsiders became alarmed, for the
assailants were violently abusive, and the Christians, taken un-
awares, hardly knew what to do. Some exclaimed:

"Put them out. It is unseemly. We must continue the service."

Others were for calling the local policeman and having the disturbers punished.

"No," said old Pastor Sung, when he could make his voice heard. "It is the Lord's table, not ours. We are only guests at His Supper. These men are defying Him, not us. The Lord must deal with them. We have no complaint."

This greatly surprised the aggressors, who had expected a very different result. They were prepared for resistance, and hoped to work up a genuine quarrel. But Sung, understanding this, hurriedly explained to the Christians:

"If we turn these men out to-day, next Sunday we shall have four times as many more. Let them alone. The Lord will undertake for us."

The attacking party, seeing the Christians weaken, as they supposed, carried things with a high hand. They cleared the chapel, and took complete possession of the premises. They were so violent that the patients under treatment thought it best to escape while they could. And soon the Refuge was deserted.

Sung, of course, and his faithful helper Chü, stayed on, and sent word to Pastor Hsi, asking him to come up as soon as possible. But Hsi, on considering the matter, wrote advising them to retire from the conflict, and leave the men in possession of the premises. He saw that what they wanted was money, and an opportunity for making further trouble, and that the only thing to do was to leave them entirely alone.

"The Refuge is closed anyhow, for the present," he said. "Just take what things you can, and go elsewhere. The Lord will not let them follow you. We shall be constantly in prayer."

This advice commended itself to Sung and Chü. And gathering together a few belongings, before the men in possession of the Refuge realised what was happening, they disappeared.

But it was not easy to find other premises. They had to put up with miserable accommodation for a long time, while hunting for a landlord willing to take them in. Plenty of houses could have been bought outright; but their trouble had been noised abroad, and no one was willing to risk a repetition of such scenes on a rented property.

"See," said their critics, "what a mistake you have made. You should not allow yourselves to be imposed upon. You are simply advertising for all the riffraff of the countryside. Respectable

people despise such weakness, and feel a contempt for your
religion accordingly. Even your God does not seem able to
protect you!"

It was a difficult situation, and many of the Christians were
puzzled. When week after week went by, and no judgment from
Heaven overtook their enemies, they too began to advise going
to law for the recovery of the Refuge property. Hsi felt the
trouble keenly; and poor Sung and his helper had hard work to
hold on. But they did their best with a few patients in great
discomfort, and gave themselves to prayer and fasting.

Meanwhile the men with the Refuge on their hands rather felt
the wind taken out of their sails. They did not know what to do.
They had no real grievance, nor would the Christians give them
an opportunity for making any. They had ostensibly gained their
point and come off victors. What more could be desired? And
yet they could do nothing with the premises, and were finding
themselves in an awkward predicament.

And then the Lord began to work on behalf of His servants. It
all came about so naturally that it scarcely seemed like the
judgment of God. But all the ringleaders who had seized the
Refuge became involved in serious trouble. Family affairs went
wrong. Some were reduced to poverty. Others fell sick. One or
two died. Gradually the opposition which had been so formidable
melted away, and in the course of a few months it entirely disappeared. Onlookers were surprised; for, as everyone could see,
not a man among the Christians had lifted a finger against their
enemies.

Meanwhile the Lord provided a place in which the Refuge
and church meetings could be carried on. The very house Sung
most desired was given them in answer to prayer. The landlord
at first would not hear of renting it. He was willing to sell, or to
lease. But this the Refuge could not afford, and Sung had almost
given up hope.

Just then Pastor and Mrs. Hsi arrived in the city under peculiar
circumstances. They were travelling homeward from Hochow,
and had to pass Chaocheng on the way. They had not intended
staying there, but strangely enough found themselves without
provision for the journey, having left their cash-bag behind. It
was too late to go back and fetch it. So they pressed on to Chaocheng, knowing there were friends there who would gladly
supply their need.

Upon reaching the city, Hsi remembered a visit he wished to pay to a former patient, and the cart was driven straight to his door. Delighted at their arrival, this gentleman received them with all hospitality; and before they could leave again another visitor was announced, who proved to be the landlord of the very house Sung was so anxious to obtain. He was far from well, and finding Hsi in the guest-hall, entered into friendly conversation, and finally asked him to prescribe for his complaint.

This was Hsi's opportunity. Listening to the medical details put before him, his heart went up in prayer to God both for the patient and the Refuge. The result was that the gentleman went away with a valuable prescription, after he had cordially expressed his willingness to let Sung have the house at a nominal rental.

It was a satisfaction not to require the new premises long. At the end of about six months all opposition had vanished. The original premises were vacant, and the landlord was eager for Sung to return.

"I so well remember," writes Mr. Hoste, "when we went back to the old Refuge. Oh, the power of God that was in that place! One felt it overwhelmingly at times. It was so easy, in the meetings there, to talk of Him. One did not need to warm things up, or labour to make an impression. The working of the Holy Spirit was manifest."

During the next four and a half years nearly five hundred men were cured of opium-smoking in those premises, many scores of whom, under the loving influence of Pastor Sung, were led to Christ.

Thus the Lord undertook for His own, turning all the troubles of those difficult years to fuller blessing. "Thou hast caused men to ride over our heads: we went through fire and through water; but thou broughtest us out into a wealthy place."

Looking back upon it all long after, Hsi wrote:

At that time the Heavenly Father allowed Satan to buffet me, and tried me with fire, in a manner quite different from anything I had before experienced. There were three false brethen connected with the Refuge work, who endeavoured to kill me. But trusting in the Lord, I escaped out of their hands. In four of the leading Refuges there were deaths among those who were breaking off opium, and in all the others we had great and special troubles. And for nearly two years this testing continued.

Each time I met with heavy trials—all of which I received from the hands of my Heavenly Father—I used to fast for three, four, or five days: and the tears that I shed were beyond knowledge. But the Lord opened a way of escape for me. And although I endured much loss of means, weariness, and alarm——still, in the end, it was peace. For, in the midst of it all, the Lord comforted and strengthened me, and kept me from growing cold-hearted and going back.

Now, thanks be to God's grace, all the Refuges are in peace.

# 30

# A Wealthy Place

BEFORE us is a list of the Refuges Hsi was enabled to open in the years immediately following 1887: a long list, and most significant; embracing city after city, town after town, province after province (see next page). Eight places on the populous plain around the capital; five cities in the far south of Shansi; five cities still farther south, in Honan; Sian itself, and other important centres in adjacent provinces—in all, more than twenty Refuges opened within six years, and every one of them in places where no missionary work was being done.

.     .     .     .     .

"For I the Lord thy God will hold thy right hand, saying unto thee, Fear not; I will help thee. Fear not, thou worm, Jacob, and ye few men of Israel; I will help thee, saith the Lord thy God, thy Redeemer. . . . And thou shalt rejoice in the Lord, thou shalt glory in the Holy One of Israel."

"When men are cast down, then thou shalt say, There is lifting up."

And all this began in the dark days of the very darkest time he was ever called to go through. For it was then, while Hsi was all alone at Hungtung, only a few weeks after the outbreak of the Fan troubles, that a messenger arrived calling him to the capital to meet Mr. Stevenson, whose visit led to these important developments.

It was August, 1887, when, sad at heart, he took that solitary journey. How changed were all his circumstances since the time, only one year before, when Mr. Hudson Taylor had come down that very road. Then, all had promised brightly for the future, and fresh opportunities of usefulness called for redoubled effort. Now, difficulties and discouragements had closed in on every hand, and nothing but a sea of troubles loomed ahead.

Wonderfully, at such a time, the Lord knows how to open new vistas of hope, fresh springs of encouragement. "His understanding is infinite." Do you feel helpless as "a bruised reed"? Is all your best nothing but "smoking flax"? Then look up, Your case is just the one for Him. Like Hsi, you shall rejoice to find He still has need of you. *There is uplifting.*

It was beautiful how it all came about. One chief object of Mr. Stevenson's visit was to discuss with Hsi plans that were ripening in his own mind for large extension of the Refuge work. A forward movement was just beginning in the evangelisation of the province; and it was felt that as an auxiliary agency in opening up new districts and gaining the confidence of the people, nothing could be more helpful than Hsi's system, under his own supervision.

One of the missionaries at the capital was ready to work with him and provide the money needful for renting premises all over the Pingyao plain. And there would be no difficulty about the initial expenses in other districts also. The suggestion was for Hsi to undertake all the responsibility, find and train workers, decide upon suitable localities, and establish Refuges as widely as possible, beginning with the above-mentioned plain; and that the Mission should follow up the openings thus made, by caring for the spiritual interests of the work. No more enthusiastic associate could have been found than Mr. Orr Ewing, already winning for

---

## HSI'S REFUGES OPENED AFTER 1887

### *Pingyao Plain, Shansi*

| | |
|---|---|
| PINGYAO | HSUKOU |
| TUNGKU | KIAOCHENG |
| LINGSHIH | SHIHWU |
| KIHSIEN | TSINGANYANG |

### *South Shansi*

| | |
|---|---|
| WENHSI | TSECHAU FU |
| PUCHAU | YANGCHENG |
| | WUCHENGTSO |

### *On the Sian Plain, Shensi*

| | |
|---|---|
| SIAN | WEINAN |

### *In Honan*

| | |
|---|---|
| YUNGNING | CHANGTE |
| HUAIKING | WUAN |
| WEN HSIEN | 110 *li* W. of Shunteh |

### *In Chihli*

NANHO

himself among Shansi Christians the beautifully suggestive name
of "Glory-face"; and no more appreciative director than Mr.
Stevenson, who had so sympathetic an understanding of Hsi's life
and work.

The plain suggested was an important region lying immediately
south of the capital. With a population of fully a million, it had
nine governing cities, and no fewer than four thousand towns
and villages, in none of which missionary work had as yet been
commenced. Chief of all these cities was Pingyao, the great
banking centre of North China, which gave its name to the plain.
Crowded with merchants and scholars, and visited by a constant
stream of travellers, this city in itself offered a most important
sphere for the Gospel. And reaching out from it in all directions
lay a perfect network of towns and villages of which it was the
governing centre.

The idea was, if the Lord opened the way, to obtain a footing
in Pingyao city first of all. The Opium Refuge as an entering
edge would soon make it possible for Mr. Orr Ewing to secure
a house and make his headquarters there. And further extension
would follow. Then, from Hochow in the south, across the whole
length of the plain, Hsi was to open a chain of Refuges, one in
each walled city if possible, many of which it was hoped would
develop into permanent stations of the Mission.

It was a large programme, and Hsi was greatly encouraged;
although for the time being his circumstances did not admit of
much advance in the direction indicated. He went back to
Hungtung richer in friends and in sympathy, with new fellowship
in prayer, and an outlook that inspired hope and strengthened
patience through dark days yet to come.

Among Hsi's most promising helpers at that time was a young
farmer named Hsü, from a village a few miles went of Chaocheng.
When the Refuge was first opened in that city, Hsü was a confirmed opium-smoker, and in course of time he was persuaded
to try what the strangers could do to cure a craving as bad as his.

With no thought of becoming a Christian, Hsü went into the
city and presented himself at the Refuge for admission. He was a
tall, fine-looking young fellow, but sadly affected already by the
degrading influence of opium. With unusual ability and a fair
education, he was a man to make his mark for good or ill: just
the sort of man most welcome in Hsi's Refuges, though he little
guessed the reason why.

Much prayer was made on his behalf, and his cure was entirely successful; though to the sorrow of the Refuge workers, he left as he came, unconverted. But this was cause for jubilation among his family and friends, whose one fear had been lest he should return to them "bewitched."

Their satisfaction, however, was premature. For a time all went well. But cold, rainy days came, and trying experiences in business. Young Hsü was out of sorts and downhearted. The old solace was close at hand. Forgetting the bitter consequences, he went back to his opium pipe. And then the descent was rapid. He relapsed completely into his former habits, and was soon worse off than before.

Months after, remorseful and wretched, he crept back again to his best friends. The doors of the Refuge were open to receive him. Love and care were lavished upon his cure. Until, broken-down, the poor opium-smoker wept his way to the feet of Jesus. Then it was that Hsi got hold of him, and brought him to his own home for further help and teaching. There Hsü found complete deliverance. His opium habit was finally conquered. And from that time he gave all his life to saving others, body and soul.

Attractive, genial, gifted as a speaker, and full of tact and courage, Hsü was well fitted to win his way in a new and difficult sphere. But more than all this, was the deep reality of his spiritual life, his love for souls, prayerfulness, and real devotion.

This was the man Hsi was planning to use as a pioneer in the new enterprise. Hsü was eager for the task. And as soon as respite from pressing difficulties made it possible, he was sent forth in prayer and faith to Pingyao. Plunged as a stranger into the busy life of that great city, Hsü needed all the help that came to him from those that held the ropes at home. "Unprayed for," said the missionary pioneer of Mongolia, "I feel like a diver at the bottom of the sea cut off from his air-supply; or a fireman on a burning building, with an empty hose." But Hsü was not forgotten, and in answer to prayer the Refuge at Pingyao soon became an established fact.

Meanwhile, in yet another direction, Hsi was being drawn into new developments as unexpected as they were encouraging. A week's journey from Pingyao, away in the south of the province, lay the busy city of Wenhsi, with its hundreds of opium-smokers but no Refuge. The fame of Hsi's treatment had made its way to this district; and during the winter of 1888, a man who knew nothing of the Christians, but was eager to be cured if possible, travelled up painfully to Hungtung.

Weary with his journey, cold and forlorn as an opium-smoker can be on wintry days, he inquired his way to the Refuge, and was directed to the handsome doorway on Grain-Market Street. This looked hopeful. And when the gate-keeper admitted him to a spacious, well-kept courtyard, on which the Refuge opened, he felt he had come to the right place. Still more was he pleased with the welcome that encouraged him to tell his story.

A hundred miles away, in Wenhsi city, he had heard of the honourable Refuge. His case was almost hopeless. But as a last resort he had made the difficult journey. He was prepared to meet necessary expenses, and hoped that the benevolent doers of good deeds would take him in.

Once at home in the Refuge, the new patient found plenty to occupy time and attention. Full of wonder, he was never tired of asking questions about all that was going on. The singing, the preaching, the kindliness of the Christians, the strange power of their prayer-answering God, all interested him deeply.

"If I had only known," he said, "I would have come years ago."

Delivered at length from his opium-habit, the time came for leaving the Refuge. But it was hard to say good-bye. And the Wenhsi patient left half his heart behind him, when he went back to the south of the province.

Not long after, two or three other strangers arrived from that distant city. "Oh, we are friends of Mr. ——. He has told us about the illustrious Refuge. We too want to be cured and believe in Jesus."

And all through the winter this went on. One after another, or in little groups, these Wenhsi men appeared, smiling and friendly; though more or less miserable, all of them, through the ravages of opium. One by one they went back; well in body and enlightened, if not saved in soul. And always there were more to follow. Until in the course of that one season, no fewer than a hundred patients from Wenhsi had passed through the Hungtung Refuge. And most encouraging of all was the interest they showed in the Gospel. Many became inquirers; and some, earnest Christians.

"Truly," said Hsi at length, "it is God that gives the increase.

While we are ready to faint through many afflictions, He is
working out in new and unexpected places His purposes of grace.
The Lord is never weary and never discouraged. Oh, that we
may more closely walk with Him."

So great was the interest in Wenhsi, that a Refuge had to be
opened there, which became a centre of much blessing. Hsi paid
several visits to the city. And later on, four other Refuges were
established in that part of the province, one of which was in an
important place on the banks of the Yellow River.

Up at Pingyao also, the work was attended with blessing. Hsü's
Refuge was successful, financially and spiritually. Hsi visited the
district often, planning for further developments. He waited
much upon God about every step, praying to be guided to the
right places and the right men for the work. And the hand of the
Lord was with him. In four of the chief cities on the plain and
several lesser towns and villages, Refuges were opened which
became centres of light and blessing. Mr. Orr Ewing came to
live at Pingyao; and other missionaries followed. Finally, three of
the Refuges developed into mission stations, which are still
carried on. Six years from the spring of 1888, when Hsü commenced the work, a conference was held in Pingyao city, attended
by over ninety church members, at which nineteen men were
baptised. And many more believers, who could not be present,
were scattered in village homes throughout the district.

Still the work grew, and Hsi grew with it. In that same winter
of 1888, tidings reached him that drew his heart very specially to
the great plain of Sian, beyond the western mountains. There,
walled about in proud exclusiveness, lay the ancient city, once
capital of China, that had never opened its gates to the residence
of foreigners. No missionaries were working there, and the bitter
opposition of the wealthy and educated classes made their
entrance impossible. And all around Sian stretched the vast plain,
fertile, populous, unreached: twelve thousand square miles of
country; with twenty-one walled cities, sixty market towns, and
almost countless villages crowded with people, among whom no
witnesses for Christ had been able to gain a footing.

"I heard," writes Hsi in his brief record of these years, "that
Sian, the provincial capital, had several times refused to allow
missionaries to settle within its walls. I therefore prayed that the
Lord would guide me, and enable me to open a Refuge in that
city; that by means of curing opium-smokers, I might lead some

to trust in the Lord Jesus, and make it manifest that the sole object the foreign teachers have in view is the announcement of good tidings, able to save the body as well as the soul."

No wonder his heart was drawn out in longing toward such a sphere. But it was one thing to pray for Sian and sympathise with the missionaries who had suffered there, and quite another to attempt its evangelisation. No city perhaps in all China, was at that time more conservative and anti-foreign. It was at a distance from his home, several days' journey across the Yellow River; and in another province, where the difference of dialect and customs would at once proclaim him a stranger. He had no friends there, no openings, no influence. And the fact of his connection with foreigners and faith in the religion they preached, would stamp the Refuge work as suspicious, and might even put his life in danger. But the missionaries could suffer for Sian. Why should not he?

On account of the difficulty of the undertaking, he had decided to go himself, whenever the way opened. And at length, sure of divine guidance, he seized an opportunity when all was going well in the Refuges, and set out on the long and lonely journey. His brief manuscript supplies but little record of his experiences, and other sources of information are few. But the fact of chief importance is that he was prospered.

On the way he seems to have met with a military mandarin, a Mohammedan, who was travelling in the same direction. Pleased with the scholarly stranger, this man made many inquiries as to his connections and the object of his journey. When he found that Hsi was a doctor, prepared to undertake the cure of opium-smokers, he promptly confessed that he himself was a slave to the habit, but most anxious to be free. With this object in view, he befriended Hsi on their arrival in Sian, and materially helped him in securing suitable premises. Then, in spite of the difference of their religious opinions, he put himself into Hsi's hands for treatment; and in answer to prayer his case was successfully dealt with. This favourable beginning did much to ensure success, for the mandarin was well known and had many opium-smoking friends.

Finding the Refuge likely to prosper, Hsi sent back to Elder Si for two reliable men; and having spent some weeks preaching and teaching in the city, he left them in charge, returning to visit the work from time to time.

A year later, when Sian was crowded with scholars for the annual examination, two wealthy young fellows, sons of a retired mandarin, came up to take their degree. Fond of gay company, they had easily fallen into the habit of opium-smoking, and were now suffering from the vice they could not conquer. On the streets of the great metropolis they met their old military friend the Mohammedan mandarin. After profound salutations, the young men, surprised by the change in his appearance, exclaimed:

"Some great good fortune has surely befallen you, General. You never looked better in your life. What accounts for this renewal of youth?"

"Good fortune indeed," replied the older man, smiling. "And good fortune that you may share. I have given up opium-smoking."

"Why! Is it possible? By what magic could you accomplish this? And did you say there is hope for us too?"

"By all means. Come, and I will take you to the place where my friend Hsi of Pingyang applies his remarkable treatment."

Delighted with all they saw, the brothers decided to make the most of the opportunity; and, released from the examination hall, they hastened to the Refuge and put themselves under the care of the Christians. Weeks went by, during which they learned much of the Truth; and when, completely cured, they left the city, it was with feelings of the deepest gratitude and interest.

But what shall be said of the satisfaction of the father who received them home again, well and strong as they had not been for years? When the old gentleman heard their story, and learned that the Christians had refused the large sum of money pressed upon them over and above the usual payment, he was so delighted that he ordered a beautiful *pien*, or presentation tablet, to be made and sent to the Refuge, with a glowing inscription in praise of the work and its virtuous promoters. This valuable gift was suspended in the guest-hall; and in a city so full of official and scholarly men as Sian, it proved of no little service.

By the blessing of God the Refuge continued to prosper. Numbers of men were delivered from the opium-habit, and not a few became interested in the Gospel. On one of his visits to the city, Hsi found four or five inquirers who had given up idolatry, one of whom was evidently a sincere believer in Jesus. This man, whose name was Chang, was most anxious to be baptised. There were no Christians in the city but the Refuge keepers; nor was there any organised church within hundreds of miles. But after prayer and fasting, Hsi decided to receive him, and Chang was baptised: the first believer thus to confess his faith in Christ on all the plain. Several others subsequently joined the little group; and Hsi was greatly helped on more than one occasion by the faith and earnestness he found among these Sian converts.

Meanwhile the Lord had been preparing His own reinforcements to take up and carry on the work. Far away in America, His hand was leading. The devoted Fransen, a Swedish evangelist, fired with missionary zeal, carried revival through the Scandinavian churches from New York to the Pacific coast. A hundred missionaries, as a result, sailed for China in two or three parties, and were received by the Inland Mission. Most of them went up north—to Shansi, to Mongolia, to the Sian plain. There they followed the pioneers who so long had held the fort alone, and entered into their labours. Full of love and zeal, they opened station after station, in which they are living and working still.

At length, with unquestioning faith, one of their brethren approached the capital itself. More experienced workers, who knew the difficulty of the task, sought to dissuade him, saying that educationally and in other ways he lacked fitness to influence the cultured classes of Sian. But Holman had heard the call of God, and was not afraid to go to that proud city with no message and no power but the love of Jesus.

He secured a house, and an attentive hearing for the Gospel. And when, roused to indignation, leading scholars and officials came to turn him out, he made no objection, but welcomed them as honoured guests; entertained them with the best he could provide; and asked if they were fond of music, and would like to hear his guitar. This was too much for their curiosity! They had never heard foreign music, and begged him to bring the instrument. Inwardly crying to God for protection, Holman sang hymn after hymn to simple Swedish melodies, until somehow prejudice was disarmed and his enemies were listening to the Gospel. The result was peace. Holman was left in possession. Half-interested and half-amused, his would-be opponents went away, won to neutrality if not friendship. Thus the Swedish mission station in the capital was established, and continues to this day.

While these events were transpiring on the Sian plain, Hsi's sympathies had again been aroused by hearing of the sufferings of other pioneer missionaries in the neighbouring province of

Honan. Due south from his own district, across the Yellow River, lay that broad, populous region, with its strong, splendid, but turbulent people. A brave attempt was being made to plant the Gospel in some of its over one hundred governing cities—all without a missionary. Riots had followed in place after place, and the evangelists were obliged to flee. Huaiking was the city in question when Hsi heard the tidings; and as it was in the northern part of the province, only just over the border, he could not but desire to introduce the Refuge work there, in the hope that it might facilitate future operations. The danger was even greater than on the Sian plain, because of the formidable character of the people. But they were so well worth reaching, whatever the cost.

After much prayerful consideration, Hsi felt he had been led to the right man, and that the time had come for this fresh advance. Cheng was more than willing to go; and, taking money and medicines with him, followed by the sympathy and prayers of the Hungtung church, he set out.

No friendly traveller joined him on his journey, nor did anyone seem disposed to help him when he reached the city. Opium-smokers were plentiful; and so apparently were houses; but land-lords wanting tenants, there seemed none. No one would rent to him; no one was interested in the idea of a Refuge. For the Honanese are reserved and cautious. At the first glance they saw that Cheng was not a native of the province; and it did not take long to discover that he had "Eaten the foreign devils' doctrine," and was thus connected with the missionaries they had driven away. Prejudice filled their hearts. And though all he said was reasonable and interesting, they did not believe his fine sentiments, and wanted none of them.

But Cheng's Christianity went deeper than they had surmised. It made him patient and persistent, for reasons they could not guess, and enabled him to bear in a gracious spirit all the rebuffs with which his advances were met. It was stronger far than all their opposition, for it had behind it the Love that many waters cannot quench.

Still the circumstances were painful enough, and sitting one day in a tea-shop, Cheng was weary and discouraged. There was no opening anywhere. The people seemed determined to freeze him out by studied indifference. Lonely and far from home, what would he have given for a word of sympathy and kindly cheer?

Just then he caught sight of a forlorn figure coming down the busy street, a man who seemed even more in need of a helping hand than himself. He was evidently a stranger, and to judge by the remarks made about his pitiable appearance, was the victim of some misfortune. Followed by a group of jeering lads, he made his way toward the tea-shop, respectable people standing at a distance to see what was going on. They all knew his story, and were ready to give information.

He was a traveller from a distance. Passing the city a few days previously, he had been attacked and robbed. Without a cash in his pocket or a decent garment on his back, who could be expected to befriend him! At first he seemed to think that Huaiking people were easily moved to benevolence. But he was finding out his mistake. No one, of course, would involve themselves in such an affair. They did not want to be drawn into a lawsuit; or to have him left upon their hands! The more sick and suffering he was, the more serious the responsibility. And so on. But Cheng could not stand it.

Moved with pity, he hastened to the unhappy stranger, who could hardly believe his good fortune when he looked into a kindly face and saw that he had found a friend. Cheng led him to the inn at which he himself was staying, and having supplied his immediate needs, set about making arrangements for the remainder of his journey. Properly clothed and shaven, with his queue freshly plaited, the stranger looked what he was, a gentleman; and people began to feel ashamed of the way he had been treated in their city. Responding in a cordial spirit to the readily proffered advice of onlookers Cheng completed his task. And by the time he had provided his grateful *protégé* with money to take him home, and had sent him off in the care of a competent carter, he was himself surrounded by a little group of respectable people disposed to be friendly.

From that moment, the tide began to turn. All over the city, the facts called forth appreciative comment. Generous, when once their hearts are touched, the people could not but feel that they had misunderstood the quiet, kindly stranger. Seen in this new light, his religion was not so bad after all! And evidently his sympathetic spirit made him just the man for the difficult work he wanted to undertake! Why not give him a house, and see what he could do for opium-smokers? Surely there were enough ruined lives in their city to make such a movement desirable.

So Cheng obtained his Refuge. And the work was made a

blessing. For difficulties are nothing. We open our own doors or shut them. And the solemn word, "I give unto you the keys of the kingdom of heaven," is more true for all of us, in daily life, than we sometimes realise. We make our own opportunities. And Christlike deeds, prompted by His own Spirit, open closed hearts to Christ.

Time fails to tell of many other developments that crowded these busy years. Hsi's life, in a very real sense, had gone down like the corn of wheat into darkness and death; and now the time had come for "much fruit" in blessing to himself and others. Six years only after the outbreak of the Fan troubles, he was carrying on Refuge work in more than forty places, scattered over an area as large as England and Wales together. His hopes had been realised as regards providing employment for Christian men needing help, for the staff of trained workers in his Refuges numbered about two hundred. And the outcome in lives uplifted and blessed, was more than he had asked or thought; for many hundreds of patients were now passing through his Refuges annually, many, many of whom were won as trophies to lay at the Master's feet.

# 31

# The Burden and Heat of the Day

MANY difficulties beset Hsi's pathway during these busy years in which he was bearing the burden and heat of the day. But what are difficulties? Are they not, to the man who prays, simply occasions for proving afresh the faithfulness of God? "I never feel a burden," said Hudson Taylor, when he was carrying the care of a Mission numbering hundreds of workers mainly dependent upon him, under God, for guidance and supplies. "Here I sit in my little room," wrote John Evangelist Gossner, under similar circumstances: "I cannot go hither and thither to arrange and order everything; and if I could, who knows if it would be well done? But the Lord is there, who knows and can do everything; and I give it all over to Him, and beg Him to direct it all, and order it after His holy will. And then my heart is light and joyful, and I believe and trust that He will carry it all nobly out."

This secret of childlike faith Hsi too was learning, amid all the perplexities that surrounded his way. Opening and sustaining forty-five Refuges in four different provinces, involved more of care and responsibility than can easily be told. Hundreds of patients at a time were under treatment in widely scattered places, anyone of whom might at any moment become a source of grave anxiety. Scores of workers were now employed, and had to be kept happy and harmonious, far from his immediate influence, and under conditions peculiarly liable to excite friction and jealousy. The financial condition of all the Refuges needed constant watching, and the mere correspondence and account-keeping for so large a business concern were a heavy burden. Four to five thousand dollars annually had to be provided, and a constant supply of helpers sought and prepared, if the Refuges were to be maintained. Friendly relations must be preserved, in the midst of communities often hostile; and suffering, persecuted Christians, succoured and guided in many a complication, that unless wisely dealt with would lead to serious trouble. Then there were endless claims upon his time and sympathy as pastor of the Hungtung church, as well as the spiritual responsibilities of his wider cure of souls. And last but not least were all the demands constantly surrounding him in his own busy home, with its manifold activities.

"Whose head would not be puzzled," says Flemming Stevenson, writing of Gossner's experiences, "if left to its own wit in such a tangle? What nicely balanced calculations would not be often rudely overturned? What peculiar doctrine of chances would cover with a uniform and calculable success the venture of twenty years? What known human power can determine that when a man receives twenty pounds he will be kept as comfortably as if he had a hundred? Yet push forward such questions and the world will set busily to answer them. It does not believe in our day that there is anything which it cannot do; it must account for all phenomena upon its own principles. It is a monstrously clever world. Steam, and telegraph, and photography, and planets discovered before they are seen, Great Easterns, and St. Lawrence Bridges are very fair credentials. But there is a kingdom into which none can enter but children, in which the children play with infinite forces, where the child's little finger becomes stronger than the giant world; a wide kingdom, where the world exists only by sufferance; to which the world's laws and developments are for ever subjected; in which the world lies like a foolish wilful dream in the solid truth of the day. Gossner had been brought into that kingdom. These questions were nothing to him; it was enough that he could kneel down and pray."[1]

In this spirit Hsi went steadfastly forward; laying each difficulty before the Lord, as it arose; seeking His guidance at every step, and then counting unwaveringly upon it; daily and hourly cast upon God by needs he had no power to meet, but always finding His grace, His power sufficient.

The steadfastness of conviction and conduct was one of Hsi's strongest characteristics. He was cautious, unusually so. He made very sure of his ground to begin with. But when once he was satisfied as to the guidance of God, he was prompt in action and unfaltering in spirit. He moved carefully, but one may almost say he never went back.

Sometimes, in the Refuge work, the temptation to abandon an unsuccessful post was very great. The Refuges did not all flourish equally. Some were satisfactory from the first, financially and otherwise. Some could never be made to succeed. Few

[1] From *Prayer and Working*, by the Rev. Flemming Stevenson, D.D.

patients came, or the men in charge proved unsuitable. But trying as the circumstances might be, Hsi felt he had no right to go back upon steps taken in faith.

"As far as I know," he would say, "I was led of God to open that Refuge. I am simply His servant. He is responsible. How dare I venture, without orders, to close my Master's business?"

So he would go on, it might be for years, subsidising the work considerably, rather than take matters into his own hands and make a way out of the difficulty. In this he was markedly in contrast with the impostors who from time to time continued to imitate his methods. Such men would borrow a little capital, go to a place where Hsi was known by reputation, and commence a Refuge under his name. For a time the fame of the medicine would enable them to make large profits, and before popularity died away they would clear out, leaving the patients to shift for themselves and the landlord to recover his property. Probably this very abuse of his system, and the dishonour it brought to the cause of Christ, did not a little to strengthen Hsi in the opposite attitude.

Of course, at times, he had seriously to consider the question of abandoning work that was unsatisfactory; but he never seemed guided of the Lord to do so. In one case, where a Refuge had been "eating up money" for years, and there was little or nothing to show for it, he prayerfully considered, more than once, whether it ought not to be closed. But on each occasion the Lord seemed distinctly to say to him, "No, let it alone. That door is not to be shut." So he kept on, quietly, in spite of financial loss; and in time the place was made a blessing, but only to a limited extent. It was one of his trials of faith, and with other similar experiences no doubt tended to keep him humble.

Once he did close a Refuge; but only once. And it is significant that that was the only place he ever opened without special waiting upon God in prayer. It was a strange story, and might have had a much more painful ending.

Fifteen miles west of Hochow lay the little city of Fensi, charmingly situated among the hills. Hsi's Refuge there had been made a blessing, several patients being brightly converted; and a general readiness to hear the Gospel was the result. After some years, one of the men in charge began to grow restless and show signs of mental weakness. He was a good man who had done excellent work, and at first no one realised that the matter was

serious. While he was in this condition, Pastor Hsi had occasion
to go up to the Pingyao plain to visit his stations; and not far
from Fensi they met on the main cart-road.

"Ah, Pastor," cried Wang, "this truly is admirable! I was just
on my way to see you."

"Is all well at Fensi?" inquired the traveller, who knew that
for some time there had been few patients in the Refuge.

"Yes, all is peaceful. But we have nothing to do. And, Pastor,
such an interesting invitation has come from over the mountains.
A number of men, twenty miles yonder, want to break off opium
and learn the doctrine. But their homes are distant, and the mountain road is bad travelling. They are most anxious for one of us
to go over and establish a Refuge in their own market-town. And
I want your permission to do so."

Hsi thought a moment. The opening seemed promising. He
knew that the work in Fensi was not more than one man could
manage. They did not propose to close the Refuge, but only to
embrace a fresh opportunity in a district not far away. And there
was the man waiting beside the cart.

"Very well," he said slowly. "You may go over and see what
can be done. The Lord prosper you, and bless the undertaking."

Wang was more than delighted. But Hsi, as the cart drove on,
felt a little uneasy. He prayed over the matter. But it was too late
then to get the guidance that should have been sought before.

The new Refuge was opened, and favourable reports were
received as to the success of the work. Hsi returned from the
north, and all seemed to promise well. But gradually disquieting
rumours began to reach him. Wang had been turned out of one
set of premises, and was trying to obtain others. Patients were
few and disreputable. No money was forthcoming; but Wang
was going into debt for all he needed; giving it out that the "Jesus
Religion" had any amount of silver, and would pay at the end
of the year.

Mr. Hoste was about to take a journey in that direction, and
Hsi thankfully accepted his offer to call in and find out on the
spot the true condition of affairs. It was the depth of winter,
Christmas, 1893, and the little town looked chill and dreary as
Mr. Hoste entered the muddy streets. With some anxiety he
inquired for the stranger who had started an Opium Refuge, and
found him only too well known in the business quarter. Followed
by an interested crowd, he was soon escorted to the house in

which Wang was living; a wretched place, tumbledown, filthy, and in the most hopeless disorder.

Knowing what the man had been, it did not take Mr. Hoste long to perceive that he had entirely lost his reason, and that the only course open to him was to close the so-called Refuge and get Wang away as quickly as possible. This, however, was difficult, if not dangerous. Wang had several patients on hand, supposed to be breaking off opium. They were in a miserable condition, sadly in keeping with the deplorableness of their surroundings. Further, it soon appeared that he had been running up bills to a considerable extent, and had given serious offence by his wild talk and conduct. Aware that his own presence would be the occasion of not a little excitement, and would give opportunity for exorbitant demands, Mr. Hoste decided to leave at daybreak the following morning and send a trustworthy native to go into the whole affair.

But this was easier said than done. Creditors began to clamour for a settlement of their accounts; the landlord wanted rent; friends of the patients came demanding reparation for the fraud practised upon them; and the owner of another house insisted that Wang had taken his premises, and must hold to the bargain. Mr. Hoste had only one small piece of silver with him, and a couple of thousand cash worth five or six shillings. It was impossible to meet all these claims, even had it been desirable to do so. And for a time it seemed as though he would be seized and held to ransom, rather than allowed to leave in the morning.

But worst of all was poor Wang's utter unconsciousness of danger. He was jubilant over the whole affair; and as a proof of the success of his mission, produced an aged man in his dotage, whom he introduced as a convert. This poor old fellow had certainly got hold of one idea; that he had only to seek the Kingdom of God, and everything else would be added to him. This meant of course that if he followed the new teaching he would be comfortably supported. And the only remark he vouchsafed upon being presented to the missionary was:

"I am going to follow him." Which he proceeded to do in the most literal manner, by clinging to Mr. Hoste like a limpet.

Happily, in connection with the other house, as the stormy altercation went on Mr. Hoste discovered that the agreement had not actually been signed. But the would-be landlord had the paper with him, and was doing his best to terrorise Wang into signing it at once. This, however, Mr. Hoste managed to prevent, keeping both parties well in sight as he disclaimed all responsibility in the matter.

No privacy of course was obtainable: everything had to be said right out before the crowd: which made it doubly difficult to bring Wang to understand that he must wind up his affairs at once and go down to see Pastor Hsi.

"What?" he exclaimed in excitement; "shut up the Refuge? Turn out the patients? Why, they are not half cured. It cannot be done."

To convince him, before so many onlookers, was a slow and painful task, interrupted by indignant cries of "Pay my bill." "Refund the money you borrowed." "Settle my claim for damages, or you shall not go."

In the midst of the disturbance, Mr. Hoste explained to the patients that they had better leave at once, as Wang was no longer responsible for his actions. He gave what little money he had toward settling up accounts, promising that Pastor Hsi would send a representative without delay. And most of the remainder of that troubled night he spent in prayer.

Early next morning the excitement began all over again. But there was nothing more to be done, and calling Wang to follow him, Mr. Hoste walked quietly and quickly away. It was a dangerous moment. But taken by surprise, the people let them go. And very conscious of the protecting care of God, they passed unhindered out of the little town and made their way down to Fensi.

A few days later Elder Sî went up to explain the situation. The visit was far from pleasant. After paying eight or ten thousand cash, he was able to pacify the people and bring affairs to a peaceful termination. But to Hsi it was a sad lesson.

"I well remember his talking it all over with me," writes Mr. Hoste. "We were sitting on the heated *kang*[1] in his own little room at home. He was deeply concerned, not so much over the loss of 'face' involved, or the waste of money, as over the dishonour cast upon the Name he loved, and the victory won by the enemy. Together we committed it all to the Lord in prayer; and recognising his mistake, but without undue anxiety, he learned the lesson. It was the only time I ever knew him to close a Refuge."

[1] The brick bed of Northern China.

Not the least of Hsi's opportunities for proving the faithfulness of God arose from the practical question of ways and means. Far from growing rich, as some of his critics supposed, he was often hard put to it to supply the needs of his own household. And yet the Refuges multiplied, and his home at the Western Chang village was never empty. Whenever he had money to spare, he waited on the Lord to know how to use it. This generally led to advance in some needed direction. Then times of pressure came; shortness of crops thinned the paying patients in the Refuges, and there was great scarcity all round. But a way was always opened for him. And he never went into debt.

The yearly expenditure in the Refuges had now reached about five thousand Mexican dollars. And in addition, the medicines he gave away gratuitously amounted to a large sum. For his fame as a doctor was considerable; many of his patients were poor; and besides native drugs, he used quinine, castor-oil, and other comparatively costly foreign remedies. Then his expenses at home continued heavy; for the missionary training department increased from year to year, and other activities were diligently kept up.

With the most careful management and economy, it was not easy to make ends meet; and as in earlier years, Hsi had now and then to part with personal possessions to provide for some pressing need. His own habits were of the simplest. The silks and furs of former days had long since disappeared. He now wore plain, blue cotton garments; cotton, instead of satin shoes; and wadding did duty for comfortable fur linings in winter.

"The money I receive for medicine," he wrote, "when reckoned up at the end of the year, is often not nearly enough to meet requirements, and during the last two years I have had to part with some of my clothing and other articles to supply the deficiency. If it were not that I trust in the precious promises of Jesus and in the Holy Spirit's leading, I should on no account dare to carry on this work. I beseech all of you, honoured missionaries, to pray for me and for the Refuges, that the Lord may bestow all needed supplies, material and spiritual, that there may be no lack."

At times when funds were low and faith was tried, he was wonderfully sustained; and the fact that the Lord allowed him to have such experiences, and did not always send immediate deliverance, made him far more help and comfort than he could otherwise have been to poorer Christians. On one occasion Mr. Hoste had to learn this lesson; and, at no little cost to himself, to leave his friend in the midst of difficulties the Lord did not see fit to remove.

It was a time of semi-famine. There had been failure of the crops, and provisions were unusually high. This meant added expense at all the Refuges, as well as fewer patients who could afford to pay for treatment. Hsi, of course, suffered with the rest; and in some way it came to Mr. Hoste's knowledge that he and his household were living upon limited supplies of coarse bread and millet gruel. Mr. Hoste's first impulse, of course, was to help; and having fifteen ounces of silver that he could spare, he slipped the package up his long Chinese sleeve and set out for the Western Chang village. It was a long day's walk, and on the way he was much in prayer for the friends to whom he was going. As he prayed, the Lord seemed to lay it upon his heart that he was making a mistake, and ought not to give Hsi that money.

"But he is in need, Lord. They are really suffering. I have come down on purpose to help and comfort him."

"You can do so by loving sympathy," came the answer. "But leave it to me to care for his needs. I have a purpose in the trial. It is meant for blessing."

Toward evening Mr. Hoste reached the familiar homestead, and was welcomed to the frugal entertainment that was all his host could afford. Hsi was full of joy at seeing him; and together they talked of the loving faithfulness of God, and committed all needs to Him in prayer. No complaint was made, and no help sought or offered. But Mr. Hoste had all he could do to keep that silver up his sleeve.

During the night he prayed still more earnestly about it, longing to be permitted to assist the friends he loved so well. But the conviction only deepened that he must stand aside, and not attempt to steady with his hand the ark of God's providence. He saw that the Lord was wanting Hsi to set an example of faith and patience that might encourage weaker believers. All around him were other Christians suffering just as he was. Mr. Hoste could not relieve them all. But the Lord could and would strengthen them to endure, and provide some way of escape that they might be able to bear it. Hsi as their pastor and leader had to ring true at such a time. All that he could say about the Father's unfailing care would have been valueless if they could answer:

"Exactly. It is easy enough for you to talk. But we happen to know that after the missionary visited your place there was a sudden influx of cash. We could trust too, under those circumstances."

Still it was very hard for Mr. Hoste to say farewell next morning, and return to Hungtung, leaving matters just as he had found them. Hsi accompanied him some distance along the road, and was never dearer to the heart of his friend than when he had to let him go back, alone, into the trial.

Long after, when it was all over and they were talking one day of the way in which God had provided, Mr. Hoste told Hsi of the real purpose of that visit, and of how nearly at the last moment he had handed him the silver that would have removed all difficulty. Hsi was deeply touched; and to Mr. Hoste's surprise, thanked him earnestly for having followed the guidance of God and refrained. He said that the many little ways in which help had come to him, as to others, had brought them all so much nearer to God; and that they had learned precious lessons in the trial that would all have been lost if by Mr. Hoste's gift deliverance had come immediately, and their eyes had been turned to him rather than fixed on the Lord.

One of Hsi's most helpful and most widely used hymns was written at a time when funds were low and there was a good deal of persecution and distress, as well as the prospect of famine. It was written in perfect peace of heart, and is still sung by Shansi Christians when amid fiery trials they are enabled to rejoice in God.

1.        Through the faith,
            Grown so poor!
        How can I but be sad?
            Think of Christ
            Born so low!
        And then my heart is glad.

*Chorus*

Jesus gives me peace,
    Jesus gives me peace
    The peace that Jesus gives
Unlike the joys of this world,
    None can take away:
    It is the peace of Heaven.

2.        For the truth
            Treated ill,
        How can I but be sad?
            Think of Christ
            Crowned with thorns!
        And then my heart is glad.

3.                           For "Good News"
                                Pass through pain;
                      How can I but be sad?
                                Think of Christ
                                Scourged and torn!
                      And then my heart is glad.

4.                           For the Church
                                In sore straits;
                      How can I but be sad?
                                Think of Christ
                                On the Cross!
                      And then my heart is glad.

This joy, that the world can neither give nor take away, was the secret of his strength. In the midst of "reproaches, necessities, persecutions, distresses," the knowledge that it was all "for Christ's sake" filled him with a gladness that only those who have felt the like can understand.

"In labours more abundant" he was now often away from home for weeks or months together, visiting the Refuges and superintending church affairs throughout his wide district. On the cover of his cart, as he travelled from place to place, he had the sentence, "Holy Religion of Jesus" in large, red characters, to draw attention and afford an opening for conversation on spiritual things. For the same reason he often wore across the front of his outer garment the six characters, *Je-su chiang shi chiu ren*: "Jesus came into the world to save sinners." Wherever he went he embraced every opportunity for talking with fellow-travellers and preaching Christ in the towns and villages he passed through. Many a Christian in Shansi was first led to an interest in the Gospel through a word thus spoken by the wayside, in some tea-shop, or in an inn at night, by the tired, travel-stained man who was never too weary to tell of the love of Jesus.

During later years he was away from home as much as ten months out of twelve, travelling and working thus. He used his own conveyance less then than formerly, and on long journeys, to save expense, travelled like any poor man of the district, walking half the time, and engaging a donkey for a stretch here and there, wherever one was available. Some of his Refuges were in remote places, and many of the hamlets he visited were hidden away among the mountains. Thus his journeys were often difficult and lonely, and he had to carry his own belongings many a weary mile. On these out-of-the-way roads there were often no inns, or only those of the roughest description. But he was content to be "as his Master," and put up cheerfully with poor accommodation and still poorer fare. Many a half-sleepless night he had to spend amid crowding, discomfort, and dirt. He was never a strong man physically, but it was wonderful how the Lord sustained him amid great and constant hardships.

At home, between his journeys, he was always busy; teaching and training his men; attending to correspondence, accounts, medicine-making, and all the business details that had to be kept right; discharging his pastoral duties in the Hungtung district; conducting weddings and funerals, or visiting the sick and dying.

"You are always hard at work," said a visitor.

"Yes," he replied. "One cannot be diligent overmuch in the Lord's harvest field. But my heart is always at leisure."

This was indeed the case, and increasingly so as time went on: at leisure from itself, to care for and comfort others.

One burden that became increasingly heavy as the work grew was the strong opposition to the whole Refuge system that developed on the part of some whose opinion he valued most. There were able and devoted missionaries in Shansi who objected to Hsi's methods, and would have preferred the Refuge work, if it must be carried on at all, to be under the direct control of the Mission. They thought that he went ahead too fast; and that the condition of affairs that gave him so much influence among the native Christians was dangerous. Some did not hesitate to express these convictions to Hsi himself, and he was aware of a good deal more than was said in his presence. All this, of course, was painful and perplexing, for Hsi had learned to value the sympathy and approval of missionary brethren.

Rumours even began to be circulated that he was making money through the Refuge work, and carried it on chiefly for the sake of enriching himself. When this was reported to Hsi, he quietly answered:

"Yes, I am engaged in a profitable undertaking. My business sign is *Tien-chao-küh*.[1] My Master, the Proprietor, is Lord of All. The profits I seek and obtain are the priceless souls of men; those who enter the Refuges, hear the Gospel, believe, and obtain salvation. They are not a few. Several thousands of men and

[1] "Heavenly Invitation Officer," the three characters he put up over all his Refuges.

women have through this business been delivered from opium-smoking. Several hundreds are at the present time standing firm in the faith: some pastors, some elders, some deacons, and many chutch members and inquirers. My hope is that when the Master returns to reckon up accounts, He may receive His capital and interest, without loss. What objection can there be to such business in His name?"

But though at times he responded cheerfully to criticisms of this sort, the distress they caused under other circumstances was very great. His brief autobiography affords a glimpse into this phase of his experience.

"Some honoured missionaries," he writes, "exhorted me very earnestly to close the Refuges, saying it was an undertaking fraught with perils.

" 'If it were a question of my own wishes,' I replied, 'I would not continue a single day. But seeing the Lord has led me into this work, I dare not withdraw. But I will pray over the matter.'

"Thereafter I kept these words spoken by the missionaries in my mind, not venturing to disregard such advice. From that time my strength of heart for work in the Refuges seemed considerably weakened, and the battle was harder to fight.

"The devil also, using this opportunity, disturbed me not a little.

" 'The task you are attempting is truly an ungrateful one,' he persisted. 'It is criticised by outsiders and disapproved of even by missionaries. It absorbs your money, your time, and your strength. To the end of your days you will never be free from care, or able to obtain rest. You and your wife seldom see each other's faces. In several of the Refuges you are losing money, and obtaining no results. Why should you toil and suffer more than other people? There is no need for you to take all this trouble.'

"Hence I was still more unsettled, and could only pray earnestly to the Lord."

It was not that he was really undecided; for the more he prayed, the more he was sure that the work was of God. But he keenly felt the weight of opinion against him; and as it was shared by men whom he respected and loved, it cast him back upon the Lord continually for reassurance.

It was, perhaps, scarcely to be wondered at that some of the foreigners in Shansi should feel as they did about the movement. They saw in it elements of danger that caused anxiety. The Refuges were numerous and widely scattered, which rendered supervision difficult. Hsi himself and his helpers were far from perfect: and it was impossible but that mistakes should occur at times. His power over the native Christians was undoubtedly very great. Had he chosen to go off on his own account and sever all connection with the Mission, he might easily have carried with him the larger part of the local church. It was difficult for those who had not lived with him, to understand his character and position, and to appreciate the enthusiastic love and confidence he inspired. They felt concerned about his being such a centre of influence, not realising that spiritual relationships are at least as strong as natural, and cannot be set aside. During ten years or more of the busiest time of his life, this misunderstanding continued. No doubt the effect was to a certain extent beneficial; for it led to more prayer and greater carefulness. But it was painful also, and cost Hsi no little exercise of mind.

On one occasion it seemed more than he could bear, and led to his making a mistake he much regretted. It was at a difficult crisis. Funds were low and discouragements many. Hsi went over to Pingyang on business, and there a missionary whose age and experience entitled him to respect, called him aside and strongly urged him to retrench and even abandon the work.

"He is my senior," said Hsi to himself. "I must reverently attend to his words."

When the missionary had pressed home all his arguments, Hsi answered respectfully:

"Your exhortation I will keep in my heart. Had it been a question of my own wishes, I should never have opened one Refuge. But if the Lord desires to do this work through me, can I refuse? I dare not say I will or will not continue. I must be quiet in His hands."

After this, troubles only increased; especially at Hochow. The work there, which had been so promising after the arrival of the ladies, seemed at a standstill. Dissensions weakened the little church, and some among the Christians had even gone back to opium-smoking. The Refuges both for men and women were almost empty. Financially they were a failure, and the expense of keeping them open was a tax upon the treasury. All this lent urgency to the temptation that assailed him:

"You see, Mr. —— was right. His words are true. You cannot get on. Better do as he said, and abandon the Refuges. He knows much more about missionary matters than you do."

Hsi fought these suggestions bravely; but at length the difficulties at Hochow reached a climax, and he decided to close the Refuges and hand over the station to the Mission. His time and resources could be better spent elsewhere.

Important affairs took him to Hungtung just at this time, and after the usual evening service he went to Mr. Hoste's room and explained the situation.

"When next you go to Hochow," he concluded, "I shall be glad if you will confer with the ladies, and let me know the result. If they wish to make use of the courtyard adjoining their own, I will arrange it so. If not, the premises can be given up. I do not intend to carry on the work any longer."

Mr. Hoste was greatly surprised, and felt that something was wrong. He saw, however, that it was no use to question or argue, and simply said:

"I will see that your wishes are carried out."

But alone that night he prayed much that the Lord would undertake for His tried servant, and not allow any mistake to be made.

Midnight came and passed; but still Hsi could not sleep. His heart was strangely troubled. At length, weary with tossing from side to side, he rose and gave himself to prayer. But the burden only increased, until the very depths of his being seemed stirred, and he broke into an agony of weeping.

"Lord, what does it mean?" he cried, "I am but a child, full of ignorance and weakness. Lord, how have I grieved Thee? Show me the reason for this distress."

"Remember Hochow," came the answer, almost as if a voice had spoken. "How dare you retreat there, because of a little trial? Have you forgotten your many prayers for missionaries to work with you in that city? I sent them. It has cost them far more than it is costing you. Yet now, because of difficulty, you are about to close the Refuges and abandon the ladies when they need you most. Where is your faith, your love?"

Overwhelmed with conviction, Hsi fell on his face and reconsidered the whole position before the Lord. Things always look so different from that point of view.

"Ah, Lord," he cried, "if it be Thy will that I should suffer on account of these Refuges, I welcome it with a willing heart. Thou canst make them prosper: and whether or no, I will not abandon one of them, if Thou dost not approve."

Early next morning Mr. Hoste was surprised to find Hsi all ready for a journey, and to hear that he was going himself to Hochow.

"I have been wrong," he said. "The Lord has showed me. Instead of giving up the Refuges, I must go over at once and help to get things on a better footing."

"Then my prayers are answered," was the cheering response. "Last night I besought the Lord to show you His will in the matter. He has surely done it."

Through the long hours of that summer day, Hsi urged his mules over the mountain road, and as evening was drawing in, he reached the gates of the city. Slowly he made his way through the streets and climbed the hill to the mission-house. There, to his surprise, all was silent and deserted. The servants were out apparently, for he knocked again and again, but could get no answer. Where were the Refuge-keepers? Where was the Biblewoman? Where were the ladies? At last his anxiety was relieved by the sound of footsteps, and a voice from within inquiring what was wanted.

"It is I," cried Pastor Hsi. "Let me in. The Lord has sent me to help you."

With surprise and thankfulness the door was thrown open, and he was welcomed to the empty house, where he found the ladies in real trouble, their helpers having all deserted them. Cook, watercarrier, woman, all were gone, and even the Christians had left them, for the night, alone.

As they answered his questions, Hsi noticed that the ladies had slipped away in turn to draw water from the well, light a fire, and prepare him a meal. This broke him down altogether. And when they urged that such services were but a small expression of their gratitude for his coming and all his care on their behalf, he had to go away to hide his tears.

That evening he did all he could to encourage the young missionaries, thus strengthening his own faith in God.

"There was a time," he reminded them, "when even the Lord Jesus could do nothing, and all His work was stopped. Oh, those dark days when He lay still and silent in the grave! It is like that just now with us in Hochow. But there will be a resurrection morning."

Next day he went in search of the Christians, and gathered together as many as possible with the Refuge-workers and servants. Earnestly he pleaded with them to return to the Lord; and having investigated the trouble, straightened out complications and set everything going on a satisfactory basis again. There was, about his appeals, a warmth of love and renewed devotion that awoke a response in all hearts. That was the turning point. The men's Refuge was reopened, and many patients applying, it soon became financially independent. The missionary work of the station was resumed with growing encouragement. Best of all, souls were saved, and Hsi never again lost faith so far as to attempt to abandon work that the Lord had given him to do.

One remarkable feature of his life, during these busy years, was the energy and endurance he manifested under long-continued strain, both mental and physical. "I always felt," said Mr. Hoste, who was with him constantly, "that Hsi had a bodily strength not his own. He was a man whom God specially sustained for the work He had given him to do. I have known him walk thirty miles at a stretch, in case of need; quite a remarkable feat for a man of his age and training; and after fasting entirely for two days, he was able to baptise by immersion as many as fifty men at one time."

Hsi himself definitely realised that the strength he drew upon from day to day was supplied in answer to prayer. He had long since learned the secret of triumphing over weakness, weariness, and physical infirmities in the power of the Holy Spirit. He believed that Christ was *life*—daily, hourly, as need arose—life in abundance.[1] At the same time, he never would bind himself to any hard and fast system of divine healing. He recognised clearly the efficacy of "the prayer of faith"; and also just as clearly that the Lord was pleased, often, to use means. There was room in his mind, as in his experience, for both sides of truth to find a place.

This was partly due to a well-balanced temperament. For Hsi was an unusual combination of faith and practical wisdom; intense devotion and common sense. There was nothing of the ascetic about him, and yet he constantly resorted to fasting. This was not with any idea of mortifying the flesh, but simply with a view to the furtherance of the Gospel. He found that in times of difficulty, his prayers were more in the power of the Spirit, and more effectual, when he was fasting than otherwise. But under ordinary circumstances, he could enjoy a good dinner and would take it gladly. In the same way he appreciated nice clothing and

[1] John x. 10, R.V. margin; see also John i. 16, and Rom. v. 17.

comfortable surroundings. He recognised that God has given these and many other beautiful things, richly to be enjoyed, and that there is no virtue in going without them for its own sake. But with him the supreme question was: "How can I make the very most of myself, my time, my resources, for the extension of the Kingdom of God?" With unfaltering determination he subordinated everything to this end, and shaped his whole life in view of eternity—his own, and that of other souls.

The welfare of those for whom he was responsible, was truly more to him than his own; for he entered deeply into the Apostolic spirit: "All things are for your sake and the Gospel's." The following instance may serve to illustrate the principles that guided him in such matters.

It was during the trying time at Hochow. Difficulties were passing away, and the number of Christians gathering for worship on Sundays was increasingly large. Many came from a distance. The services were long, and they could not get back to their homes until evening. Seeing this, the ladies in the station had been in the habit of providing a simple mid-day meal. But though harmless in itself, this custom had given rise to a great deal of criticism. The Christians were spoken of as beggars and impostors.

"You only believe in Jesus for the food you get," became a common reproach.

Under these circumstances, Pastor Hsi and the ladies felt that they must make a change. The country Christians saw that this was right and necessary, though it came hard on many of them, who were so poor that the only food they had was of the coarsest description, and they preferred to go hungry all day rather than bring that with them and eat it among their friends in the city. Here then was a difficult position, and one that Hsi felt keenly.

Soon after the custom was given up, he decided to go over to Hochow for the sake of spending Sunday with the Christians. A long day's journey brought him to the city at nightfall. He had been fasting since the previous evening, that he might specially wait upon God for blessing. For the same reason he went without supper. And the next day he would touch nothing, on account of the Christians who were gathering for the services. He truly loved them, and wanted them to feel it. Morning, afternoon, and evening he preached with unusual power; and there were few dry eyes when he spoke of his joy that so many had come in from the country though it meant being hungry all day.

"As you have nothing," he said, "how could I eat? We must stop this evil-speaking, for the glory of God."

Was it any wonder the people loved him? He taught them by his life. He lived, indeed, for them. This was the spirit of all his self-denials: "I endure . . . that they may obtain."[1]

Some things in the experiences of Pastor Hsi that, looked at superficially, may seem extravagant, are simple and natural enough when one remembers how absolutely he lived his whole life with and for God. Mr. Hoste was interested to observe, for example, that he was not infrequently warned of danger by a curious, sudden failure of physical strength.

"I often know," Hsi would say, "when special trial or temptation is at hand. I become so weak in body, that it is necessary to stop whatever I am doing, and cry to the Lord."

This was no unusual experience. In the midst of the day's work, even when absorbingly engaged in business matters, his strength seemed unaccountably to ebb away. It was not faintness exactly; but overpowering weakness, with a sense of great apprehension. There was nothing to be done. Rest and food did not relieve it. But prayer always did. And usually it transpired that prayer had been specially needed just at that time, to prepare for some exigency in the work. So often was this the case that Hsi came to regard the experience as a call to prayer, and always gave himself to waiting upon God until it passed away. Sometimes no indication followed of what the danger had been; but more often it came to light, and he was able to praise God for deliverance.

It was wonderful how closely he was guided, and how in times of peril he was protected and spared for further service. One instance may stand for many.

In the province of Honan, across the Yellow River, lay the city of Yungning, in which Hsi had a Refuge. It was a long journey from his home, part of the way over lonely mountain roads on the border. One day while Hsi was praying for Yungning, he was impressed with the conviction that trouble threatened the Refuge, and there was urgent need for care. He could not go down himself, but sent a Christian man named Wang, without delay. Wang crossed the mountains and the mighty river, and after about a week's journey reached the Refuge. He found the

[1] 2 Tim. ii. 10.

men in charge, on the point of receiving a new patient, who seemed most anxious to break off his opium-habit. Wang carefully examined the man, who was weak and emaciated; and as he did so, he felt sure that he had found the danger of which Hsi had been forewarned. The man was already dying. But Chang, the Refuge-keeper, could not see it, and nobody else would allow that he was even seriously ill.

Wang, however, took the matter into his own hands. He had come from Pastor Hsi with full power to act as might seem necessary. He knew the peril involved, should the poor fellow die on the premises. Chang was bent upon admitting him, and it required no little firmness to withstand them all. But seeing that Wang was resolute, the patient and his friends retired. They managed to get him home, but that was all. For that very night he died. A profound impression was made in the city, where the matter became widely known. Had the man died in the Refuge, the work might have been hindered for years, for the people were turbulent and unfriendly. As it was, they were inspired with awe for the God of the Christians, and regarded the Refuge-keepers as men of supernatural wisdom.

A little later Hsi himself went down to Yungning. On the way he called in at Pingyang to see Mr. Hoste, who was visiting there, and shared his room in the mission-house. Far into the night they sat talking of many matters, and especially of Hsi's journey and the work he was leaving behind. At length, as they knelt in prayer, a strange and solemn sense came over Mr. Hoste that Hsi was going into unusual danger. He was praying for his friend at the time, and, so great was the burden, that he could not but speak of it to the Lord, and in a special way implore His protection and aid.

Next morning Hsi set out on foot for Yungning. He reached the city in safety, and found good opportunities for preaching the Gospel. In the home of one of the Christians, he met with an old man who had been suffering for eight years from what was believed to be demon-possession. His condition was very pitiful, and the moment Hsi saw him he felt conscious of the presence and power of the devil. The strange, wild look in his eyes, and his uneasiness and furtive movements, plainly told their own sad tale, though he was not then in one of his violent paroxysms. With such an object-lesson, Hsi preached Jesus, calling the people to witness whether the devil were a hard taskmaster or not, and telling of the power of Christ to save and deliver. Then, in the name of that wonderful Saviour, he called upon the evil one to depart, charging him to trouble the old man no more. The change was instant and complete, filling the Christians with joy and the heathen with wonder.

On his homeward journey Hsi was much in prayer for the people of Yungning. Here and there, in lonely hamlets, were a few scattered Christians to whom his passing brought welcome cheer. But for the most part it was a solitary road, and he was glad of the companionship of Wang, who was travelling with him.

A little north of the border, they were right in among the mountains, when he sighted four men of alarming appearance coming towards them rapidly. A second glance sufficed to show that they were robbers of the most dangerous type. Armed with foreign pistols, and with drawn swords in their hands, they had just accomplished some deed of violence, and were carrying off their booty.

Seeing that escape was impossible, Hsi dismounted from the hired animal he was riding, and quietly waited their approach. With savage cries the band fell upon their prey, seized the donkey, the cash-bags, and the little clothing the travellers had with them, and demanded silver. Hsi could do nothing but pray. The next thing he expected was that the men would search them, strip them of their clothing, and probably half kill them in fury at not finding enough silver to satisfy their greed. But, without offering any resistance, he and Wang stood quietly waiting, conscious of the nearness of God.

Suddenly the men stopped They seemed uneasy in some way. The one who had seized the cash-bag flung it across the donkey's back, and tossing the reins to Hsi, simply said: "*Tsiu-pa!*" (Be-gone). Then with one consent they dropped the things they had taken and went off hurriedly, soon disappearing among the mountains.

Hsi and Wang could not make out what had frightened them, and half thought they meant to return. As they went on their way, thanking God for deliverance, they soon came to the spot where the brigands had just been at work, and found two men robbed of everything and badly injured. But it was not until later they learned that the band was captured that very day, and two of them killed in the encounter.

But of all the trials incidental to his work there was none Hsi felt more keenly than constant absence from home and separation from Mrs. Hsi, who had come to be so dear a companion and friend. The tie between them was very close and helpful.

It had not always been so. In earlier years, when he was an opium-smoking Confucianist, the usual wrangling and bitterness prevailed. Mrs. Hsi, though bright and attractive, was narrowed down to the ordinary routine of a Chinese woman's life. She could not read, much less write, and was in no sense the equal of her lord and master. But when the great change came, the reality of his conversion was attested by earnest desire and effort for her enlightenment. And when she too was brought to Christ, a new home-life began. Eager to understand the Bible, she soon learned to read. Other books followed. Her mind matured rapidly, and before long she was her husband's efficient colleague behind the scenes.

It was a wonderful development: just one of the countless, priceless blessings enfolded in the Gospel. But even then, and for many years during which they were growing in grace, Hsi was tried and humiliated by a tendency to jarring that it seemed nothing could conquer. He could keep his temper and control his natural irritability with almost anybody else. But with her——! How was it? Why could he not overcome? It seemed all the more strange because he truly loved her, and she was devoted to him. Few things are more humbling to a Christian who really seeks to live near the Lord, than failure in this direction; and it certainly had one good effect, in keeping Hsi from pride of heart in a very practical way. He prayed about it constantly. Alone and together they cried to God for grace; and by degrees the difficulty was so completely conquered that their lives became a consistent testimony to the power of God in this respect.

As time went on Mrs. Hsi grew in faith and devotion, and came to take her place more and more independently in his work. From superintending domestic affairs, she rose to the full charge of everything, indoors and out, during her husband's absences from home. With a household of fifty or sixty people, patients to care for, medicines to compound, Sunday services to be kept up, as well as the daily instruction of workers in training for the Refuges, it was no small responsibility. But she was a calm, clear-headed little woman, with a quiet way of managing people and things that was effective. And she was a woman of prayer. While intensely loyal to her husband's wishes, she was by no means pliable in his hands. And he came increasingly to value her judgment in important matters. As they drew nearer to the Lord, they became more dear to one another; and, absorbed in living for His service, they lost sight of little things that had been trying between themselves.

At length the day came when Mrs. Hsi faced the great sacrifice of her life, and passed with him into blessing so full and deep, that the cost seemed small in comparison. For years it had been coming. They had laid much upon the altar. Time, strength, comfort, possessions, privacy, all had been given up, as need arose. But there was something more.

"In the work of curing opium-smokers," writes Hsi, "and leading them to trust in the Lord, we meet with great difficulties, and it often happens that men who have been delivered, and promise well, are ensnared again when they go home and find their wives still smoking, so that they have no escape from the seductive fumes even in their sleeping rooms at night.

"For long we desired to open Refuges for women, but had no one to undertake the work. Therefore I have consecrated my wife to the Lord for this service. She first opened a Women's Refuge at Hungtung, before any lady missionary came to live there. Concerning this matter both my wife and I have endured great suffering and temptation. Often it seems like a sword pressing against my heart, and I have found it almost unbearable. But praise the Lord, the devil has been defeated, and the work goes on."

Much lies behind these words. Only those familiar with the East can know what it would mean to a woman brought up in an Oriental home and surrounded by the facts of heathenism, to step out into such a ministry. No sacrifice of social standing or public opinion a woman could make for the sinful and outcast in Christian lands, could compare with what was involved for Mrs. Hsi when she left her home and husband to go to distant places, among unknown people, and devote her life to the rescue of opium-smoking women. But she did it, and he encouraged her. And as they trod this pathway, they found their immediate reward in a love so deep and tender that all that had ever come between them was forgotten.

Throughout the last five years of her husband's life, Mrs. Hsi was almost constantly engaged in this difficult work. Her sister, the wife of Elder Si, was able to fill her place at the Western Chang village, so that she was practically free from home ties. Hsi himself, of course, looked after her and travelled with her whenever it was possible; but often he was called in one direction while she was needed in another, so that for months they hardly met. But the brave little woman kept on. Loneliness, hardship, misapprehension surrounded her. She put up with discomfort, poor fare, trying and anxious duties, and the companionship of heathen women degraded by opium. She toiled for them night and day, lovingly and patiently winning them to better things. She conducted Sunday services, taught the children, gathered the converts round her, helping them to read and pray, and was always and everywhere ready to lead a soul to Jesus and tell of His mighty power to save.

The Lord greatly blessed her efforts. City after city was reached. Quite a chain of Women's Refuges resulted, from Ki Hsien on the Pingyao plain almost down to the Yellow River. Over this wide district Mrs. Hsi travelled, superintending the Refuges and encouraging the women she had trained to carry on the work. Sometimes on the main road through the province she would meet her husband's cart, or at one of the larger Refuges she would find him announced to lead the Sunday services. Those were little foretastes of heaven. Sometimes they would spend a week or two together at home, and almost forget, in the joy of such reunion, that they were pilgrims and strangers. But that would not be for long.

"Do I not love my wife?" wrote dear Pastor Hsi. "Often she is in the north, and I am in the south; and for several months at a time we are unable to see each other's faces; and can only mutually weep and pray, seeking those things which are above and the reward promised to every man according as his work shall be. The Bible says: 'The time is short; and it remaineth that both they that have wives be as though they had none.' My wife and I, remembering these words of Scripture, are comforted, and our hearts are kept in peace."

# 32

# The Refuges as Mission Stations

IT was the summer of 1893. Hsi was on his way to Hochow to conduct a conference among the Christians of that district, where the work was going forward with much blessing. As he travelled, many thoughts were in his mind, with regard especially to a new departure that for some time had been under consideration.

Years before, in the early beginning of the Refuge work, how little could he have anticipated all that God had brought to pass. Then it had been a question of saving a few opium-smokers in one country district, without any thought of the development of an organised church or a mission station, much less several. But as the movement spread and the blessing of God rested upon it, souls were saved and whole communities interested in the Gospel, until a wide field seemed open before the Refuge-workers, wherever their patients were scattered.

At that time the question had arisen as to whether these opportunities should be embraced, and the Refuge-keepers permitted to enter upon general evangelistic work. And just there Hsi's wise judgment, under the guidance of God, came in to prevent what might have been a serious mistake. It is no use pushing people beyond their capacity, or hurrying them into responsibilities for which they are not prepared. These men were themselves, in most cases, only young converts, saved from lives of open sin. They had all they could do, in their busy days, to find time for prayer and Bible study, without which their own spiritual life could not develop; and among the patients under their care and the people who thronged about them, they had all the opportunity they could improve for living and preaching Christ. Hsi was practical and thorough, and was concerned about doing well, as well as doing much.

"After prayer and fasting," he writes, "I drew up rules for the Refuges, including the regulation that those in charge should preach only on the premises, and not attempt to evangelise in the surrounding country. This seemed to me necessary because the workers were, for the most part, inexperienced and weak in the faith; and because they were not as yet familiar with the dialect and customs of the new localities in which they found themselves. But in travelling myself from place to place, visiting the Refuges, I have embraced every opportunity of preaching the Gospel, both in cities and villages, frequently healing the sick and casting out demons. So that in this and other ways many believers have become connected with various Refuges, and attend the services on Sundays, though they have never been smokers of opium."

But as time went on conditions began to change. The Refuge-workers grew in grace and in experience. Their labours were made a blessing, and established them in the regard of even un-friendly communities. Every one could see the good they were doing, and feel the sincerity of their motives and the devotion of the lives they led. In all directions they had friends; and many were the grateful patients who would willingly open their houses for meetings. If only the staff in each Refuge could be increased, so that the more experienced workers might be free to go out for days or weeks at a time, preaching and teaching the Gospel, much good might be accomplished in districts where there were no other missionaries.

This was a different proposal; and coming as it did from friends whose judgment he valued, could not but have weight with Pastor Hsi. He saw the need and the advantages; and felt the force of the argument that no preachers could be more welcome or have more influence than the men who were known to be giving their lives to a difficult and trying task, in such a way as to win the gratitude of all classes. But there were serious questions in-volved, and Hsi was cautious, and had to be very sure a thing was of God before he went into it. Sad experience in the Hung-tung district had convinced him that people may be thrust out too quickly into public work. Many a promising young convert had been encouraged and even urged to preach the Gospel, whose life was not sufficiently under the influence of the truth to make his testimony effective. The result was failure in case after case. Exposed to the temptations of a position for which they were unfitted, they were carried away by pride or self-seeking, the occasion for which need never have arisen.

But quieter years followed; and undoubtedly, now, many among the Hungtung Christians were ready for such work. They were not only preaching the Gospel naturally, of their own accord, but were living consistent lives, full of helpfulness for

others. Some had acquired a fair knowledge of Scripture, and
showed ability as preachers that made them welcome among their
brethren. These men, added to the staff of the Refuges, would
both increase the value of existing work, and make possible an
aggressive movement that might lead to widespread blessing.

It was characteristic of Hsi that he generally knew when the
right time had come for doing a thing, as well as the right thing
to do; and also that, when he knew, he stopped at nothing. Early
in the year he had come to feel clearly that the plan was of God:
and now, as he travelled to Hochow, he was thinking out the
necessary steps for carrying it into effect. It was practically,
though he little realised it, putting a finishing touch to his life-
work.

"At Hochow," he writes, "during the conference, I was led to
draw up new regulations for the Refuges; in the faith that the
Lord would send forth additional workers, that henceforth there
might be two responsible men in each place—one to care for
internal arrangements, and the other to preach the Gospel in all
the regions round about. It seemed right, and was decided, that
these evangelists should take no provision for their journeys;
because, seeing the Refuges distributed medicine freely for the
cure of various diseases, not only would patients who had been
delivered from opium-smoking willingly receive them, but many
others also would gladly offer entertainment free of charge.

"Some of the brethren were afraid that, with such an increase
of workers, there would be an insufficiency of means. But I took
the words of Scripture, and exhorted them, saying: ' "Seek first
the kingdom of God and his righteousness," and your Heavenly
Father will certainly supply all your need.' I also will constantly
trust the holy words of Jesus, and press onward without fear."

Thus it was that the Refuges grew into regular mission stations.
For the plan worked well by the blessing of God. Not a few of
the men in charge developed considerable preaching and pastoral
gifts. And the last years of Hsi's life, that were slipping away so
fast, were gladdened by seeing little churches spring up and
become a blessing, where otherwise there would have been none.

.        .        .        .        .

And now come, let us visit in thought at any rate, one of these
Refuge centres to gain some idea of what is going on. Let us
choose Chaocheng city, an excellent example, as we have

already watched the progress of things there more or less from the beginning. It is a long journey from your distant home: a month or more by steamer to Shanghai, and then some six weeks inland. But one of us has travelled the road before, and knows pretty well how to manage in native inns at night, in boats, and carts, and even mule-litters over the mountains. It is a beautiful journey too, in some places, and full of interest everywhere. And as of course we are wearing native dress, we shall not attract too much attention.

Weeks have passed, and now we are in Shansi. The capital is lying far behind us. We have crossed the Pingyao plain green with summer crops; followed the Fen River into its beautiful valley; climbed the Lingshih Pass; spent a Sunday at Hochow; and after a long morning's journey—yonder, shimmering in the heat of noon, stretch the north wall and massive gate of Chaocheng.

Now we have entered the city. Crowded and busy are the streets through which our cart jolts slowly. There is no difficulty in finding the Refuge; every Chaocheng man knows it. There it is: that wide doorway round which the people are standing. You must expect a throng, for a "great gathering" is being held to-day, in honour of missionary travellers passing through the province.[1] Here we descend from our clumsy vehicle with what grace we may, and pass into a large square courtyard round which the rooms open.

What a company of men. Every corner is packed and crowded. And the guest-hall seems overflowing with women and children. No room for us there, evidently; nor under the blue awning that covers the centre of the court. Every seat is filled already, and the meeting is about to begin. What delightfully hearty singing. But the sunshine is intensely hot. Let us take shelter here in this dark kitchen, it seems comparatively empty.

Alas the reason is not far to seek. Dinner is preparing for a hundred guests, and the place is a perfect oven. Still, from the brick bed we can see through this little window all that is going on, and it will be a new experience, for you at any rate, to sit cross-legged on a Chinese *k'ang*. It is certainly a drawback that this particular *k'ang* should be heated from the cooking range,

[1] What follows is a description, written on the spot, of a visit to this Refuge in the summer of 1894, when Mr. and Mrs. Hudson Taylor were travelling through Shansi, and Dr. and Mrs. Howard Taylor were among those that accompanied them.

instead of separately in the ordinary way. It must be comfortable in winter; but to-day, with the temperature well over 100° in the shade, and a huge fire to heat the flues, it is distressing. However, there is nowhere else to go; and the bricks are not unbearable through this thick matting.

How pleasant it looks out there in the courtyard, where the trellised vine casts a green shade, and ripe grapes hang just out of reach. Flowers in abundance lend colour to the scene; and the white garments, shaven heads, and long black queues of the men —rows and rows of them under the awning—make a picture not easily forgotten. Faces young and faces old are there; some fresh and full of promise; some wrinkled and seamed with care; a few bearing sad traces of the havoc wrought by opium; others showing marked signs of the transformation made by grace.

Pastor Hsi is speaking. No wonder these people leave their farms and workshops, and come through the heat of a mid-summer day to hear preaching like this. He is giving a heart-stirring address on The True Vine, showing the secret of a life always fresh and full of power, because hidden with Christ in God. Tears in many eyes, and the look on these eager faces, tell of a fresh vision of things unseen.

Now comes our opportunity. The meeting is over. Half the people, living in or near the city, are going home to dinner; only a hundred or so remain. We shall be able to move about a little, and ask questions to our heart's content. But first will you not take a basin and chopsticks, and try some of this Chinese macaroni stewed in gravy? Quite appetising, I assure you.

Here from the doorway of the women's room we can see to better advantage, and it is not quite so hot as in the kitchen. What a bright, interesting scene it is. Such greetings, laughter, friendly conversation; such busy preparations for the meal! Mats are spread under the awning, upon which, grouped around little tables, the older men are seated; and the rest, supplied with basins and chopsticks like ourselves, sit comfortably on the ground, or perch on the steps of the side houses. And there, in the midst of them all, under the spreading vine, is dear old Pastor Sung, manager of the Refuge, and spiritual father of almost everyone in this large company.

What a picture he makes, surrounded as with a halo by their loving reverence, seated on that low wooden bench, with the flowers behind him and the cool green leaves overhead, his face all aglow as he looks from one to another of his large, happy family. Dear old man; small, spare, and stooping, with a little whitey-brown queue, and a strongly marked, benevolent face: dear old wonderful man, who, without learning or special gifts, simply by the power of the Holy Spirit in his loving heart, has drawn all these to Jesus—he is worth coming to China to see.

But let us ask whether all these men are Christians; there may be a good many outsiders here to-day. Elder Liu is coming. He can tell us.

"Christians?" he responds with surprise. "Why, certainly; without exception. And all brought to the Lord here in this Refuge."

"But surely these men cannot have been opium smokers? Some here and there show signs of it; but the majority——"

"Do you not understand?" he interposes eagerly. "*All these men have been opium-smokers, every one.* They have all been delivered and brought to Jesus, here in this Refuge; and twice as many more, who are not with us here to-day."

The busy hours slip by; most of the guests depart; the missionary travellers set out again upon their journey; but we linger to spend a quiet evening with Sung and his helpers, and learn more of this story. At last the duties of the day are done. In the guest-hall Sung has gathered round us all the comforts his simple *ménage* affords. Supper over, he lights the fragrant incense to keep tormenting flies away, draws up the best chairs to the open doorway, pours boiling tea into his china cups with bright brass saucers, and forgetting his usual shyness sits down to answer our questions as if we were old friends.

Silently the shades of evening draw around us and a cool breeze replaces the burning heat of day. The low hum of countless mosquitoes sounds through the open doorway, and one and another of the household gather to hear what is being said. But the dear Pastor's shining face is the thing to see, as he tells us his story.

Long years ago he was himself a confirmed opium-smoker, hopeless of deliverance. Trouble had brought him to it. In the terrible famine-time, he lost all his relatives; wife and children starving to death before his eyes. Lonely and suffering, opium was his only comfort; and as the famine passed away and he was able to earn a little money again, it all went to keep the pipe burning.

There were plenty of other opium-smokers like himself in the village. Their condition was truly pitiable. The longer they smoked the worse they became. But not one of them could give it up. The daily misery of living under the tyranny of the habit was one degree better than the agony of trying to get free.

But a strange thing happened in their village. A man named Fan brought back from the city tidings of a new and wonderful doctrine; something about Someone named Jesus, who could deliver people from their sins. This man was full of it. He could talk of nothing else. He even went so far as to say that Jesus could save an opium-smoker, and take away all craving for the drug.

Certainly Fan's own life was different since he believed in Jesus. He was a new man. Everybody could see it. And when at last he gave out that the Missionary was coming to stay in his house, and was bringing medicines with him, to help any man who wished it to break off opium, Sung was the first to decide that he would make the attempt. Tremblingly, he came and put himself under treatment; not at all reassured by the fact that he was the only one to venture, and that he had never seen a foreigner before.

He suffered terribly; for his craving was great, and but little medicine was given. But he kept on; cheered by the things the Christians had to tell, and by the hymns they were always singing. Day by day more men came to the Refuge; and as Sung began to get over his worst experiences, he found many little things he could do to help newer patients. His craving cured, he could not bear to think of leaving. He had no home, no friends. Nobody cared what became of him. There in the Refuge he had found love and sympathy, and heard of things that brought new life and hope. Would they not let him stay and work for his living? He would cook, carry water, attend to the patients, do anything.

So it was arranged. And Sung became the first helper in the Opium Refuge work.

Still he was scarcely to be called a Christian. Hard at work from early childhood, he had never been to school or learned to read. He was slow and dull and sad; bad-tempered too; and in fits of passion would use terrible language. But he was feeling after better things: longing to find what the Christians had, that made them seem so happy.

One day alone in the East Room, he saw the Missionary's New Testament lying on the window-sill. It was a large book, attractively bound, and Sung went over to look at it. Reverently he took it in his hands. The characters were clear and beautiful. Even his dim eyes, half-blind with weeping, could make out many of the easy words. Long he stood pondering, and turning the pages. That wonderful Name came so often. He could find the characters on almost every leaf—*Je-su*, Jesus. It was his first Bible study.

Very gradually the change came; but it was complete. From the Refuge he was promoted to help in Hsi's medicine shop, and then to a position in his home in the Western Chang village. There, as a member of Hsi's household, he came out brightly as a Christian; and his growth in spiritual things was so marked, that when a helper was needed for the ladies at Hochow, Sung was chosen. Eight months in the hallowed atmosphere of that home, left him for all life a better man.

Finally, through many vicissitudes, Sung was led "by the grace of God," as he loves to put it, to the Refuge in this city of Chaocheng. After helping for some time in a subordinate position, he was put in charge of the whole concern. Six hundred patients passed through his hands in six years. Many of these, not becoming Christians, relapsed into opium smoking, but fully two hundred were saved men who became members of the church.

"It is almost always the case," explains Sung, "that unless a man truly believes in Jesus, he will sooner or later go back to his opium. Illness or trouble comes, and at once he turns to the enticing fumes to drown his misery. Then truly his last estate is worse than the first."

"But it is not hopeless," adds the old man, with a smile. "Then is our opportunity. 'Alas', exclaims the poor victim, 'this surely has come upon me because I did not believe in Jesus when He was so near.' This will draw him back again to the Refuge. And he comes in a different spirit; his heart is ready to receive the Lord. Many believe at the second time."

"But do you take them in again, if they have once gone back?"

"Take them in? Why, of course we do! And we love them, and deal with them more tenderly and prayerfully than ever, for perhaps the fault was partly ours. Oh, we are glad to welcome them back the second time. So many will then give their hearts to the Saviour, without whom they cannot stand."

"Yes, I know all that is true," puts in a deep, manly voice at our side.

"How do you know?" we ask, turning to the speaker; a fine young fellow, and, as we have been told, a gifted preacher.

"I have good cause to know," Hsü answers gravely; "for I was one of those saved the second time."

"Hsü, is it possible? Were _you_ ever an opium-smoker?"

The strong, handsome face is shadowed with deep feeling; and we think with wonder of the work God has done through this man, and the many souls saved in his Refuge on the Pingyao plain. Oh, what a story is in dear old Sung's face, as we look from one to the other, and Hsü replies:

"Yes, I too was saved from the depths. It was all through the loving tenderness of my father here."

Silence falls in the twilight. A number of the Christians have gathered. All hearts are one in love and sympathy too deep for words. A flickering candle lights the finely contrasted faces of the old Pastor and young Hsü, close beside us, and behind them the listening group.

"You have told us the story. Tell us now the secret. How is it that here you have such fruit for your labours? It is not always so."

The old Pastor pauses a moment; but the young man begins eagerly to speak.

"No, no! wait, brother. Let us hear the Pastor first."

But the old man has not much to say by way of explanation. He himself is the answer. And this he does not perceive.

"Let me tell you," Hsü continues. "For I was saved here and I know. It is all his love that does it, by the grace of God"; and the young man puts his arm around the old Pastor, to whose eyes the tears have come. "He not only preaches for us. He lives it. He cares for his patients with a mother's tenderness, night and day. He cheers them when they are sick and troubled; reading, talking, singing to them; never leaving them till they are better. And best of all he prays for them, often with long fasting: and his prayers have the real power. The more miserable and degraded the sufferer, the more his heart goes out to him with the very love of God. Do you wonder we poor hopeless, helpless opium-smokers respond with all our hearts—'this Gospel truly is good: we too would believe.' "

"And do the patients suffer much at times?" we query, anxious to hear more.

"Oh yes," exclaim many voices. "Often the Pastor is up six or eight times in the night. Some of the men, in their anguish, almost give way; others become so exhausted that it seems as if they must die. At times we have even thought that they were dead. And in their extremity he never leaves them. He thinks nothing of being up all night if necessary, praying for them, preparing food and medicine, and as they get better, singing and comforting their hearts."

"Oh, that singing," puts in old Li, a deacon of the church, "how well I remember it. The only hymn that used to comfort me was 'Je-su ai O.' He must have sung it for me a hundred times 'Jesus loves me, this I know.' "

Just a rough, weather-beaten old Chinese, his neck and face one unbroken succession of wrinkles, his back bent, his queue reduced to a few grey hairs. But such a spirit in him; such glowing love for Jesus. He had been a desperate character before Sung found him and led him to the Saviour.

"It was the singing that did it."

And even as he spoke, Sung softly started the dear old hymn, soon joined by all the rest. It seems to be the old man's habit to fill up all the intervals of life with singing, which no doubt partly explains his cheery brightness and power to help.

"And do you never weary in the work, dear Pastor?"

"Yes, sometimes," is his quiet answer. "And then I pray; asking the Lord to forgive my cold and sinful heart; and I have peace again."

The moon is setting now, and it is late. As we retire for the night they are singing still, having an extra meeting out in the cool courtyard.

Dear Sung. Did you hear his last request? He declined all compensation for our entertainment to-day, or that of the missionary party.

"Oh no," he said, "I cannot take it. It has been the Lord's goodness to send you here. All we ask is that you will pray for us, that we may be truly filled with the Holy Spirit."

# 33

# The Middle Eden

THEY called it simply "Eden" at first; that dear old home in the Western Chang village. And for years it was known by no other name. But when the troubles broke out in 1887, some of Fan's people appropriated the title for a Refuge of their own in the neighbourhood, and it became necessary to make a distinction. So Hsi added the one word *Chung*, so full of meaning to every Chinese, and after that it was always known as "The Middle Eden."

It was there one had to see him, really to know him best. Some people do not shine at home. But Hsi did. And even a brief sojourn beneath his roof was never to be forgotten. It enabled one to understand the devotion he inspired, and the power of his life in its wider activities.

At The Middle Eden, affairs moved with great regularity. Everything was planned with system; well thought out, and diligently put into practice. Hsi's loving, vigilant attention to the best interests of all entrusted to his care, recalled the divine commendation of Abraham, "the friend of God":

"I know him, that he will command his children and his household after him, and they shall keep the way of the Lord."

As the work grew, and he was more frequently away from home, he drew up a set of Rules for the guidance of his helpers, that occupied a prominent position in the guest-hall. Beautifully written, in fine "grass characters" or running hand, and mounted on a board, this document looked like an official proclamation. But it differed materially from most proclamations, in that it was carried into effect.

"By the grace of God," it began, "these Regulations are appointed for learning the Heavenly Doctrine; for conducting business affairs; and for the proper entertainment of guests. They must be faithfully obeyed."

## RULES FOR THE MIDDLE EDEN

I. On the Lord's Day all must attend public worship three times. The Communion Service shall be celebrated once a month. Some Pastor or Elder shall arrange for this, and entertain Members from the surrounding country. Any who have fallen into sin and not repented, may not be entertained.

II. No work may be done on Sunday. In the families of the worshippers, all indoor and outdoor work must be completed in six days. Only the labour of serving-men for God is not forbidden; feeding and watering the cattle, and tending the sheep.

III. During the week, each one shall rise at daybreak. All are to watch and pray; and having combed hair and washed faces, must diligently sweep out the rooms and courtyards, set the children to work, and go to their own occupation, not daring to be lazy.

IV. Every week-day evening, a service will be held. In summer the hour is changed to noon. In the hottest weather the meeting may be conducted out of doors, until autumn, when again it will be held in the chapel at night. For if arrangements are convenient, it is helpful to the worshippers.

The Order of the Services shall be as follows:—

On Monday, Exposition of the Scriptures: each one reading a verse in turn.

On Tuesday, Prayer Meeting: first reading a few verses about the Gospel or on prayer. A Member may be invited to conduct the service, or several may be asked to lead in prayer. Pray that labourers may be multiplied in China and abroad; that blessing may be given in our Church and Refuges in all the provinces; and also for our Middle Eden.

On Wednesday, Singing of Hymns: ten hymns shall be practised, new and old.

On Thursday, Gospel preaching: the speaker shall catechise men, women, and children alike; that they may more easily understand and remember: from shallow going on to deep, from less to greater, making daily progress.

On Friday, Prayer for All Men; asking a gracious outpouring of the Holy Spirit, to lead men everywhere to believe and obtain salvation.

On Saturday, again practise ten hymns: and unitedly pray the Lord to grant blessing on His own day, and to preserve the Refuges from calamity.

Then follow detailed regulations for the conduct of domestic affairs; affording a glimpse into what went on daily at The Middle Eden. For example:

Brother Yü is to look after matters of husbandry, feeding the animals, the use of mules and carts, drawing water, collecting manure, grass-cutting, etc.; seeking in all, God's protecting care.

He will employ some of the children to help him in odd jobs. He may not allow the children to fight and quarrel. If they are disobedient, upon returning from the fields Elder Sï is to see that those under ten years of age receive twenty blows on the hand, those over ten, thirty. If any boy will not submit to this castigation, two able-bodied Members are to hold him, and administer a bare-backed flogging; twenty blows for those under ten, thirty for those over.

This regulation is necessary on account of the universal Chinese weakness of discipline. But the exhortation is added:

You must love the children for the Lord's sake, and it is certainly your duty thus to correct them.

When the sheep come home from grazing, brother Ti-teh will look after their welfare. He will carefully supply water and salt, praying God to keep the beasts in health. Two other Members are deputed to attend to the stables, the cow-byre, and the farm gate; also to sweep the road; and in their leisure to study the Scriptures.

Elder Sĭ, trusting in God's great power, will see that these regulations are carried out during the Pastor's absence from home. With Cheo and Yüen, he will also make up the various pills, not omitting united prayer that by the help of the Holy Spirit the medicine may be properly prepared, may be able to rescue people from opium-smoking, and lead them to believe in the Gospel; also that the pills may be well-made, smooth, and attractive-looking.

The children's time is so regulated that half of them study while half are at work.

If they disobey the heavenly laws of God, they are to be beaten with sticks according to the above regulations.

Gentle Princess [the Pastor's little niece] in the morning is to sweep out the three rooms on the south of the courtyard; after breakfast she will spin thread; after dinner study, and feed the chickens; waiting until the hen has left the nest to pick up the eggs. If she does not do all this properly, her old Aunt with a small stick is to beat her five strokes on the hand.

Little Silver Bells is to take care of her small sister. She is not to let the baby rest on other people's beds, nor to give it into other people's care. If she does not properly look after it, she is to have three stripes from the old Aunt.

The old Aunt is to be responsible for rice, flour, salt, vinegar, and other pro-visions, and to keep the keys. She is constantly to pay attention to household affairs; also to beat the gong, look after the women, and make up the medicine into packets, ready to be sent out. In managing these affairs of the Lord she is to be thoroughly trustworthy.

The Elder's wife, in Mrs. Hsi's absence, is to care for indoor matters; keeping all the house nice and tidy. She is also to consult her old Aunt in controlling the women. They are to pray together and be at peace, and in all things to work harmoniously.

Wang and Yüen are to be responsible in this household of God for preparing the food. They must be diligent, and have their dishes well cooked and fragrant. God's things cannot be thrown away or wasted; and dirty water must not be cast out into the road, to the inconvenience of passers-by.

Another Member is to prepare coal and water sufficient for use on Sunday.

Mr. Ch'i [a good and gifted brother] is to be free to follow the Spirit's guidance; sometimes working in his own home, and sometimes helping at The Middle Eden.

Mr. Cheo is responsible for all the farming implements, oiled baskets, sieves, etc., when he is not making medicine.

Then follow special injunctions respecting an adopted son of Pastor Hsi, who turned out a prodigal, and almost broke his heart.

If my nephew Kuen-hu comes home, he is to be treated kindly. Give him medicine if he is ill. Send to the town and buy fine flour and bread. I cannot but love him, although he gives me sorrow.

Finally, no one is permitted to attend fairs, or theatricals; no one may smoke either the dry pipe or the water pipe; and on no account is wine to be used. Members of the household may not sleep in the daytime, save in harvest (the 4th moon), when days are long and work heavy; then a little rest may be taken at noon. Gossiping is not allowed from door to door.

Any unwilling to follow these regulations will be earnestly exhorted to repent. If they choose rather to leave The Middle Eden, they are at liberty to do so.

Regulations in force A.D. 1894.

Trusting the Lord, Hsi, Overcomer of Demons.

All this reads quaintly to our Western ears, but it illustrates the way in which Hsi carried his Christianity into daily life. There were no unimportant matters with him. "Everything has a great truth underlying it," was one of his characteristic sayings. He believed that the highest principles should be applied to the smallest details of everyday affairs, and that the true state of the heart shows itself in just these little things. It is a deeply earnest view of life, and means, "whether ye eat or drink, or whatsoever ye do, do all to the glory of God."[1] Thus it is possible to be *filled* with the Spirit; because nothing is kept back from His control. Hsi was remarkable for discernment in the matter of character, that amounted almost to intuition; and his judgment of those with whom he had to deal was largely based upon such indications.

It was this genuine consistency in little things that gave his own life its practical power. For he was more strict with himself than with anyone else; and strove, unremittingly, to attain the ideals he set before others. At the same time there was nothing forbidding about his presence. Children loved him. He had a genuine sense of humour, and a pleasant laugh. Genial and bright at all times, he was specially so at home; and to none did he give himself more freely than to the members of his own large household. In later years he adopted the precaution of receiving those who wished to come to him, for a probationary three months to begin with. This conquered many difficulties, and made matters work more smoothly all round. But though his requirements were rigorous—no fairs, theatricals, wine, smoking, gossip, or resting in the daytime—few, if any, desired to leave The Middle

[1] I Cor. x. 31; and Col. iii. 17.

Eden at the close of that period. They had found practical Christianity at work in a Chinese home, and were glad to be under its loving, wholesome influence.

Even the heathen who looked on as outsiders merely, could appreciate much that took place at the Western Chang village. Years had passed since his own neighbours had insisted upon making Hsi headman of the community, in spite of his change of faith. They were willing even to let the idols starve, if only they could secure his prayerful management of their affairs. And subsequent developments had not shaken that early confidence. Of course those who did not become Christians were often bitter in their opposition. But on the whole Hsi's character was regarded with respect, even by those of "his own country." And far beyond the village, the power of his prayer-hearing God was widely known, so that from distant places sufferers were brought to be prayed for.

"For many years past," he writes in his own brief sketch of things, "there have been both a Refuge and a Gospel Hall in my own house, where through the power of God I have healed diseases, cured opium-smokers, and preached the Gospel. Also in my absences from home this work has continued.

"There was a man named Liang, who for a long time was violently possessed of the devil, and could not be restrained. His mother prevailed upon certain of their relatives to come to our Middle Eden and beseech me to go and heal him. Some members of the household declined, saying: 'The Pastor is not at home. But Mrs. Hsi exclaimed:

" 'We save men through faith in God! Are we dependent on the Pastor? If his mother is willing to believe in the Lord Jesus and put away her idols, she may bring her son here at once. We will pray with them; and the Lord will certainly restore him.'

"The mother, upon receiving this message, did put away her idols, and expressed a desire to believe. Her son forthwith became a little better, and they were able to bring him to my house. Mrs. Hsi and the other Christians prayed much for him. And in about a month, his opium craving was cured; the devil was cast out; and he was entirely healed.

"There were also several others, both men and women, who had diseases that no man could cure; but by regularly attending the services in our home, they gradually recovered, and were led to trust in the Lord."

Here is another quotation: the last paragraph of his too brief manuscript.

"Whenever there is a season of drought, neighbouring villages worship the Dragon King (Satan) in order to obtain rain. Our village never joins with them. But our Heavenly Father in His grace hears and answers prayer, and for several years has given us more rain than has fallen in other villages of the neighbourhood. So that even the heathen are beginning to say:

" 'The people of the Western Chang village certainly reap great benefit from the Jesus Religion.'

"This is because in our village we do not reject the Lord. Therefore we obtain blessing. Does not this prove the truth of God's Holy Word?"

Such testimony is needed among the heathen. And which of us does not feel the power of a life of prayer? Hsi prayed about everything; seeking the help of God in business matters and family life just as simply and confidently as in spiritual things. He believed, for example, that the Lord understood farming much better than he did, and was as truly interested in the care of his land and crops as in the ordering of the spheres. Just as the greatest ruler on earth, if he were a father, would be sure to care for the needs of his little one no less than for affairs of state. And our Father is infinite: that is, without any limitations. So Hsi prayed "without ceasing," because he prayed about all things, from moment to moment, day by day. As an instance of the way he was guided, the following facts speak for themselves.

It was the summer of 1894, and Hsi had just got in his early autumn crops from land that in a few weeks' time was to be sown with wheat for the spring harvest. The Chinese farmer follows well-nigh unalterable usages in all matters pertaining to agriculture. It would never occur to him to change them; for how could he be supposed capable of improving on the wisdom of the ancients? When, therefore, the early autumn crops are gathered in, the ground is roughly ploughed, and left to bake in the sun until the latter half of September. Then the autumn rains fall; and it is an easy matter to harrow the soil and sow the seed in time for it to strike root strongly before the frosts commence. That is how it always has been done, and no one would attempt the slightest change. And yet there often comes a difficult moment; especially on a farm like Hsi's, where irrigation is impracticable and the land is entirely dependent upon rainfall for its fertility. For the wheat cannot be sown until the rain has softened the ground; and yet, if it is not sown before the end of September, there is very little prospect of a harvest in the spring.

On this occasion, Hsi was praying as usual for guidance, and a question seemed to be raised in his mind as to whether that land should be left to wait as usual. For several days he prayed earnestly about it. Would the rainfall be late? Should he make any change, to secure a better harvest? At length the answer seemed to come very definitely:

"Harrow the land at once, but sow late."

He told his men forthwith; and in spite of the ridicule involved, they set to work while the land was yet moist from summer rains, and harrowed it thoroughly, until all was soft and ready for sowing. Of course this meant putting on one side pressing work that other farmers were doing, and seemed to onlookers a preposterous vagary—just like those unaccountable Christians. But Hsi and his helpers took it pleasantly; and by working a little harder in other ways, they soon caught up with their neighbours.

Then came the critical season. Day after day went by, and no rain fell. The third week in September passed; the fourth drew to a close; and farmers everywhere were almost in despair. Just at the last moment, however, the showers came. Hsi's land quickly absorbed the grateful moisture, and all that was necessary was to put in the seed. Full of thankfulness, he quickly accomplished this task, while his unhappy neighbours were trying in vain to break up their hardened soil, and one by one abandoning the attempt as hopeless for that season. When asked, almost indignantly, how he could have known, Hsi readily explained that it was in answer to prayer. The moral needed no pointing.

One outcome of this habitual prayerfulness, was the attitude so natural to him of seeing God's hand in everything. Just as in earlier years, so still the Lord spoke to his heart through all circumstances; and he learned many a lesson where others might have been wholly occupied with second causes.

> Earth's crammed with Heaven
> And every common bush afire with God;
> But only he who sees, takes off his shoes;
> The rest sit round it and pluck blackberries.

Not only in the constant miracle of nature, above and around him, was Hsi aware of God. When was he not aware of Him? It almost seemed as though nothing were too commonplace, too trivial to have some message from the Father in Heaven who undertakes to make *all things* work together for good to His children. Take quite a homely illustration.

In that same winter of 1894, which was unusually severe, a number of his sheep died, apparently of cold. Of course his neighbours were quick to say:

"Oh, why didn't your God protect you? You say the idols are no good. Now it is our turn——" and so on.

It was trying, and the loss was serious. But more than this, Hsi felt it was not for the glory of God. So he gave himself to prayer and fasting about this ordinary matter. Can anything be unworthy of our earnest attention that affects, however remotely, His honour? Perhaps, he felt, the Lord had a purpose in it. Was there something in himself, or any member of the household, displeasing to God? Was it a rebuke; a warning?

After a time, as he prayed, he began to see lessons that might not occur to us, but that proved to be most timely for himself and those about him. It undoubtedly was the thin sheep that had died. In summer time, when there was abundance of pasture, they had neglected to feed properly, and now had succumbed to the rigour of the season.

That was enough. Calling the household together, he put the circumstances before them; specially emphasising those two points. He then explained the internal mechanism of the sheep; and how by feeding when there is abundance, it can lay up stores of fat that act as a reserve supply when less nutriment is obtainable. Finally he applied the whole matter in an earnest exhortation to himself and others, not to do as they had done.

"Here we are in the green pastures of our Middle Eden," he said, with truth. "Every opportunity is given us for feeding on the Word of God and for growing strong in spiritual things. It will not always be so. This is our year of grace. The time will come when we shall be scattered, and exposed to persecution and trial in the cold world without. Those who are careless now, and slothful, will then inevitably fail. How are we using our opportunities? You who neglect private prayer, and are inattentive at worship, what will happen to you later, when trouble comes? Your souls, half-starved, will be unable to sustain the cruel frosts the devil is sure to send."

It was a solemn warning. But it was the way in which he brought it home to himself at the close that melted all hearts.

"Brethren," he said, "the Lord has spoken to my soul also. I have been most to blame. Why did those sheep die? It was the cold. Perhaps we might have taken better care of them. They were weak, even if it was their own fault. And brethren, I have been too severe with you. I have not loved you and watched over you all tenderly enough. The Lord is reproving me for my cold heart and want of gentleness in dealing with the erring. The Chief Shepherd is not like that. I too repent; and with you will seek to live nearer to His heart."

How ready he was, in those later years, to see his own mistakes and learn to do better. Even before the heathen he was willing to make open confession of failure or wrong: the last thing a man would do in China, apart from the grace of God.

On one occasion he was asked by a heathen relative for help in reaping his harvest. Hsi had plenty of men to draw upon at the time, and thinking only of the claims of kinship, he at once offered to send over eight or ten. This was probably more than the man had expected, and well satisfied, he went his way. But Hsi had not prayed about it. And he was painfully reminded of the omission when, that very day, three of his men fell ill. He at once sought the Lord about the indisposition of these helpers, and then it was the conviction came that the matter was displeasing to Him.

"The man is a heathen. You are lending them solely because he is your relative. And these are Christian men: My servants."

Immediately he confessed his mistake; telling the Lord he would not send the men.

"But you have promised," came the answer.

Deeply convicted, for a time he did not know what to do. Then he decided to go to his relative and tell him all the truth, asking him under the circumstances to accept five men instead of ten. This done, his heart was at rest; and the men who were suffering quickly recovered.

It was a busy life he led, especially at The Middle Eden. His many-sided ability made him always in requisition. Whatever was going on, if he was anywhere within reach, "Our Pastor" was sure to be wanted. He could cook a good dinner; cut a coat nicely; see to the making of a complete suit of garments, inner and outer; or a pair of shoes that would fit without pinching. To eminent capacity for directing large operations, he added an unusual mastery of detail. And all that he was, or by the grace

of God could be, was at the disposal of every one he could
help.

It was a great change, most noticeable to those who had known
him from the beginning. Not to override others, but to bear their
burdens; not to rule, but to serve, had become his ideal. For had
not his Master said: "I am among you as he that serveth." In later
years he was much impressed with the thought that just as God
in Christ had laid down His life for us, "we ought," not we may,
but we *ought*, "to lay down our lives for the brethren." And this
seemed to him to apply to little things as well as great. Was not
the Lord Jesus always laying down His life for others, long before
He came to the cross?

In the matter of time, for example, the way in which he
patiently submitted to the most trying interruptions, was just
part of this spirit. Burdened though he was with serious responsibilities, he was always at the disposal of those who came to him
with even the smallest need. His time was thus constantly broken
in upon, and he had to make it a matter of prayer that the Lord
would save him from unnecessary distractions. But when the call
came, he would respond at once; not with remonstrance, but in a
loving, sympathetic spirit; even if it were some needless question
of a blundering helper, or the outpouring of a mother's anxious
care. Of course he tried, as far as possible, to organise the work
so that each department should be carried on by its own responsible head. But there were all the extra things that could not be
foreseen and provided for, and all the personal difficulties that
could be brought to no one else.

The writer well remembers learning one lesson from him that
will never be forgotten.

It was during an important conference, and Hsi was just about
to take one of the principal meetings. He had been fasting and
waiting on God in prayer, and when the audience had assembled,
he came out of his room, books in hand, ready to go on the
platform. His mind was full of his message, and crossing the
courtyard he scarcely noticed a woman who was waiting, until
she intercepted him. No one else was present, and he had not the
slightest idea that the little scene was watched from behind an
open window.

"Oh, Pastor Hsi," she exclaimed, "I have been waiting for you.
My baby boy is poorly. Please give me something for his cough.
Your medicine is sure to do him good."

The case evidently was not urgent. But without the slightest impatience, he paused and said kindly to the woman:

"Do not let your heart be anxious. As soon as the meeting is over, I will prepare something. If you cannot stay just now, send someone later to fetch the medicine."

The woman, comforted, sat down to wait. Hsi spoke that afternoon with great power. And when the service closed, he slipped away to find the mother and patiently explain to her just how that medicine was to be given, and what to do for the child.

"It was really wonderful," said Mr. Hoste, after the close observation of years. "He used often to remind me of Mr. Hudson Taylor in this respect. Amid all the press of work that was upon him, really important affairs claiming attention, his patience and courtesy, toward even the most unreasonable intruder, seemed unfailing. He was deeply imbued with the spirit, the conviction, that he really was their servant for Christ's sake, and that so it ought to be."

At the same time, he felt these interruptions keenly, and longed for more leisure that he might give himself to prayer and spiritual ministry. Toward the close of 1894, he wrote:

During the fifteen years that have elapsed since I first believed in the Lord Jesus, I have sometimes been engaged in leading the Christians of our Middle Eden in farming; sometimes in helping to cook in the kitchen, in preparation for a feast; sometimes in assisting with the manufacture of our medicines; sometimes even in domestic work; as well as in travelling from province to province arranging for the Refuges, preaching and healing diseases, or assisting to govern the affairs of the Church. All the year round I am exceedingly busy: and in consequence of this have come very far short in my duties toward the churches at Pingyang and in the Taning district, so that I am not worthy to be called their pastor.

I humbly beg all the foreign missionaries and native pastors to pray for me, beseeching the Lord to grant me more helpers, who will be able to undertake the responsibility of my household and Refuge matters, in order that I may give myself unremittingly to prayer and the preaching of the Gospel. This is what my heart truly longs for. Amen.

# 34

# Ready to Depart

FIFTEEN years had passed away since in the old home at Pingyang, David Hill led Hsi, his opium-smoking teacher, to the feet of Jesus. They had never met since then, though each had followed with deepest interest the career of his much-loved friend. Together they were nearing the end of the journey. But the last years were the best. Each was ripening in spirit for the glorious translation; growing in love and in humility; crowding the closing hours of life with richer, fuller service: as Paul, "ready to depart on the morrow," gathered the believers round him on that Asian coast, and continued all night comforting and exhorting those who should see his face no more, "even till break of day."

One source of constant joy to Hsi during these later years was the manifest deepening of spiritual life among the Hungtung Christians, and the development of gifts that proved the Holy Spirit's working and did much to strengthen the church.

Limits of space and of the reader's patience forbid our dwelling upon the simple but effective system of church order that had grown up under the special conditions existing in that district. It was quite *sui generis*; in many respects the outcome of Hsi's own life and influence. The missionary colleague with whom he was associated had been guided, through constant prayer, to interfere as little as possible with the natural development of the work of God around him. He might have sought to mould the ideas of his fellow-workers in strict conformity with the practice of one or other of our denominational systems at home. But he saw that Hsi was being taught of God, and that excellent as our established usages may be for the old country, there is no need to limit brethren surrounded by such different conditions to exactly the forms we have inherited. "If you have a live thing, it will grow; and grow after the order of its own life." There is infinite variety and adaptability in nature; why not also in the spiritual creations of God? Was it not in a similar connection that our Lord Himself said: "New wine must be put into new bottles"?

So the missionary felt it more important to minister to his

Chinese brethren in spiritual things, seeking to deepen their knowledge of God and understanding of the Scriptures, than to regulate for them the precise methods they should follow in the management of their own church affairs. He saw that the only way to develop the native leader was to leave responsibility upon him; and that in the long run better results could be obtained for the Chinese church, by the direct working of the Holy Spirit through the heart and mind of such a man, imbued with the teachings of the Word, than by the *ex officio* control of any foreigner.

A brief outline of the facts, as they existed at this time, may be of interest.

"As years went on," writes Mr. Hoste, "I am thankful to say that my relations with Pastor Hsi grew more and more close and helpful to ourselves and to the Church. The work also steadily increased; the village gatherings growing both in number and in the Christian character of their members: until, at the time of his decease, some seven hundred persons had been baptised, or whom five hundred were still living and in good standing. The work had spread its branches over hundreds of miles, and had just succeeded in touching the three adjacent provinces of Shensi, Honan, and Chihli (Hopei).

"There were four subordinate pastors or presbyters, exercising control over wide portions of this field; and some fifteen or twenty other brethren who had been set apart to the supervision of local centres. Over the whole Pastor Hsi, advised by myself, exercised what in its essence was episcopal authority.

"None of these men were receiving any salary or pecuniary support from the Mission of which I am a member, or from any foreign source. They were all self-supporting; either having means of their own, or, as was the case with most, working for their living.

"These brethren, in the first instance, had been private members of the church; and in their own local centres had developed the spiritual qualifications needful for the care and leadership of other Christians. For the village gatherings, necessarily only visited by us at intervals, were thrown on their own resources; and in this way any latent gifts among the members had an opportunity of coming into requisition and being increased by use. As such brethren showed themselves, they became the objects of our special attention; and when they seemed ripe for it, and the needs of the local church called for such a step, they were formally set apart by the laying on of hands, as deacons of their own churches. Among these again, as time went by, it was not difficult to perceive one and another whose character and influence pointed them out as fitted for wider control; and in due time such men were set apart as elders.

"The principle upon which we acted in this important matter was never to appoint a man to church office until he had proved himself capable of exercising its functions with acceptance and profit to his brethren. The teachings of such Scriptures as the twelfth chapter of First Corinthians, appeared to indicate that wherever the Spirit of God was gathering out a company of believers from among the heathen, He would develop of their own number individuals able in their several degrees and various ways to contribute to the well-being of the whole. Our circumstances admitted, indeed almost compelled, a very simple and direct application of this truth. We did not lose sight of the fact that human agencies of special training are part of the means for perfecting the usefulness of these men. And for ministry in the churches among which they were labouring, a knowledge of Scripture, especially of the New Testament, and power of expounding it in a helpful, practical fashion, was the great thing to be aimed at as far as public worship was concerned.

"It should be added that while they were responsible for all the public meetings, they were free, and were expected to invite any of the members to conduct services who had a measure of fitness for doing so; and to encourage the development of such usefulness amongst others. In the matter of their temporal support, it seemed to us best for the present to let them earn their own living. Any who, through the growth of the work under their care, might in the future find their time wholly absorbed by their ministry, should be supported by those amongst whom they were labouring, rather than become dependent on funds from the missionary.

"Similarly, when through the number of worshippers it was no longer suitable or convenient to hold the services in the private house of any of the members, a hall was secured in the village for the purpose, the expense being met by the subscriptions of the natives themselves. In this way there had come to be more than a dozen meeting-places in various market towns and large villages; while in the capital cities of half a dozen counties, the Mission had premises that were available for occasional united gatherings, and served also as administrative centres. There were also, in twenty-five or thirty other villages, small groups of converts and inquirers who held daily evening meetings in private houses, and who on the Lord's Day would, in most cases, attend at the nearest village in which there was a 'worship-hall.'

"Once a year a general meeting of the church officers, and representative members from all the centres, was held in the city in which I resided. This lasted three or four days; and the time was spent in devotional meetings and deliberation about the work, when such matters as the appointment of church officers, the framing of church rules, and the like, were gone into. Voluntary offerings for the church fund were also made, for the relief of the poor and the support of 'worship-halls.' By this means the unity of the work was maintained, and much spiritual refreshment afforded.

"In addition to this annual gathering, Pastor Hsi and myself were habitually meeting with the local church officers, as occasion arose. All questions connected with baptisms or church discipline were decided by us, in consultation with the elders and deacons.

"During those years of intimate association with native workers, one or two thoughts were impressed upon me that it may be well to refer to.

"The first was that there may be a close walk with God and real spiritual power, in a convert whose Bible knowledge, through lack of opportunity, is very slender; and that such a man may be much blessed to the conversion of his fellow countrymen. One's attitude toward him must be that of Aquila and Priscilla with Apollos, rather than that of Eliab toward David.

"Again, a man in some respects a spiritual giant, may be long in shaking off the influence of mistaken views imbibed before conversion. Martin Luther in history, and the Apostle Peter in Scripture, are instances of this. And there have been many since the latter, who have needed a threefold vision from heaven, before their 'Not so, Lord,' of previous prejudice and training, has been swept away."

Our Lord's most precious gifts to His Church are men; next to the supreme Gift:

"Some to be apostles; and some, prophets; and some, evangelists; and some, pastors and teachers; for the perfecting of the saints, unto the work of ministering, unto the building up of the body of Christ."

And the right men come as His gift only. Paid helpers are easily obtained; but for the truly God-given man or woman, one must wait: wait upon Him who alone can raise them up. Ishmael may be got by other means, but not Isaac. And Ishmael is more easy to get than to get rid of.

One of the chief difficulties in missionary work lies just here. The right man often seems so hard to find; and for us it is so hard to be patient. But may we not, *must* we not believe that if the Holy Spirit is unhindered, the right worker will assuredly be given wherever needed, in answer to effectual, earnest prayer? Oh, how many more soul-winners, and Spirit-filled men and women we might have in China, if we prayed more.

Such a man, for example, was old Deacon Li of Yohyang in the eastern mountains: simple, homely, uneducated; but a man of real faith and spiritual power.

It was at Fan's village, in the early days, that Hsi first met him. Li was a travelling doctor then, just an elderly countryman who went about selling medicines. In his village home, thirty miles to the east, he had never met a Christian or heard of Jesus. It was a lonely, out-of-the-world spot. No missionary had visited there, or was likely to for a long while to come. But in those scattered hamlets, the Lord had not a few of His "other sheep," waiting to be brought home. He knew the man whom He could use. And so, guided doubtless by the Spirit of God, Li made his way over the mountains to the very spot where he could find the Saviour who was longing to find him.

It was a wonderful change when the old medicine-seller left his drugs, and charms, and all the rest, to become a "fisher of men." He was no scholar, and could not even read; but he drank in the truth with avidity; and went back, his heart so full of the Saviour that it had to overflow.

One by one up in the mountains, other souls were drawn to the living Christ; and the news spread from village to village that old Li had found a God who answered prayer. His faith was so simple and unquestioning that when they sent for him in different directions, to pray for their sick or demon-tormented relatives, he went without hesitation, and laying his hands upon them in the name of Jesus, claimed perfect healing. Wonderful things happened in those remote little places, where the old man and his Master went together from home to home: wonderful things, known only to a few country people, and the watching angels;

but it will need eternity to reveal all the results. In those low-roofed cottages, with the little children round him, Li would sit down as one of the family, and tell them simply and lovingly of Jesus. With true sympathy he listened to their troubles, spoke faithfully of their wrong-doing, and led them to confess their sins. Then, when they were ready to put away their idols, he would kneel down on the mud floor beside the sufferer, and talk to the Heavenly Father about all their needs. His prayers were so real and full of power, that many a time the heathen felt that the mighty God to whom he spoke so earnestly, must indeed be there, beneath their roof.

Numbers were healed of all sorts of troubles, among whom not a few gave their hearts to the Lord. Later on a Refuge was opened under Hsi's direction, which became a centre for the Christians and inquirers. Old Li was put in charge, and many a man saved from opium-smoking bears witness to his loving, skilful service. It was so characteristic of his spirit that he would receive no payment even for this exacting work. At first, in connection with the Refuge, he did draw a small salary. But one Sunday at Hungtung, he heard Hsi preach a sermon on the sin of "covetousness, which is idolatry" in the sight of God. This greatly disquieted the old man; and rather than run any risk of even appearing to serve the Lord for money, he refused from that time forward to take a single cash in the way of remuneration. He could afford to trust his Heavenly Father for daily bread; but not at any price could he afford to grieve Him

When it became necessary to organise a little church in that district, there was no question as to who should be put in charge as deacon. Li felt very keenly the responsibility of this new office, and more than ever devoted himself to the welfare of his flock. When a "worship-hall" was needed, in a village where the Christians were too poor to meet the entire expense, he rejoiced even to sell his wadded gown and suffer the lack of it all winter, that he might make up the sum. "As poor yet making many rich," he often went short of what most people would consider necessaries, that he might minister to the wants of others. On his journeys round the district, he carried no money or provisions. He felt it better and more Scriptural, that the Christians should have the opportunity of entertaining him as he laboured in their service. And in places where there were no Christians, he just went as guided of God, doing His work, and trusting for needed supplies. Sometimes on evangelistic tours of this sort he would plan to be absent three or four days; but not until half a month had passed would he turn up again at the Refuge, weary and travel-stained, but radiant with joy, explaining that the Holy Spirit had not permitted him to return before.

The chief inspiration of his life, and his strongest reason for faith, was the fact of the resurrection of our Lord and Saviour from the dead. This comforted him under all circumstances, and seemed a truth especially his own. Whatever happened, he returned to it again and again, with perfect confidence: "Jesus lives. He rose from the dead. Therefore nothing is impossible."

No wonder Hsi rejoiced in such fellow workers: men after his own heart. No wonder that up to and beyond the limits of his strength he was unremitting in prayer and labour on their behalf. It was a beautiful thing to see him at the yearly conferences, drawing them all together, finding out their difficulties, strengthening them with sympathy and counsel, and seeking to deepen their faith in God and zeal for souls.

Time fails to tell much about the women. They seem almost forgotten in our pages. Not because they were less interesting or earnest than the men, but their part of the story would want a volume to itself: and we hasten to a close. One old lady must be referred to, however, who played an important part even in church affairs at this time, and helped to solve a perplexing situation.

In one of the village gatherings, Chentsun, quite a leading centre, a difficulty arose about the appointment of a church officer. A deacon was needed; and the trouble was, not that a suitable man was hard to find, but that there were too many. For at any rate three good men, substantial farmers, were forthcoming; any one of whom could have filled the office. They were all loved and valued, but it was impossible to choose between them; for though totally different in character, they were strangely equal as regards weight and influence. To have raised one above the others, would have been unreasonable; especially from a Chinese point of view. It would have been disastrous also; for merely calling him a deacon would not have added to his fitness for the office. As Mr. Hoste said:

"You can never go against facts. Try as you may, it is impossible to add to a man's stature. You may put him on a pedestal, but it does not really make him any bigger."

On the other hand, to have appointed all three would have provoked endless factions in the little church: "I am of Paul, and I of Apollos," and so on.

"Well," said Hsi, "we must leave it for the present. It is clearly a case in which we do not know the mind of the Lord."

And then it all came right so simply, as they prayed about it. There was this dear old lady in the village, mother of one of the men in question. She had, in a quiet way, done useful work among the women; and was quite a power. The Christian men valued her judgment, and were in the habit of consulting her upon important matters. They were all feeling rather badly, up there, on account of having no church officer. And it occurred to Pastor Hsi:

"Why not recognise the position the Lord has evidently given this woman, and let her be set apart as a deaconess?"

After prayerful consideration there seemed no reason against it; and when the idea was suggested, the Christians were more than pleased. The three men especially approved the step. Thus the difficulty was met. For the plan worked admirably, and no other appointment was made or desired. As a matter of fact, the position remained pretty much as it had been before. The men managed business matters, and carried on the meetings. But the old lady was more openly consulted, and had more responsibility among the women. And the Chinese word for deacon being equally applicable to a deaconess, the little church no longer felt neglected.

We may smile; but the suggestive thing is that a woman, without any education or special training, should have the capacity for exercising so much influence in religious affairs. That they are by no means rare in China, bodes well for the future of that great country; and indicates possibilities that should not be lost sight of in our life-decisions and our prayers.

As evidencing real progress among the Hungtung Christians, one forward step must be referred to that greatly rejoiced Pastor Hsi during later years; the resolve unanimously taken by the church, to appeal no more to legal protection in times of persecution, or any difficulty with heathen neighbours. It was no hurried action; indeed it could not be. The issues involved were too serious and far-reaching. For such a decision simply meant that for themselves, their homes and families, whatever happened, they would from that time forward look to God alone for succour and defence. Amid the surroundings of a heathen land, such an attitude implies a depth of inner conviction that grows up slowly.

In early days it had been very different. Then Hsi, with much of the old self still about him, felt that his zeal and energy must be employed to clear the way of the Lord, sweeping aside all obstacles and hindrances, with the means whereby he had hitherto successfully dominated those around him. Thus when troubles arose, and believers were persecuted contrary to treaty rights, he even went up to the capital and interviewed the Governor of the province, setting on foot legal proceedings that covered their enemies with confusion. For as followers of the Western faith, he and other Christians could claim the protection assured to foreigners.

It was only when he found to his sorrow that such victories tend to deaden spiritual life, and put the Christians in a frame of mind wholly contrary to the love and self-sacrifice of their Master, that he saw something must be wrong. As at Yangtsun, over and over again, a successful lawsuit meant a declining church; and the more Christian people sought to defend themselves from the reproach of the Cross, the less power they possessed for saving and blessing others. So manifestly was this the case, that Hsi was led seriously to reconsider the whole question; seeking from careful study of the Scriptures to find out the mind of the Lord.

But it was not until the time of his own worst troubles that the truth became clearly apprehended. In those closing months of 1887 he was called to go alone, into "the thick darkness, where God was." And there he learned that not human help, so often unavailing, is the real need of the soul; but the all-sufficient Presence—"the God that is Enough." He came to see that nothing can touch the life committed to Him, without His express design or permission; and that even distresses deliberately planned by the devil, "the messenger of Satan to buffet me," may be turned into occasions for the fuller outshining of His glorious power, "made perfect in weakness." Then the glad pæan of the Missionary Apostle became the language of his heart also:

"Therefore I take pleasure in infirmities, in reproaches, in necessities, in persecutions, in distresses for Christ's sake: for when I am weak, then am I strong."

To have gone back, after that, to heathen mandarins for help and protection, would have been impossible. For himself, the question was finally settled; and by the end of that year he confessedly abandoned the course of lodging complaints of any kind with Government officials. He found it so much more blessed, and effective too, to lodge them with the King of Kings.

But in this position Hsi stood almost alone among his brethren. There was a considerable element then, in the Church, that inclined to make the most of this world, while still hoping to stand well in the next. But in the Fan troubles, much wood, hay, and stubble burned away. And as time went on, true believers were more prepared to commit themselves to a spiritual line of things. Then a higher standard became possible; and prayerful thought was given to this important subject. No doubt the way in which the Lord undertook for the Refuge work, delivering Hsi and his helpers in many a danger, in answer to prayer alone, was the best comment on Scriptural teaching that could have been afforded, and had not a little to do with the final result.

But the action of the Church was unhurried and voluntary. For some time there had been a conviction that such a step would be for the glory of God, as well as for the best interests of the work. But the laying aside of all treaty rights, and the protection to be obtained through the influence of foreigners, meant renouncing very tangible benefits: and the step was not taken lightly.

But when at length the decision was come to, it was wonderful how the Lord immediately put forth His power to protect from persecution and trial in quite a new way. From the very first He gave most gracious deliverances, and unmistakably espoused the cause thus committed to Him. Afterwards, as the faith of the Church grew stronger, this was not so markedly the case. Then persecution was allowed to come; though manifestly overruled for blessing. But until they were established in this new position, entered upon with a measure of fear and trembling, the Lord undertook for them so remarkably that the missionary who watched it all was filled with wonder and thanksgiving. In this whole matter, he and Pastor Hsi were deeply one; as the following page from our Chinese manuscript indicates:

After united prayer and consultation, Mr. Hoste and I decided to bring before the next conference (early in 1891) a resolution that in future all members and inquirers connnected with any of the churches in the Hungtung district, who might suffer persecution, should trust only in the Lord for protection, and not depend upon their treaty rights. This, after full discussion, was unanimously approved by the Church, and became a fixed rule. Now, it is clearly explained to every candidate before baptism; lest afterwards, when tested and tried by persecution, he should repent.

During recent years [written in 1894] the Lord has preserved the Church in much greater peace than we formerly enjoyed.

In all matters connected with the Church or Refuges, Mr. Hoste and I have united in prayer and consultation, and are thus enabled to arrange things happily. We mutually help one another, without any distinction of native or foreigner; because the Lord has made us one. Mrs. Hoste, thank God, also loves Mrs. Hsi; and is of one heart with her husband. May the Lord continually make us of one mind, and give us grace upon grace, that we may glorify our Heavenly Father.

Strangely enough, after this resolution was taken, Hsi himself was among the first to be put to the test. The circumstance, though comparatively trivial, is noteworthy as showing how completely his own character and attitude were changed by the grace of God. Even outsiders could see that he was no longer the same man. In former days, most people dreaded the thought of offending him; and so far from taking liberties, were rather thankful if he did not come down upon them. And even after his conversion, no one would have cared to interfere with his rights. But now, nothing seemed to rouse the old, fiery spirit. And gradually it dawned upon his heathen neighbours that he was harmless, and might be taken advantage of with impunity. He would do nothing worse, at any rate, than pray.

And so, with perfect coolness, a man in the Western Chang village annexed a portion of his property; a little patch of nice, watered land. He quietly altered the boundary marks, and took over this valuable addition to his own farm.

The news, of course, was soon carried to Hsi, who could hardly believe it, until he saw for himself what had been done. Then, after praying over the matter, he went round to his neighbour's house, and in a friendly spirit remonstrated at such a proceeding. But he was at once attacked with a storm of abuse and defiance, and saw that the man intended to bluff the matter through.

Under these circumstances there was nothing to be done, if he intended to recover his rights, but go to law and have the aggressor punished. But this, of course, was just what Hsi would not do. As he thought and prayed about it, he saw that the Lord was giving him an opportunity for living out the great principle of not resisting evil, and that it was a case that might be specially useful to others, for there was not a man in the Church who would not be tempted to resent such an injustice.

"It is my Master's land," he said quietly. "I hold it only for His service. If He wants to use it thus, to illustrate the spirit of the Gospel—let it go."

This attitude, needless to say, aroused much amusement and curiosity in the village. Could it be that the Christians were as foolish as all that! But ridicule was checked somewhat suddenly, when the man who had wronged Hsi was taken violently ill. Nothing did him any good; and in his distress he begged, at last, that Hsi would come to him, for there was no such doctor anywhere else to be had. Hsi gladly undertook the case, and did all he could for the poor fellow, earnestly pleading with him to turn to God and seek the blessedness of sins forgiven.

The man was greatly impressed. He took the medicines provided, and was soon restored to health. The more he thought of it, the more he wondered at Hsi's kindly spirit. And finally he began to attend the services at The Middle Eden, and showed no little earnestness in inquiring about the Gospel.

"Now," thought Hsi, "is our opportunity. I will say nothing about that land. If he truly gives his heart to Christ, the first thing he will do will be to make reparation. We must show that to us, at any rate, his soul is worth more than the property."

But the man held back. He could not make up his mind to face the cost of becoming a Christian. Not even that one little bit of land was he willing to part with. Nothing was said. But he ceased coming to the meetings; and, before long, had relapsed completely into his former life. It was sadly evident that the strivings of the Holy Spirit had ceased, or almost so, in his heart.

And then, only a short time after he had turned his back upon Christ, he was suddenly taken ill, while Hsi was away from home, and died.

A profound impression was made in the village, where the whole matter had been closely watched. An impression that was not lessened, when upon Hsi's return he declined to take any steps for recovering the land, and left it in the possession of the family, who were even then unwilling to give it up. He was permanently the loser to that degree. But what an opportunity it gave him for preaching the Gospel. And what an incentive it proved to other Christians to pray for their persecutors and seek to win them to repentance, in view of that solemn word, "I will repay, saith the Lord."

Our Master nowhere promises that those who put their trust in Him shall not suffer loss of property. On the contrary, His servants are spoken of as men "Set forth . . . appointed unto death . . . made a spectacle unto the world, and to angels, and to men."

"Being reviled, we bless; being persecuted, we suffer it; being defamed, we intreat: we are made as the filth of the world, and are the offscouring of all things unto this day."

While one prays for deliverance and peace, and it is right to desire such blessings for ourselves and others, the only way for real heart-rest is to be willing, at any moment, to lay down life itself for His sake. And the moment of our deepest fellowship with His sufferings, may be the moment also of our richest fore-taste of His joy.

But not only in these matters of Church order and witness-bearing in the midst of persecution, was progress made. Hsi came to see more and more, as time went on, the importance of keeping the Lord's Day, and of bringing the Christians to understand that they must live for God and with God in everything. Heart and soul he threw himself into all that concerned their well-being. He was with them constantly in their homes; conducting weddings and funerals, visiting the sick, inquiring after the children, pray-ing with and helping them in times of difficulty. He knew all that was going on; and had as quick an eye for all the good points and blemishes of his flock, as any Eastern shepherd. This famili-arity with their needs gave him great power in prayer for them, and made his preaching and private exhortations very practical. His zeal on their behalf reminded one of Paul's fervent cry:

"My little children, of whom I travail in birth again until Christ be formed in you."

"I am jealous over you with a godly jealousy . . . that I may present you as a chaste virgin to Christ."

To this end he sought in every way to bring the Word of God to bear upon their lives, in the light of the Holy Spirit's teaching. He had a most searching, helpful way of unfolding Scripture. In public meetings he did not merely take a text and preach an eloquent sermon; though it would have been easy for him to excel in that line of things. His heart was far too conscious of the needs of the people before him, and of the Master's need of them. With simple directness he endeavoured to bring home to his hearers a realisation of the claims of God upon their lives, and the possibilities open to them in Christ Jesus. He would take a passage of Scripture, a dozen or twenty verses, and expound the leading thoughts, sentence by sentence. He did not refer much to other passages; for he found that turning from one to another was apt to distract attention. But he frequently took some Old Testament story, to illustrate the point he was making, and related it with a graphic interest that made it live before the people.

"It was all so practical and vivid and full of spiritual power," said his missionary colleague, recalling those days.

And in his own study of Scripture, Hsi followed the same principles. He was a man who read and pondered the Bible a great deal, and had an unusual grasp of its teachings. But it was his experimental method that was characteristic. To him the message seven times reiterated in the Upper Room, by our Lord's own lips, was of supreme importance: "He that hath my commandments, *and keepeth them,* he it is that loveth me."

In this connection is it not true—as Mr. Hoste said, speaking of his friend:

A well-taught Christian is not necessarily one who has acquired an extensive knowledge of Scripture. Though such knowledge may be a means to the end of becoming a well-taught Christian. The Bible, I often think, is like a map; in that it shows us the way to be brought into, and to maintain, a walk with God. I may have an excellent acquaintance with the map of Africa, and yet be a very poor explorer. Just as people may possess a great deal of Bible knowledge, and be able to talk beautifully about the deeper things, and the higher life, when all the while their experience may be shallow, and their life dishonouring to God. "If ye know these things, happy are ye if ye do them."

The teachings of our Lord in the Sermon on the Mount, for example, are not hints to candidates, that we may take or leave. Christ Himself *acts* on these principles. His Word must dwell in us; steadily controlling our lives. Then, and not till then, are we abiding in Him.

It is so important in Bible study to remember that we must aim at more than clear views of truth. I may perceive a great deal of inward significance in Abraham's sacrifice of Isaac. But in my own life, I have a Mount Moriah too. And that is for me the really important matter. Similarly I may understand the progression in Jacob's experience: that Bethel marked one stage and Peniel quite another, and that much lay between the two. But then, I also must travel that same road.

As to Hsi, he did love applied Scripture; and was in this sense an eminently well-taught Christian. The Word of God was the man of his counsel all the time. Not to copy but to reproduce the Truth, was his constant aim. He never encouraged those who came to him for training, to pile up Bible knowledge, and think that because they knew a great deal, they were able to others, who might have studied less. Yet that delusion is common; and not in China only. But mere teaching never feeds the soul; any more than reading a bill of fare can provide a hungry man with a dinner.

"The *tao-li* (truth or doctrine) must have full play," he insisted, "in your lives. God will always be putting you into circumstances in which His principles will test you. The path that Jesus follows, leads to the Cross. And the question, right along, will be: Are you going to take that road with Him? It means death to self, daily. Are you willing to let Him live it out? There is no other way of bringing life and blessing to others."

This was the real thing in Hsi's own life; the one thing he increasingly desired: so to preach, and so to live, as to bring others into touch with God.

It was in keeping with his own spiritual life that more and more, toward the close, he sought to turn people's eyes away from himself, and lead them to deal with God directly. He was more careful too, as time went on, about laying his hands on sick or demon-tormented people, and praying for their immediate healing. Not that his faith was less. But he came to see that to be right with God is the chief thing; and that sickness may be a means the Lord is using to draw the soul nearer to Himself. When people were truly seeking the Lord, he was just as ready as of old to pray for them and claim deliverance. But he had learned through several remarkable experiences, that if this was not the case, he dared not, as he expressed it, "misuse the power of the Gospel." In the same way he was less inclined to resort to medicine than formerly; and in his own case often preferred to wait upon God alone, for healing. He made no hard and fast rule about it. The Lord seemed to guide him as need arose, in ways that suited the occasion.

In the autumn of 1893, for example, he visited the Refuge at Chaocheng, and was immediately appealed to by some of the Christians, on behalf of sick friends. Deacon Liu, in the village of Nanshihling, was suffering much. Both his eyes were badly swollen, and nothing seemed to relieve the pain. Would Pastor Hsi make time to go over there and pray for him? And then Brother Tsao from another village was in trouble. His wife was seriously ill. He was so thankful the Pastor had arrived; and besought him to come at once to their home and heal her. Tired and busy as he might be, Pastor Hsi always responded to such requests. But on this occasion he felt that something was wrong. He prayed and thought over the matter; then calling in the men who were waiting, he said to them:

The Lord does not give me liberty to go with you. Deacon Liu is the leader of the Church in that village. I fear he has been working on the Lord's Day, and so breaking a most important commandment. If this is the reason of his affliction, it is that he may be a warning to the whole flock.

And Brother Tsao, it may be that your wife has been too busy with family affairs, and has grown cold-hearted. I fear she has been careless about prayer, and learning from the Word of God. It is more important that our souls should prosper than that our bodies should be in health.

Now you have Brother Sung here, the pastor of your own church. He is responsible for these things. Ask him to go with you. If the deacon and Mrs. Tsao will confess their sins and return to the Lord, your pastor will lay his hands on them and pray for them, and they will certainly be healed.

This unexpected answer astonished all present, who knew that in both cases it was even as he supposed. Pastor Sung went out, and was enabled to put matters right. His prayers for healing were graciously heard; and the Chaocheng church was all the stronger for the lesson.

A little later, a Christian man named Chou was so seriously ill that Pastor Hsi gave himself to fasting and prayer on his behalf. Medical treatment had been tried, but without success; and it seemed as though he could not last much longer. As he prayed, Hsi felt quite clear that the Lord had sent this sickness in mercy to his soul. Very solemnly he urged him to make a full confession to the Lord Himself, and pray for spiritual healing. This he did; and without any further treatment, the serious symptoms abated, so that that very day he was comparatively well.

But Hsi was just as tender with those who needed comfort, as stern in cases where rebuke was called for. And for comfort also, he directed their hearts to God. Nothing could be indifferent to the Heavenly Father that concerned the welfare of His children; and His resources were always sufficient for His own.

In the summer of 1893, for instance, a drought destroyed the wheat harvest, and great distress prevailed throughout the district. Hsi was travelling up from his own home to Hungtung, and a few miles south of the city came to the village of Yanghai, where lived a family of earnest Christians. In the hope of bringing them a little cheer, he stopped to pay a visit, and found that his coming was most opportune.

Like everyone else, Shao had lost his spring crops; but, as if to rectify matters, his peach trees promised an unusual yield. From day to day they had watched the little orchard; counting upon the sale of this beautiful fruit to provide means of subsistence through the winter. What was their dismay, therefore, a few days previously, to find traces of the most deadly enemy of the young peach—a worm that now, alas, had covered all the trees. Evidently the crop was doomed; and little or nothing stood between them and absolute want.

Hsi's heart was deeply moved. With real sympathy he comforted his friends; assuring them from his own experience, that the Lord had many ways of providing for His children, and would never let them lack daily bread.

"But come," he said, "let us go out into the orchard, and tell our Heavenly Father all about it."

Under the spreading peach trees, they knelt down that summer evening, and prayed that even now the ravages of the worm might be stayed, if it were the Lord's purpose to use that fruit in providing for their needs. They had no means of checking the trouble. But He could easily deal with it. And if not, they trusted Him to care for them some other way.

Then Hsi went on his journey. And much comforted, the Shaos continued looking to the Lord. A day or two later their prayers were answered. For on going to the orchard as usual, they found the ground under the peach trees strewn all over with dead worms. Apparently not one was left alive. The trees remained in good condition, and later on produced a fine crop.

But it was in dealing with business affairs, and the difficulties that came up among his Refuge workers, that perhaps the greatest change was seen in Hsi during these later years. "The meekness and gentleness of Christ" had so mellowed his spirit, that hardly a trace seemed left of the once imperious, self-confident Confucianist.

In those old days it had been second nature to insist upon his own way; to lead and manage, and put things through, regardless of the interests of others. But now he had, in no small measure, grasped the principles that lie at the root of all true spiritual directorship. His fellow-workers were no longer subordinates, serving or helping him; but brethren whom it was his privilege to help in a common service to the Lord. The work was God's work; and the men engaged in it were called of the Divine Master, each to their several posts. His business, as a faithful steward, was to see that all were arranged for as helpfully as possible, and strengthened in every way to do their best. So he sought rather to put responsibility on them, than to keep

everything in his own hands; and realised the importance of
seeking their welfare in each appointment, that he might truly
carry out for them the will of God.

He tried as far as possible to send his men two and two, that
there should be in every Refuge, beside the brother in charge, a
second reliable man to help among the patients and keep all the
accounts. This left both a measure of freedom for more directly
spiritual work. Then there was usually a third man, also a Christian, who was cook and servant in a subordinate capacity. It was
not easy, always, to find suitable men for these posts, who could
work happily together; and Hsi felt it one of his chief duties, so
to wait upon God that he should be guided to wise selections,
and not make mistakes that would afterwards cause trouble.

And then when difficulties did arise, he was learning to deal
with them in a patient, humble spirit. This was perhaps the
greatest change of all. For he had naturally a hot temper; and in
virtue of his early training as a Confucianist, very clear ideas as
to the way in which things ought to be done. He was so efficient
himself, that stupidity tried him dreadfully in others; and so
thorough, that against slackness or neglect his whole being rose
in revolt. Sometimes, even long after he had seen the sin of
impatience, he would be betrayed into the old hastiness of speech,
showing an inward irritation that left him deeply repentant.

"I so well remember," said Mr. Hoste, "seeing him in my room
one day, with a deacon from one of the country places. He was
a good brother, but slow and heavy, and had been getting into
difficulties up there about a 'worship-hall.' Instead of coming at
once to Pastor Hsi, as he should have done, he had been blundering along by himself, and had involved us all in quite a tangle.
But the thing was, he could not be made to see it. As he went
over his view of the matter, again and again, Pastor Hsi had hard
work to keep his temper. But he did want to be gentle and
loving. And once more, as patiently as possible, he put the whole
case before the man, and said:

" 'Now really, do you think that was the wisest thing to do?'

" 'Yes,' said the other earnestly, 'I am sure I did quite right——'

"But poor Hsi gave a gasp, and came out with something, quite
sharply, that made the deacon start and shook his complacency
not a little. And then, in a moment, he was so sorry he had
done it.

" 'Oh,' he said, 'let us pray. We must ask forgiveness.' And then, as the tears came into his eyes: 'Truly, I am nothing. I am unfit to shepherd the flock of God.'

"It was very characteristic of his attitude during those riper years."

One other incident must be given, as showing the principles on which he acted when troubles arose between his Refuge workers. It occurred about the beginning of 1893.

Up on the Pingyao plain, two hundred miles from his own home, Hsi had an important Refuge in the city of Kiehhsiu (see next page). The two brethren in charge had not been working happily together, and at length matters reached a climax. They were both, sad to say, in a wrong spirit; and after an open rupture, full of mutual indignation, they left the Refuge, and came down post-haste to the Western Chang village, each intent upon laying before Pastor Hsi the delinquencies of the other.

When they arrived, of course, everyone could see that something had happened; and Hsi divined at once the true state of affairs. But he received them kindly, and without giving any opportunity for disclosures, attended to their wants himself; meanwhile instructing those in charge of the household that no questions were to be asked as to the reason of the visit. When they were comfortably provided with all they could need after their long journey, he excused himself, and went away alone for prayer.

Deeply distressed, he saw far more in what had taken place than a mere quarrel between ill-assorted brethren. For as years went on, his conviction only deepened that in cases of this kind the real power at work is that of the great enemy, who had succeeded in bring dishonour upon the cause of Christ. A spiritual force lay behind the difficulty; and only spiritual power could overcome it. He saw that any persuasion or diplomacy he could bring to bear would be useless, and indeed could only make matters worse. The men were so enraged against each other, that all they wanted was an opportunity for "having it out" in the most public manner. And if once they began, there was no knowing where it would end. Their own characters, at any rate, would be so defamed that they could no longer continue in the work. And others would be drawn into the trouble. So for two days Hsi fasted entirely, and gave himself to prayer. He could not be content to make the best of a bad job, but felt he must lay hold upon the power of God for complete deliverance.

Meanwhile, he was specially careful to treat the brethren with more than ordinary kindness, waiting on them himself, and showing equal cordiality to both. The rest of the household following his example, there was no opportunity for strife; and the would-be disputants began to feel somewhat ashamed of their unreasoning anger.

On the third day, still fasting, Hsi received the assurance that his prayers were answered. Then, without delay, he went in search of the brethren, and bringing them together into his own room, in a few loving words besought them to lay aside all bitterness and mutual accusation, and each confess his own fault to God and one another.

"Brethren," he said, "the blame is chiefly mine. If I had been more prayerful and considerate of your welfare, I should probably never have put you in the same Refuge. I feel that in this matter, I have sinned against God, as well as against you both. Shall we not forgive each other; and seek His forgiveness?"

The men were completely broken down. They had not a word to say of complaint or accusation. Hsi, full of love and of the Holy Spirit, prayed with them; until with many tears they were reconciled, and the trouble conquered.

"I never knew a man," said Mr. Hoste, speaking of this occurrence, "who trusted less in his own powers in any direction. It was a constant lesson to one who was much with him. For if anyone had reason for 'confidence in the flesh,' it was dear Hsi. But he was entirely weaned from that spirit. He placed no reliance on his own judgment even, apart from the guidance of God. One might ask him about quite a simple matter, and he would say: 'Let me pray about it. I do not know just yet.' Or, 'I will tell you later, when I have asked the Lord.'

"He realised so clearly that no human power can accomplish spiritual ends: and that our Lord's own word is literally true—

"WITHOUT ME YE CAN DO NOTHING."

# 35

# Higher Service

IT was the summer of 1895. In the sunny days of August, after the wheat harvest had been gathered in, Hsi called a special conference at The Middle Eden, to consider plans for strengthening and extending the Refuge work. Much was in his mind with regard to future possibilities. The Lord had wrought wondrously in the past, setting before them an open and effectual door; and he was full of hope and confidence for days to come.

From far and near the Refuge-workers came, joined by leading members of the Church, until two hundred guests overflowed the old home in the Western Chang village. Hsi was thoroughly in his element welcoming these well-loved friends and caring for their needs. But still more was he full of glad enthusiasm when the meetings began. Many matters affecting the work of the Refuges needed prayerful consideration. With growing experience it was natural that improvements should suggest themselves; and ways in which mistakes and friction could be avoided, and the spiritual usefulness of the work increased. Though Hsi was very far from considering their methods perfect, he did believe in them; and felt even more than at the beginning, that they could be made increasingly effective as a soul-saving agency, by the blessing of God. One thing he clearly recognised was the need for more supervision, and that the time had come to associate with himself, experienced brethren as superintendents over various portions of the work. And with no little thankfulness he watched the development of several who seemed to be growing in fitness for such responsibility in the near future.

One is tempted to linger over the bright days of that summer gathering: the joyous faith; the love and unity; the work accomplished by the grace of God; the lessons learned; and the maturer powers. Hsi had reached his sixtieth year, and in spite of incessant and exhausting toil, was full of vitality. It was good to see him there, in his own home, surrounded by friends and fellow workers to whom he was endeared by many a sacred tie; looking back with thankfulness, and forward with renewed devotion.

On one of the closing days of the conference, Hsi preached a

sermon that will never be forgotten. Many inquirers were present
and Christians from the neighbourhood, as well as the Refuge-
workers. He took as his text the parable of the Rich Man and
Lazarus: the "every day" of this life; and the "great gulf fixed"
beyond. As he spoke of the eternal issues of all our living here,
a light as from that other world seemed to illuminate the message.
It was full of solemnity and power. If he had known that it was
the last time he should speak to the Church he loved so well, he
could not have pleaded with them more earnestly to turn with
an undivided heart to God. And so with quickened longing to
live lives that should tell for eternity, that little company dis-
persed to take up their work again.

A few days after the conference Hsi went up to Hungtung to
see Mr. Hoste, in his usual health and vigour.

The day was hot and the journey tiring, but he scarcely seemed
to feel it, and that evening was just himself, full of interest in all
that was going on. Suddenly, however, those around him noticed
a change; he fainted, and before anyone could reach him, fell
unconscious to the ground. After a little while he came to, but
seemed strangely weak. And when a day or two went by and
he did not rally, Mr. Hoste thought it wiser to take him down to
Pingyang to see Dr. Millar Wilson.

There in the old mission-house he was received with kindest
sympathy. They put him in a quiet room, hoping that a few days'
rest would revive him again. But in spite of all that could be done,
he seemed unable to recover strength.

But perhaps he would be better at home. At any rate, he felt
he would like to take the journey without delay. So his own cart
was sent for, and with every care they carried him back to the
Western Chang village. "Whatever comes," he said as he left the
mission-house, "it is just—trust in the Lord."

At first there seemed no reason for anxiety. He lay still and
quiet in his own room looking out on to the sunny courtyard,
and things went on as usual, except that Mrs. Hsi remained at
home and was with him all the time. He did not need much
nursing, for he suffered no distress or pain. But it was good to
be together: and he was very weak. Mr. Hoste was often there,
and though too feeble to talk much, Hsi loved to have him come.
Elder Si looked after everything; and much prayer was made
throughout the district, that the beloved pastor might soon be
well again.

But weeks slipped into months; autumn tints crept over the plain; and still he was no stronger. Dr. Millar Wilson and Dr. Hewett came over from Pingyang, and did all that love and skill could do. But without avail. Medically it was a case of utter prostration, following upon years of over-strain; and there were serious heart symptoms. But it was long before they could bring themselves to believe that he would not recover.

How gladly would he have rallied if he could, to toil a little longer where the need seemed so great. Since the old dark days in that very room, when he lived only to smoke opium, how wonderful the grace of God had been. But it had all passed so quickly. A little had been done, a few life-lessons learned, some opportunities embraced of growing in His knowledge and His likeness, of sharing "the power of His Resurrection and the fellowship of His sufferings, being made conformable unto His death": but oh how much remained. Some souls had been saved, and thousands of opium-smokers rescued. But it was only a beginning, and wider opportunities seemed at hand. And so they were. But not here; not in that way.

Worn out: yes, but in the service of the Lord he loved. Broken: but at His feet. All the strength and sweetness lavished there. Oh he was rich and blest. Those around him might turn away and weep; but if angels can covet the bliss of human hearts, surely they must have envied that dying man—knowing the welcome, the rapture that waited just beyond the shadows.

Before he became too weak to make the effort, Pastor Hsi gave directions for the temporary closing of some of the more distant Refuges. He knew that a time of difficulty must come after his removal, and tried to prepare for it as far as possible. He asked after matters that were causing anxiety, and showed the same deep interest in the work, and assurance that the Lord would care for and continue it, as long as it was for His glory. But the exhaustion was very great, and he was not capable of much emotion. At length he could no longer kneel for prayer, and even speech became impossible. There was no disease or suffering; it was just the gradual withdrawal of life, before the vital powers failed.

"The Lord is taking away my strength," he said. "It must be because my work is done."

For just six months he lingered; latterly in semi-unconsciousness at times. The house was full, but all was very quiet: and there was much prayer. Toward the end of January he began to suffer from sore throat, brought on by a cold, which led to great distress in breathing. Then the conviction forced itself on those around him that the end was near. Long as they had been expecting it, the blow was terrible; for to hundreds he was unspeakably dear. Strong men could not restrain their grief, and were shaken with sobs like children. But Mrs. Hsi was enabled to say through her tears:

"I think of Jesus—and He is enough."

.     .     .     .     .

And so on the morning of February 19, 1896, he was translated to higher service.

One cannot think of him as dead: rather incomparably more living—in that land where His servants serve Him, seeing His face. Down here amid the darkness, he gave all. Nothing was too precious, if it could be used for Jesus; no labour too toilsome, if it could save a soul for whom He died. No cross seemed heavy, if carried for the Master; no pathway difficult that His blessed feet had trod.

> If any man serve me, let him follow me;
> And where I am, there shall also my servant be:
> If any man serve me, him will my Father honour.

And so he passes from our sight, into the fuller life of perfect union with the Lord—to all eternity, on and on, expanding in rapture infinite, fulfilling His glorious purposes, sharing His victory and love, of the increase of whose government "there shall be no end."

.     .     .     .     .

One last fact remains concerning the life we have followed to its close, or its completion rather; one thought I fain would leave upon your heart.

In the early summer of 1896, just three months after Pastor Hsi was called home, the Rev. David Hill of the Wesleyan Mission, Hankow, was also taken to be with the Lord. What a meeting for those friends long parted! Seventeen years before, the missionary had won that heathen Chinese to Jesus, little thinking how many he in his turn would win. With what joy and praise to God they would go over the long story, tracing His hand in ever-widening blessing.

But was it David Hill who won Hsi to Christ? Or was it he alone? Long after both were gone, the writer received the following letter, penned by one of his colleagues at Hankow:

May I give you an unpublished incident, told me by Mr. Hill himself.

Mr. Hill had a dear friend in England, who was distinguished for her power in prayer. When she died, an unfinished letter was found upon her desk intended for Mr. Hill, and was forwarded to him by the family. In it this lady told Mr. Hill how she had recently been much drawn out in prayer on his behalf, and had specially been led to plead for an extraordinary blessing to be given to him in his work at that time. She felt distinctly that she had been heard, though she knew not what form the blessing would take. The date of this letter was found so closely to correspond with the conversion of Pastor Hsi, that Mr. Hill never doubted but that that was the extraordinary blessing given in answer to his friend's prayers.

Dear Reader, is your life so in touch with God that you can really pray? Are you using this mighty power? Are souls being saved in dark places, in answer to your pleadings? The deepest need of missionary work in China to-day is prayer; more prayer in the power of the Spirit; effectual, fervent prayer for all missionaries and native Christians, that they may be brought into contact with men and women everywhere, made ready by the same Holy Spirit to receive the truth; and that their lives, like that of David Hill and Pastor Hsi, may *win* souls to the Saviour.

# A Song of Sacrifice

HYMN BY PASTOR HSI

**1**

When Thou wouldst pour the living
stream,
Then I would be the earthen cup,
Filled to the brim and sparkling clear.
The fountain Thou and living spring,
Flow Thou through me, the vessel
weak,
That thirsty souls may taste Thy grace.

**2**

When Thou wouldst warn the people,
Lord,
Then I would be the golden bell,
Swung high athwart the lofty tower,
Morning and evening sounding loud;
That young and old may wake from
sleep,
Yea, e'en the deaf hear that strong
sound.

**3**

When Thou wouldst slay the wolves,
O Lord!
Then I would be the keen-edged sword,
Clean, free from rust, sharpened and
sure,
The handle grasped, my God, by
Thee—
To kill the cruel ravening foe
And save the sheep for whom Christ
died.

**4**

When Thou wouldst light the darkness,
Lord,
Then I would be the silver lamp,
Whose oil supply can never fail,
Placed high to shed the beams afar,
That darkness may be turned to light,
And men and women see Thy face.

**5**

When Thou dost sound the battle-call
Thy standard-bearer I would be.
With love for shield, and right for
spear,
I'll sound Thy praise from East to
West.
From Thy high throne speak forth the
word,
And sin must yield before Thy praise.

**6**

When Thou wouldst write the records,
Lord,
Then I would be the ready pen,
A medium subtle for Thy thought,
Desirous to write it true.
That when the Book of Life is read,
Therein those names be found in-
scribed,
Which hell nor death can e'er blot out.

**REFRAIN**

*My body's Thine, yea, wholly Thine; My spirit owns Thee for its Lord.*
*Within Thy hand I lay my all, And only ask that I may be,*
*Whene'er Thou art in need of me, Alert and ready for Thy use.*

Translation *by* MISS FRANCESCA FRENCH.